Using Biographical Methods in Social Research

Barbara Merrill and Linden West

Los Angeles | London | New Delhi
Singapore | Washington DC

First published 2009

SAGE Publications Ltd
1 Oliver's Yard
55 City Road
London EC1Y 1SP

SAGE Publications Inc.
2455 Teller Road
Thousand Oaks, California 91320

SAGE Publications India Pvt Ltd
B 1/I 1 Mohan Cooperative Industrial Area
Mathura Road, Post Bag 7
New Delhi 110 044

SAGE Publications Asia-Pacific Pte Ltd
33 Pekin Street #02-01
Far East Square
Singapore 048763

Library of Congress Control Number: 2008939384

British Library Cataloguing in Publication data

A catalogue record for this book is available from the British Library

ISBN 978-1-4129-2959-2
ISBN 978-1-4129-2958-5 (pbk)

Typeset by C&M Digitals (P) Ltd, Chennai, India
Printed in Great Britain by MPG Books Group, Bodmin, Cornwall
Printed on paper from sustainable resources

IN MEMORY OF OUR PARENTS

Contents

Acknowledgements

The writing of this book has been influenced by many colleagues in research organisations, such as ESREA and SCUTREA, whom we have worked with over the years. Their ideas and stories have helped to shape the way we think and feel about biographical research. Help has also come from those we have interviewed for research, or taught, using biographical methods. We would also like to thank Patrick Brindle, our editor, for his encouragement, patience and support. And we are grateful to Brenda Wilson and Charmian Cowie for helping with the presentation of the text and translating it into the Sage style. Finally, many thanks to some of our students who read and commented on draft chapters. The book is, because of all these people, a product, like life itself, of profoundly auto/biographical processes.

1

Introduction

Setting the Scene

The finest-meshed sociological net cannot give us a pure specimen of class, any more than it can give us one of deference or of love. The relationship must always be embedded in real people and in a real context. (E.P. Thompson, 1980: 8)

From the outside looking in, an observer might see a 'common' condition: a son is killed in Vietnam, a daughter's mind is destroyed by LSD, a woman is divorced, a man becomes subject to mandatory requirement, there is a divorce. Yet, in interior life, what happens to one is unique. Life histories, like snowflakes, are never of the same design ... (Audrey Borenstein, 1978: 30)

Overview

In this chapter:

- We explain the relevance of the book and introduce the biographical turn.
- We introduce ourselves.
- We identify who the book is for and what we seek to achieve.
- An outline of the chapters and structure of the book is provided.

Why did we write this book and who is it for? The answer to these questions lies in our belief, based on extensive experience of doing biographical research, that such methods offer rich insights into the dynamic interplay of individuals and history, inner and outer worlds, self and other. We use the word 'dynamic' to convey the idea of human beings as active agents in making their lives rather than being simply determined by historical and social forces. Such an idea – with immense implications for the way we think about research – has, from time to time, been lost or marginalised in social science. Yet it has recently found renewed impetus, and if we think of people – like you and us – as actively experiencing, giving meaning to and creating their worlds, we need to know more about how this happens, how it is understood by those concerned, and how it can be made most sense of.

We think this is an opportune time to produce such a book: we are all, it seems, biographers now and want to tell our stories. The genre is pervasive throughout our culture. A glance in most bookshops will reveal the extent to which biography and autobiography serve as prime vehicles for self and social exploration, or maybe self promotion. This is an age of biography, and telling stories seems ubiquitous in popular culture: we consume the stories of celebrities, are fascinated by stories on reality TV, and are constantly intrigued by wartime narratives, as witnessed by various series being repeated on television (Goodley et al., 2004). Gossip and celebrity magazines, fun-based websites, podcasts, blogs, biopics (film) and biodramas (theatre) are all sites for biographical expression and experiment, by ordinary people as well as celebrities. New biographies of celebrities appear, it seems, almost daily. Jerry Springer, the American chat show host, is using television to explore his own story and family history – including of grandmothers murdered in the Holocaust – as part of wrestling with questions of identity. Oprah Winfrey has helped create an intimate confessional as well as controversial form of media communication, which, among other things, is said to have allowed gays, transsexuals and transgender people to tell their stories. We are all, as stated, biographers now or encouraged to be so.

Very serious writers are using a biographical approach in diverse, even surprising contexts. The universe, for example, has a recent biography, as have a number of cities (Ackroyd, 2000; Gribbin, 2007). Peter Ackroyd has employed the biographical form to weave greater understanding and connections between apparently disparate aspects of London's history. The genre allows him, he says, to do this: 'if the history of London poverty is beside a history of London madness, then the connections may provide more significant information than any orthodox historiographical survey' (Ackroyd, 2000: 2). Connecting disparate social phenomena and personal experience and weaving understanding between them in new and sometimes surprising ways characterises, as we will illustrate, a great deal of biographical research.

Biographical methods have claimed an increasing place in academic research and are alive and well (if sometimes marginal and contested) in various academic disciplines such as literature, history, sociology, anthropology, social policy and education, as well as in feminist and minority studies (Smith, 1998). There is a mushrooming of PhD and Masters programmes, dedicated research centres and conferences which, in various ways, are concerned with researching lives and the stories people tell about them. The words used to describe such methods can vary – autobiography, auto-ethnography, personal history, oral history or life story, as well as narrative, for instance – yet as Norman Denzin (1989a) has observed, there are many similarities (if also differences of emphasis). There can, for instance, be shared interest in the changing experiences and viewpoints of people in their daily lives, what they consider important, and how to make sense of what they say about their pasts, presents and futures, and the meanings they give to these in the stories they tell. There can be sensitivity towards the uniqueness yet also the similarities of lives and stories, like the snowflakes referred to above. Biography enables us to discern patterns but also distinctiveness in lives. The relationship between the particular and general, uniqueness and commonality, is in fact a central issue in biographical research.

The pervasive interest in biography may be understood by reference to living in a postmodern culture in which intergenerational continuities have weakened and a new politics of identity and representation has emerged among diverse groups. Women and men, gay and lesbian, black and white, young and old, may increasingly seek to live lives in different ways from parents or grandparents and doing biographical work has been one means to this end. The self and experience become a sort of reflexive life project, a focus for reworking who we are, and communicating this to others and for challenging, perhaps, some of the dominant stories told about people like us in the wider culture. Such a phenomenon can also be understood by reference to profound economic and cultural change over the last few decades, including the rise of feminism. These processes have provided more opportunities for self-definition (in the interplay of the global and local via mass communication technologies and in the celebration of diverse lifestyles, for example). Yet this historical moment, as commentators like Anthony Giddens and Ulrich Beck have observed, seems riddled with paradox: new opportunities for self-definition co-exist with deep-seated anxieties and existential doubt about our capacity to cope. The biographical imperative, at all levels, may be fuelled by the necessity to compose a life and make meaning in a more fragmented, individualised and unpredictable culture where inherited templates can be redundant and the nature of the life course increasingly uncertain in a globalising world.

A turn

There has, as indicated, been a major turn towards biographical, autobiographical, life history or narrative approaches in the academy over the last 30 or so years (Chamberlayne et al., 2000). The turn has many labels – the narrative or subjectivist turn – and encompasses different academic disciplines, including many of the social sciences. There are new journals devoted to the field and books have proliferated. In the United Kingdom, Miriam David, an Associate Director of the Economic and Social Research Council's Teaching and Learning Programme (which has sponsored a major study of 'learning lives', using biographical methods (Biesta et al., 2008)), has welcomed the increasing use of these approaches in the study of education, higher education and lifelong learning. They offer, she states, potentially important insights into the complexities of learning across the lifespan that currently dominant evidence-based approaches, with their preoccupation with what is most easily quantified and measured, often miss or neglect (David, 2008).

The turn, in conceptual terms, has been a response to a long-standing omission or marginalisation of the human subject in research, under the banner of objectivity and generalisability, modelled on the natural sciences. The dominant story science has told itself – of objectivity, of the need to focus on the directly observable and of a methodological transcendence of the human condition in sense-making processes – came to be questioned to the core (Roberts, 2002). Social science was reconceptualised, for many, from the 1960s onwards (but echoing older themes), as a human practice, shaped by power, dominant interests and/or powerful myths, which required interrogation. The growth of feminism and oral history was especially influential in challenging the neglect of the human subject (Chamberlayne et al., 2000; Plummer, 2001). Both were concerned to engage with personal accounts in a manner respecting and valuing what people had to say. They were also about finding some means to elicit and analyse the spoken and written records of people who, more often than not, had been neglected in the mainstream social and historical record. Feminism and oral history represented, at times, a radical, questioning edge, which continues to shape the thinking and practice of many biographical researchers. Moreover, biographical researchers may frequently, if not exclusively, engage with marginalised peoples, seeking to give voice and to challenge dominant assumptions, as part of a humanist project to build a more just social order.

We should add that biographical methods, and the desire to place people and their humanity at the core of social research, are not new either. They reach back to Max Weber (a German sociologist who focused on people's actions rather than structures) and a need for understanding in social science – by reference to the people concerned – rather than observing and measuring behaviour without engaging in dialogue with those most intimately concerned. The emphasis on engaging with people, and with understanding how they make sense of their worlds, was similarly at the heart of what was called the Chicago School. This has a central place in the history of the biographical research 'family'. Chicago School sociologists and social psychologists, in the 1920s, developed the notion of symbolic interactionism to capture the dynamic, learned, malleable and constructed quality of human identity and society, not least through the medium of language. Symbolic interactionists treat the things that members of society do as being performed by them, as actors, rather than as if done by something called the system itself. The social order, in short, is dynamically created in, through and from the interactions of its members. The task for the researcher is how to chronicle such processes and to explain them theoretically: using a repertoire of psychological, sociological, historical, literary and narrative theories. Furthermore, symbolic interactionists believed that only particulars, and people, have real empirical substance. They saw grand theoretical abstractions – like class, progress or even love – as having no real solidity outside people, their lived experience and stories. The idea of grounding understanding in such experience and of using theory respectfully in its light, remains, for many, a core value in biographical research. Human beings – rather than overly abstract categories – are at the heart of the project.

The British social historian Edward Thompson made this point in his seminal study, *The Making of the English Working Class* (Thompson, 1980). 'Making' was central to his ontology, or theory of being. Class was not so much a structure, or even a category, but something that is made in (and can be shown to have happened in) human relationships. Class is embodied in real people in real contexts, as in our opening quotation: 'the finest meshed sociological net cannot give us a pure specimen of class, any more than it can give us one of deference or of love' (Thompson, 1980: 8). You cannot have love without lovers or have deference without squires and labourers. Class happens when some men and women, as a result of common experiences (shared, inherited and even imagined), feel and articulate – to which we would add reflexively 'learn' – some identity of interest in comparison to another group. How people actively 'learn' their world, and their place in it, as well as how this may be challenged, is at the heart of much biographical research.

Bringing us into the text

We want, at this early stage, to introduce ourselves and bring our work, lives and orientations directly into the book. The book, in a sense, seeks to combine notions of biographical research as a personal journey with being a textbook of how to make good and meaningful research. The business of doing research is, we believe, made more alive in such an approach. Liz Stanley (1992) also draws attention – in her use of the term auto/biography (with a slash) – to the inter-relationship between the constructions of our own lives through autobiography and the construction of others' lives through biography. We cannot, in a sense, write stories of others without reflecting our own histories, social and cultural locations as well as subjectivities and values. Moreover, choosing a topic for a biographical study tends almost always to be rooted in our own personal and/or professional biographies (Miller, 2007). A topic we choose in others' lives may be motivated by or raise profound issues in our own. We, therefore, argue the case for bringing the researcher, and processes of relationship, into the research frame – and for interrogating this quite explicitly – rather than pretending, as many researchers do, that our interests and ways of making sense of others is, or should be, divorced from the people and experiences we are.

Barbara

Barbara's interest in using biographical approaches is rooted in her own life history. As a sociologist, Barbara writes, working in adult education, I am interested in researching the stories and experiences of adults who decide to return to learning later in their lives, in community, further or higher education. In particular, I am interested in looking at marginalised groups of adult learners whose life histories have been shaped by inequalities of class, gender and race. The latter have been central concerns throughout my life. Being female and working class, I soon became aware of class and later gender discrimination and inequalities in society through my own experiences and those of my family. Later, as a teacher in a multicultural comprehensive school, I became very conscious of the pervasiveness of racism in society through the lives of the black pupils.

My life experiences of being female and working class drew me towards Marxist and feminist politics at the age of 17 in the early 1970s. Studying sociology at school and university enabled me to articulate, understand and politicise my life experiences. Like many young people at that time, I was optimistic that the injustices of capitalism could be challenged and that through collective political action society could be changed. It was a belief in the importance of subjectivity in building agency and in overcoming the determinism of structural forces. This is probably one reason why, in relation to the biographical research I undertake, I am interested in the dynamic of structure and agency in people's lives.

However, despite my political awareness as an undergraduate student at the University of Warwick from 1973 until 1976, I felt overwhelmed by the middle-class culture and the privileged lives of the majority of its students, and the culture of the institution. This led to feelings of not always belonging – of being an outsider – despite enjoying my academic studies and having a circle of friends, as well as being involved in political groups. My confidence was occasionally undermined despite this political background and sociological knowledge.

My first experience of doing biographical research was in the mid-1980s when I was studying part-time for a Master of Philosophy degree in the Sociology Department at the University of Warwick, while also teaching at a school. The topic of my research was racism in schools and involved interviewing black pupils and getting them to talk about their life experiences. Looking back on my first encounters with life history interviews, my approach was not embedded in any particular theoretical underpinning. It was more about taking the plunge and engaging with people in what may have been a naive way. Luckily, all the pupils were willing to talk and talk intimately about how racism affected their own and their family's daily lives. What struck me was how articulate they were in discussing personal and political issues of racism and what they felt about other pupils, teachers and the school. They illustrated how powerful biographical approaches could be in understanding everyday lives.

Later, I made a career change from teaching 14–18 year olds to teaching adults at the University of Warwick. I entered academia feeling excited about the opportunity to undertake research but also experienced some trepidation. Echoing my earlier time as an undergraduate student, I was concerned about whether or not I would be good enough to work in the academic world. It was hinted to me that if I wanted to remain at Warwick I would need to obtain a PhD. My biography helped me to choose an area of study. I, therefore, became interested in how working-class adult students who had been out of the education system for a long time coped with the middle-class environment of a 'traditional', although relatively young university like Warwick. I reflected back on my pupils at the school where I had taught because many of them had been alienated by the middle-class and white school system and, as a result, left school having underachieved. Did the adult students at Warwick share similar life experiences? If so, why had they chosen to return to learn and why at this moment in their lives?

Here was my second encounter with using biographical approaches. However, this time I was part of a research team and environment. Although the focus was on mature women students, I also interviewed male adult students to explore differences and similarities. The process confirmed my belief in the value of the life history in enabling the social science researcher to gain an in-depth understanding of social life as well as revealing how past lives impact upon the present. The stories were often painful but also filled with resilience in a determination to juggle lives and struggle on in order to get degrees. Such narratives illustrated how education could be empowering and change lives for the better.

Furthermore, my own biography was implicated in developing a particular orientation in research: employing life histories to examine collective experiences and possibilities for change in people's lives. My family life history also led me to be aware that in using biographical research, we have to remember that there are stories which some people never tell or reveal only partially, because, perhaps, they are simply too painful or even traumatic.

My father had a story which he never really shared because of painful memories. The untold story affected the life of my family as a whole. My father was a British prisoner of war at Auschwitz III camp (E715) – the fact that there were such prisoners is not well known. Auschwitz III (Monowitz) was located near the IG

Farben chemical factory where British prisoners of war, alongside Jews and others, were used as forced labour in the factory. They were witnesses to many atrocities committed against Jews and others. The camp was the target for a bombing raid by the Americans. It was a Sunday, I subsequently discovered – their day off – and they were playing football. My father survived but friends were killed. He spoke a little about these events but not in detail: it was too painful. After my parents' deaths, I found out more about his story by seeing a picture of him at Auschwitz in a British war veteran's magazine, as well as in documentary evidence in a letter from another British prisoner there. More recently, I have found reference to him in a book about the experiences of British prisoners of war at Auschwitz. It refers to an episode, which I did not know about, whereby he and a friend attempted an escape during an air raid in 1944. I talked to his sister and visited Auschwitz with two friends. The site of Auschwitz III could not be visited at the time, nor was it easy to find out much detail about the camp, but I want to go back in the near future to complete an aspect of my life history. Biographies, and researching others' lives, can affect us in profound, interconnected ways.

Linden

My biography (Linden writes) has pain, puzzle and sadness too – like everyone's – and led me towards doing biographical research. This includes, professionally, a disenchantment and frustration with conventional research methods. I directed a study, in the mid-1980s, to examine the impact of second-chance educational pro-grammes on the lives of adult learners. These programmes were designed to enable working-class people to return successfully to education. The research was mainly quantitative in design, using standard psychological instruments, which, on the face of it, were well tested for rigour and reliability. Structured into the design were diverse and well-tested procedures for asking the same questions in different ways. The particular instruments sought to measure changes in the locus of control (the extent to which people feel they may shape their own lives or whether these are determined by external forces), as well as in self-concept and health and well-being, over the period of the programmes.

Some of the 'instruments' (the language of psychological research can have the ring of the laboratory to it) were, in fact, resented by a number of students, especially some working-class women, towards the end of their programme. They felt empowered by the programmes and encouraged to question what academics did and said; they dis-liked feeling forced to tick particular boxes. 'But it is not like that at all, it is more com-plicated', they would say (Lalljee et al., 1989). They could feel, they elaborated, empowered and more in control of their lives but also less in control at the same time. The locus of control, in certain regards, had shifted in positive ways – via access to a good and supportive group as well as feminist ideas – but this was only part of the picture. If they gained new insight into how a deeply gendered and classed culture could make them feel inadequate, and were empowered, in turn, to question what had been taken for granted, they also learned the pervasiveness of social and cultural inequalities with a corresponding sense of pessimism. Struggles to change a world seemed hard and illusive. I wanted to find ways of researching more of this complexity and nuance of how people thought and felt, and in more collaborative ways.

In 1990, I moved from an administrative post in adult education to a university lectureship. The transition was traumatic, partly for personal and family reasons. I was uncertain about the new post and my own credentials for doing it. I wanted to write about adult education, to make sense of professional experience. But I was distracted as I spent unexpectedly large amounts of time developing a new Diploma and Masters degree in Continuing Education for people working with adult learners in different settings. The range of students on the Diploma was more diverse than anticipated, including nurse educators, police, counsellors, social workers and teachers in higher, further and adult education. Their needs were varied and I struggled to cope.

Students found some of the psychological literature remote from their experience and concerns. Particular academic conventions compounded the problem: a number of students wanted to understand and establish a more reflexive and even biographical focus to their work, but was this permissible, they asked, and could they use their own experiences in academic writing? Dare they even introduce the personal pronoun 'I' in written assignments or were they supposed to be more objective? These may appear naive questions now (although students still ask them) but I worried about the codes and conventions of academic writing and research. In fact, I encouraged students to adopt a more experiential and autobiographical approach in their writing.

Some resolution of these tensions was found in becoming part of a community of biographical researchers. The literature on biographical research, and the writing of various colleagues, offered conceptual and methodological links between the personal and academic, the psychological and social, self and others. I also came to understand how I could relate burgeoning psychotherapeutic ideas – I was training as a psychotherapist at the time – to teaching, research and academic writing and learned that others were doing the same (West, 1996). If I was mad, there were others who were equally mad; moreover, I came to see psychotherapy itself as a form of biographical enquiry, a theme taken up later in the book.

The desire to connect social and psychological levels of explanation in the study of lives was profoundly rooted in my autobiography. I was one of a small number of working-class children going to Grammar School (for those who passed an exam at the age of 11: mostly middle-class children) from a public housing estate called Abbey Hulton on the edge of the industrial Potteries, in the English Midlands. I left close friends behind in negotiating, in effect, the contours of the English class system. Brian Jackson and Dennis Marsden's seminal study of education and the working class made use, in part, of the biographical approach in documenting the lives of working-class children struggling with issues of origin and destination, and of identity and where they really belonged (Jackson and Marsden, 1966). The book spoke to me, and still does, because this was my story too.

Yet making sense of my own experience required psychological insight alongside a sociological understanding of class and the workings of the educational system. Although my parents were working class, my mother's father had been a pottery owner between the two wars although the business had collapsed in the Great Depression. Mother, as I now see it, resented the insecurity and social inferiority brought by a lost status and was affected by the immense emotional impact on my grandfather, who was never quite the same man. I came to realise how she invested energy into my education partly as compensation for her own frustrated ambition and loss, and that of her family. My relationship with my own father was equally complex. We grew apart as I got older and as I moved into adolescence we lost some of the intimacy of earlier times. An uncle moved in to live with us and my father felt squeezed out. I got caught up, later, in seeking the trappings of academic success – on behalf of my mother – and rejected part of my background and my Dad (who was from an ordinary working-class background) in the process. The Oedipal and social were deeply entwined.

Psychoanalytic psychotherapy gave me a way of thinking about biographies, combined with sociology, in writing my first book. Psychoanalysis places the making and meaning of subjectivity – as well as its contingency – at the core of its work. Subjectivity and selfhood are forged in the quality of our interactions with significant others and the extent to which these encourage a more or less open, more or less curious, engagement with experience. We may learn to become defensive about who we are and what we may desire, for fear of rejection. We may learn to tell stories that are partial and shaped by a need to appease powerful others. Such patterns can continue across a life and even find expression in research, as we may invest others, unconsciously – including researchers – with some of the characteristics of significant people in earlier periods of our lives (Hollway and Jefferson, 2000; West, 1996). I came to realise that I was part of a growing movement to redraw the boundaries between personal experience and research, between psychological and sociological forms of understanding, in biographical enquiry. The present book is, in fact, born of the desire, for both of us, to develop this interdisciplinary project and conversation. Biographies, we argue, require an interdisciplinary spirit, which can give interpretation and understanding great richness and vitality.

There is something too, in my case, about becoming 60 in 2006, which added to the interdisciplinary impulse. Like Barbara, I was thinking a great deal about my father's life and the period in which he lived. He was born in 1905 and was nine at the outbreak of the First World War. He was 34 when the Second World War began and was badly injured in 1944. History matters. He volunteered to join the National Fire Service during the Blitz and a shard of glass cut though his helmet when a bomb hit a factory in Maidstone, Kent, in the south-east of England. To understand my Dad required a sense of history, alongside sociology and psychology. Like many men of his time, Dad was uncomfortable with intimacy, shaped as he was by social class and dominant constructions of masculinity. When I first went to university, he came to visit me and gave me a hamper of sausages, bacon and fruit. He did not mention the shortages during the war and how precious such food had been; and he would have been uncomfortable in exploring the symbolic meaning of the gesture in 1965. Dad said little about many things and meaning was more implicit. Yet his gesture was pregnant with historical, sociological, psychological and relational significance.

A question of terms and cross-cultural perspectives

We need to make clear that our use of the term biographical method denotes research which utilises individual stories or other personal documents to understand lives within a social, psychological and/or historical frame. One of the problems is the bewildering use of different labels such as life history, narrative, life writing, autobiographical and auto/biographical research (use the Glossary, at the end of the book, whenever you feel unsure). We employ 'biographical' as a convenient term to encompass research that can have different labels. We are aware of the dangers of this, that descriptors like narrative or biographical research may denote different meanings and preoccupations as well as things in common. Narrative researchers, for example, tend to focus on the nature and conventions of the stories people tell. Narrative is understood to indicate a temporal sequencing of events, including having a beginning, middle and end. Considerations of time lie at the core of narrative research as does the idea of accounts of events being like fictions, a creative means of exploring realities rather than being fixed and objective, in some absolute sense (Andrews, 2007). Narrative research can also encompass how the myths within a wider culture infuse and shape individual narratives. Witness, for example, the heroic myth of the adult student in the literature of adult education, who journeys from poor beginnings towards glimpses of light – through knowledge – onwards into suffering and yet achieves some final redemption. See too the myth of the adult teacher who can, potentially at least, be redeemed by students, from cynicism and despair in the academy (the film *Educating Rita*, with Julie Walters and Michael Caine has some of these qualities). We may barely be conscious of how we may use a range of myths, or how they use us, in our stories.

The words biography and life history can also have quite distinct meanings. In Denmark, for instance (West et al., 2007), a distinction is drawn between biography or life story as the told life, and life history, in which the researcher brings his or her interpretations and theoretical insights into play. This distinction has influenced biographical researchers in other countries (Roberts, 2002). We recognise how the varying terminology is confusing and have tried to simplify the use of language in the book. Where we feel it necessary to make explicit use of other terminology – such as auto/biography – we do so but try to keep this to a minimum while always remembering that terminology can be a contested field.

Cross-cultural perspectives also inform the book as we deliberately draw on examples of biographical research from across Europe and America as well as parts of the southern hemisphere, illustrating research in diverse contexts. We include studies of people in professional settings, or in varying forms of work, in education, in local communities, as well as in families and therapeutic processes. The book encompasses political and social action and the use of biography to chronicle and interpret social movements – such as the rise of feminism – and the critical learning and consciousness raising at the heart of certain biographical projects (Ollagnier, 2007).

Opposition

We illustrate throughout the book the peculiar power and potential of biographical research to generate novel perspectives on important social phenomena and to challenge a tendency in social research to over-simplify complex problems – such as the fear of crime – by insufficiently engaging, in a lifelong and lifewide way, with those most directly concerned. But biographical research, as well as other forms of qualitative enquiry, has its critics, including powerful interests who fund research, even though, as noted in the United Kingdom, biographical methods have begun to receive more substantial funding (Biesta et al., 2008). The United States government, for instance, has gone so far as to legislate that what counts as fundable research needs to be grounded in positivistic traditions, which favour scientific and quantitative rather than qualitative paradigms (Davies and Gannon, 2006).

Biographical research has academic critics too. Some historians question the biographical turn as a sort of retreat into 'fine, meaningless detail', which obscures the big picture and important social policy questions (Fieldhouse, 1996: 119). Researchers get lost, in this view, in the detailed description of lives, even in a narcissistic way perhaps, without helping people understand how society works or how it can be changed for the better. A different criticism comes from certain 'post-structuralist' perspectives, influenced by, among others, the work of the French philosopher Michel Foucault (1979a, 1979b). Foucault conceived human subjectivity as forged in the play of various power–knowledge formations: human beings become positioned by language in ways they may only be dimly aware of, if at all.

Focusing on biographies risks missing a bigger point about how power permeates knowledge and knowing at every level. Power works to control, not least in what has been termed our confessional society. At earlier times, the body was regulated but now it is the soul that is the target, via technologies of the self, expressed in a range of psychological, medical and professional practices. Power, in this view, circulates in and regulates subjectivities, which includes the stories people tell, whether to Oprah Winfrey or researchers. Mention should also be made, however, that Foucault and other post-structuralists have inspired various biographical researchers, including in feminist collective biography, where attempts are made to articulate the discourses through which selves and bodies may be shaped. This can challenge the tendency to think of the individual who exists independently of discourse as well as of time and place (Davies and Gannon, 2006).

We believe that biographical methods offer rich rewards in making sense of self and others in social and historical contexts but that such research raises many questions, which researchers – new or experienced – must consider. In fact, a major reason for writing the book is to share our work, and what has inspired it but also some of the insights we have gained into diverse theoretical, interpretative and practical challenges, and about the relationship between the stories people tell and the realities they purport to represent: between 'realists' at one end of the spectrum and some post-structuralists, at another. Can we in truth talk about reality at all? There is also a question about the nature and status of theory in biographical research. This is considered essential by biographical researchers, yet with a note of caution: that its development should be grounded in an engagement with real people and their complex experience and stories. Overly abstract theorising tends to be treated with suspicion.

At another level, there are questions about how to do interviews and what makes for good or rich interview material. (Our main interest is the biographical interview, given its central place in social research, but there are many other ways of doing biographical research, using diaries, letters, autobiographies and memorabilia of various kinds. There can be visual biographies, using photography and video. Interviews can be combined with these other sources of evidence.) How should we conduct interviews and what might be meant by a good interview and why? How should we transcribe interviews as well as interpret and code the material? How then to employ the material in our writing or other forms of representation: how do we balance quotations with our interpretations, for instance? Crucially, what of the ethics of biographical research, given that we may engage with difficult, emotionally charged and potentially vulnerable aspects of people's lives? (This is an important issue which we consider later in the book once you have some understanding of biographical research.) Is there a danger of voyeurism, of being over intrusive, or of meddling with people's souls? Finally, what makes such research valid and on what terms? Such questions – both theoretical as well as practical – inform our writing.

Our aim has been to set the biographical method in context, to illustrate its range and potential, but also to engage with the many questions surrounding its use. In the process, we make clear our stance and values as researchers. We favour, under the influence of feminism, more collaborative approaches to research, including interviewing as well as interpretation. We tend, because of our own backgrounds and values, towards working with marginalised peoples or at least to challenging dominant orthodoxies. We favour interdisciplinarity as well as engaging with our own role in the construction of the other's story. And we think it possible to build a convincing sense of the realities of others' lives, of what it is like to be in someone else's shoes, albeit necessitating reflexive understanding of how we, and other influences, may shape the other's story. In charting aspects of our journey, alongside those of others, and by making clear where we stand, and why, as well as by chronicling mistakes and wrong turns, we believe we can help you find your own distinct way.

Who is the book for?

By 'you', we are referring, especially, to students in higher education – both graduate and undergraduate, researchers in academia – but also many professionals, given the burgeoning interest in employing such methods in diverse professional contexts (Chamberlayne et al., 2004; Dominicé, 2000; West et al., 2007). The book represents a sort of invitation to enter a conversation, involving a diverse community of scholars. We seek to offer an informative, comprehensive, accessible and practical guide for university students, as well as professionals interested in doing research and engaging with others having similar interests.

The structure of the book

In Chapter 2, we place the development of biographical approaches in historical context, tracing its origins back to the oral tradition and oral history. In doing so, we connect the use of oral reports from the French Revolution to the Polish tradition and the emergence of the Chicago School in the United States, and on to more recent developments, particularly feminism. We introduce some of the resistance to biographical methods in disciplines like psychology. We note how the more contemporary burgeoning of interest in biographical research, and the interest in biography per se, may be located at a point of time, at least in the 'developed' West, where the social scripts that once shaped people's lives, as in earlier agrarian and industrial societies, have weakened and where the necessity of doing biographical work has increased.

In Chapter 3, we map the application of biographical methods across a number of academic disciplines: in sociology and social policy; in studies of education and life-long learning; and in psychology, psychotherapy, medicine and health care. We note that biographical researchers often work with marginalised peoples and provide examples of such work. In mapping the territory, we note the interdisciplinary shape of some of the terrain, including the emergence of new, psychosocial perspectives.

In Chapter 4, we introduce some of the diverse theoretical and methodological roots of biographical research and note how researchers have drawn on interpretivism, hermeneutics, symbolic interactionism, critical theory, psychoanalysis, feminism, narrative theory and post-structuralism in their work. However, for the purposes of our book, we give particular attention to those perspectives which have influenced our work: such as symbolic interactionism, feminism, critical theory, and psychosocial and psychoanalytic thinking. We introduce some of the dialogue between sociologists and psychologists as well as the role of reflexivity and subjective and intersubjective insight in doing research of this kind. We develop a provisional framework for categorising different theoretical and epistemological positions and you are asked to consider where you might stand in relation to these 'positionings'.

We offer, in Chapter 5, case studies of different ways of using and conceptualising biographical research. We include some of our own work at this point, as part of sharing what we have done and why. This encompasses research among families living in marginalised communities, and into changing identities among adult learners as well as professional learning and struggles to be an authentic doctor or teacher in demanding inner-city contexts. We consider the role of the researcher in shaping the subject of enquiry and raise some ethical issues. As a pedagogic device, we invite you to reflect on aspects of your own autobiography and how this might shape your interest in others' lives.

In Chapters 6, 7 and 8, we address the specifics of how to do biographical research, which includes generating, analysing and presenting data. We consider how to choose a subject to research. We think about questions such as 'why this topic, why me and why choose a biographical approach in the first place?' We pay attention to working as an individual researcher or as part of a research team. We consider selecting a sample and discuss a question that students often ask: 'can you really work with only one person or a very small number?' Chapter 7 focuses on the interviewing process and we consider the nature and role of description, and how important our sensitivities as well as conceptual understanding can be in generating what we term 'good stories'. We highlight some differences in approach, especially between the narrative and the interactive interview, which reflect contrasting perspectives on the role of the researcher in the interview process. We illustrate some debates about this in the context of a new trans-European research study of non-traditional learners in higher education and offer examples of interviewing from our own work, as well as looking at the different approaches to transcription.

In Chapter 8, we provide an overview of different forms of analysis, from grounded theory to computer-based, as well as more dialogical styles, and explain our own methods in detail. In Chapter 9, we consider the processes of writing biographical research and how it can tend to blur the boundaries between creative and analytic forms of writing. Ways of representing the self and others in stories are also examined. We discuss the practicalities of and the preparation needed in starting to write, such as creating a good environment in which to work. We consider the creativity but also discipline at the heart of good research writing and provide examples. We introduce different styles of writing for different audiences as well as discussing different ways of presenting biographical material. In Chapter 10, we return to the important issues about the validity and ethics of biographical approaches and explore differing notions of validity, and how validity claims for biographical methods are often rooted in notions of verisimilitude, or lifelikeness – and in the peculiar power of biographical research, like good literature, to bring experience to life in intelligible, even profound ways. The chapter further examines the ethical questions raised throughout our text, which includes the boundary between research and therapy.

In the final chapter, we summarise the key themes of the book, such as the place of subjectivity and detachment in research and the nature and status of theory in biographical studies, as well as the relationship between the particular and the general. We ask what it means, or might mean, to be a biographical researcher, and the shifts of identity that can be involved. We consider the doubts and anxieties as well as rewards research can bring and revisit the excitement and benefits (as well as difficulties) of engaging in academic conversations, across disciplinary and cultural boundaries. We ask what makes a good researcher and discuss the importance of belonging to a research community, and of developing the capacity to engage with and learn from others and otherness. We conclude the book by referring to wider issues and social policy as well as by reflecting on the process of writing this book and what it has meant to us.

Key points

- There is renewed interest in biographical methods in social research.
- It is important to think about how our own biographies may shape our interest in others and their lives.
- A range of different terms can be used to describe the sort of research encompassed in the book. We use the term 'biographical method' as a convenient label to cover a range of approaches with many similarities but also some differences.

FURTHER READING

Chamberlayne, P., Bornat, J. and Wengraf, T. (2000) (eds) *The Turn to Biographical Methods in Social Science.* London: Routledge.

Plummer, K. (2001) *Documents of Life 2: An Invitation to Critical Humanism.* London: Sage.

Roberts, B. (2002) *Biographical Research.* Buckingham: Open University Press.

DISCUSSION QUESTIONS

1. What do you understand by biographical research?

2. Have you ever studied a relative's life or even your own? In one sense, we 'do' biographical research all the time, when, for instance, composing a Curriculum Vitae. What can be important is what is missing as much as what is included. Write a paragraph on your experiences of doing research and/or of composing a CV.

3. Have you read a biography or autobiography? If so, who was it about and what were the key points in that person's life?

4. What do you consider might be the strengths and weaknesses of the biographical method?

ACTIVITIES

1. Select an artefact/object that has some significance to you in your life and explain why.
2. Draw your timeline and mark key events in your life on it.

2

Biographical Methods

An Introductory History

… we are concerned with understanding the three components harboured in the word [auto/biography]: autos (what do we mean by the self?), bios (what do we mean by the life?) and graphe (what do we presume in the act of writing?). Finding answers to such questions is not easy and they have been the basis of philosophical reflections for centuries. Yet they are returned to over and over again in the musings over telling a life. (Ken Plummer, 2001: 86)

Overview

In this chapter:

- We see how the origins of biographical methods can be traced back to oral traditions and the use of oral history.
- We examine the central place of the Chicago School of sociology in the history of biographical approaches.
- We look at how biographical methods have been greatly influenced by feminism, and to an extent critical theory and post-structuralism.
- We consider how psychology, in its mainstream guises, has often been unsympathetic to biographical and narrative methods. Yet there has been a subsidiary strand that has adopted a more sympathetic view.
- We note that the popularity of biographical methods has ebbed and flowed and that, at the present time, there is flow once again.

Introduction

In this chapter, we locate the development of biographical methods in an historical context by tracing their roots back to the oral tradition and oral history. Oral history has made a significant contribution to the field, reaching back to accounts of the French Revolution. Likewise, the Polish tradition and the Chicago School of sociology, which emerged after the First World War, have been important influences. We examine the significant contribution of feminism and consider the development, sometimes uneven, of biographical research in specific disciplines, particularly sociology, psychology and education. Undertaking a biography of biographical methods is useful in painting a backcloth to contemporary debates and methodological issues. Questions about the nature of research, the meaning of a life, and the problems of representing lives, as Plummer (2001) states, have been around for centuries.

The biographical turn

The present popularity of biographical methods in social research – the biographical or subjectivist turn (Chamberlayne et al., 2000; see also Bertaux, 1981a; Rosenthal, 1995) – denotes, as mentioned in the first chapter, a reaction against forms of social enquiry that tended to deny subjectivity in research and to neglect the role of human agency in social life. The current resurgence may also be understood by reference to a late or postmodern culture in which some of the social scripts that shaped people's lives in earlier agrarian or industrial periods have weakened or have been rejected, at least in the 'developed' world. Many women, for instance, because of feminism and profound labour market changes and increased educational opportunities, may strive for lives quite different from their mothers or grandmothers. There is a broader sense that people may want to compose (and/or may be forced to, because of social and economic change) their biographies on different terms, in what the British sociologist Anthony Giddens terms 'the reflexive project of the self'. Of course, others may find the loosening of intergenerational continuities difficult and there can be nostalgic yearning for past certainties, expressed in the rise of various fundamentalisms (Frosh, 1991; Giddens, 1991, 1999).

We should emphasise, once more, that not all social researchers have been influenced by the subjectivist turn and some are actively hostile to it. Many psychologists, for instance, can work from different assumptions: that subjective accounts are too amorphous and unreliable as evidence, as well as beyond systematic observation and measurement. Their approach to research is often rooted in experimentation and observation (in the manner of the natural sciences), and in quantification and statistically validated propositions. They seek to identify the precise impact of particular variables on a specific phenomenon (like group pressures on individual behaviour) using controlled experiments (which can be directly observed and measured) – stripping away, as they see it, extraneous socio-cultural or subjectivist dimensions (Frosh, 1989). Social research can move in varied directions.

Oral traditions and history

Story telling has been an important dimension of human communication in all societies: serving to generate and pass on meaning and guidance in what could be a chaotic, brutish, unpredictable world. Stories were a vehicle by which collective histories, shared values and prescriptions for living were communicated intra- and intergenerationally. Pre-literacy, using the voice to tell a story was the key means of communication. Stories were also represented in earlier centuries through art, including prehistoric cave paintings. The collective history, myths and legends of a people were later written down in epic poems such as *The Iliad* and *The Odyssey*. In the oral tradition of passing down stories across the generations, stories became refined, re-interpreted and reconstructed.

Jan Vansina's (1985) work, *Oral Tradition as History* charts the development of the oral tradition. Vansina defines oral traditions as being, 'all oral testimonies concerning the past which are transmitted from one person to another' (1985: x). They serve as a prime historical source of information. For example, we know the history of native American tribes such as the Sioux and Pueblo Indians largely through the oral tradition; yet for some historians this raises questions of validity and reliability. What credence can be given to the stories people tell, riddled as they could be with self-justification or even illusion as to some idyllic past? Such questions have echoes today among social scientists opposing the turn to subjectivity in research. Notwithstanding, oral history was and is used by historians to tell the history of ordinary people and to explore what life was like for them, on their own terms. Paul Thompson stresses this point, arguing that 'the challenge of oral history lies partly in relation to this essential social purpose of history' (2000: 3):

> Oral history by contrast makes a much fairer trial possible: witnesses can now also be called from the under-classes, the unprivileged, and the defeated. It provides a more realistic and fair reconstruction of the past, a challenge to the established account. In so doing, oral history has radical implications for the social message of history as a whole. (P. Thompson, 2000: 7)

In a similar vein, Raphael Samuel emphasises how:

> Interview and reminiscence will also enable the historian to give an identity and character to people who would otherwise remain mere names on a street directory or parish register and to restore to some of their original importance those who left no written record of their lives. (Samuel, 1982: 142)

Oral history claims an egalitarian purpose in that it can bring to life people's social worlds in ways which much documentary evidence rarely does, other than diaries and personal testimonies (P. Thompson, 2000). As with the biographical interview in social research, the oral history interview can be conceived as an interaction and dialogue – generating what Frisch (1990) calls 'shared authority', lending to it a particular legitimacy and a wider social purpose. Many biographical researchers have inherited this social purpose commitment in their work, using it to question dominant myths or challenge some of the stories told of marginalised peoples by powerful others.

The French Revolution: a case study

The French historian, Jules Michelet, based at the Sorbonne, wrote a history of the French Revolution, drawing partly on oral accounts of life at the time. Michelet described his research approach as follows:

> When I say oral tradition, I mean national tradition, which remained generally scattered in the mouths of the people, which everybody said and repeated, peasants, townsfolk, old men, women, even children; which you can hear if you enter of an evening into a village tavern; which you may gather if, finding on the road a passer-by at rest, you begin to converse with him about the rain, the season, then the high price of victuals, then the times of the Emperor, then the times of the revolution. (1847: 530)

The use of the oral tradition is not confined to the world of historians, as anthropologists employ similar approaches. Today, the oral tradition continues to be of significance in many cultures, and sub-cultures, as the work of Elizabeth Tonkin (1992), an anthropologist, illustrates.

A definition of oral history

Tonkin defines oral narratives as being 'social actions, situated in particular times and places and directed by individual tellers to specific audiences' (1992: 97). For Tonkin, it is a dialectical process between structure and agency so that memory becomes 'a key mediating term between the individual and society' (1992: 98).

Oral history developed out of the oral tradition and oral historians have engaged in lengthy debates about the nature of memory and truth in oral accounts, or the interplay of past and present, as well as about processes of interpretation (emphasising that oral narratives, like written texts, are always and inevitably interpretations of events rather than representing the events themselves) (P. Thompson, 2000). Oral historians have raised fundamental issues that biographical researchers also address. Al Thomson, for instance, in developing a theory of memory within oral history, suggests that experience never ends and is open to constant recreation in the light of the present (Thomson, 1994).

Thomson interviewed a number of Anzac veterans about their private experiences of war, comparing the material to the powerful tribal mythologies of Anzac legend. The interviews led to a recovery of lost, even repressed memories, which could, on occasions, be at odds with dominant public accounts (of, for example, a classless, egalitarian army in comparison to the British). The processes of revising stories could be painful because the public myths served, partly, to legitimise a present way of life (in Veterans' Organisations, for example). Thomson also made use of psychoanalytic ideas on repression to develop his theory of selective memory. An individual may feel too vulnerable to integrate certain experiences within their story at a particular time and survives by denying or repressing them, such as in the case of horrific incidents in war.

Oral historians, such as Luisa Passerini (1990) and Alessandro Portelli (1990), have raised similar questions about the selective nature of memory and story telling. Passerini has focused on the nature and power of myth in people's stories. (Myths can be defined in various ways – historically, they were concerned with the nature of the divine or transcendent in human life; in a more psychological vein, they may be a product of frustrated desire, or of social alienation, which finds expression in the imaginary, in dreams, fantasy and story telling.) Myths can be a way of dealing with collective alienation or disappointment. Oral histories of British and Italian car workers, for example, have illuminated how myths of the car as a means to equality and affluence or sexual potency can permeate the stories workers tell. Myths may find expression in the perceived failures or frustrations of radical organisations, like the Red Brigade in Italy, in their stories of small communities against the world or of heroic struggles of revolutionaries in other countries. The myth, in these terms, is a means of handling difficult pasts and uncertain presents. Portelli (1990) recounts some of the myths of the 1940s generation of communists in Italy who, as hope for a new order, post-liberation, faded, became frustrated. As they grew older, history could, in some cases, be reinterpreted in dream-like ways, giving vent to frustration. Narrators might exaggerate their role, as a way of managing disappointment and disillusion. The past may be a painful place of lost hopes and frustration and the stories we tell of it can be shaped by a need for self-justification.

Portelli (2006) is, nonetheless, the author of a powerful defence of oral history, especially in an Italian context. There is, he insists, in the academy and beyond, a range of criticism of history from below: that once the 'floodgates of orality are opened, writing (and rationality along with it) will be swept out as if by a spontaneous uncontrollable mass of fluid, amorphous material' (2006: 33). This echoes the 'fine meaningless, detail' accusations of certain British historians. Portelli, in fact, takes on 'traditional writers of history' and the 'omniscient narrator'. 'They appear to be impartial and detached ... oral history changes the writing of history ... the narrator is pulled into the narrative ... the telling of the story is part of the story being told' (Portelli, 2006: 41). Oral historians deliberately allow more of the people to tell their story, which helps create confrontations of different partialities rather than a transcendental account. This, he insists, is what makes oral history (to which we can add biographical research) interesting and important.

Michael Roper (2003), an oral historian, has used psychoanalytic ideas, alongside insights from feminist research, to argue that researchers need to focus on the present as well as the past: in particular, what might be happening, unconsciously, in the relationship between researcher and researched. Knowledge produced by researchers, he insists, is always situational, the product of an interaction. The oral historian is inevitably caught in a transference situation in which the degrees of empathy between people will be shaped by emotional residues from the past, including the past of the researcher. Roper concludes that if 'we seek to do more than explain our subjects' behaviour in terms of economics, social forces or conscious intent – if that is we seek a serious engagement with subjectivity – we have to consider the subject's relationships', including with the researcher (Roper, 2003: 30). Rigid distinctions between past and present, self and other, memory and immediacy, begin to unravel as we think seriously of research as a human encounter.

A strong movement

Oral history became a strong movement in various countries after the Second World War. An Oral History Society was established in the United Kingdom and an Oral History Association in the United States, both of which remain popular, with important international interests, as exemplified in the *Oral History* journal. There are many and diverse localised groups worldwide, involved in school oral history projects, oral history workshops and community education/development. Oral history offers a grassroots approach to historical research, focusing on the memories of marginalised peoples who might otherwise be forgotten. Oral history methods have been used within community development/education to confront and heal painful past memories. In Germany, such an approach has been employed to enable the older generation to come to terms with the Nazi past, while educational and community projects on Nazi Germany and the Holocaust have brought different generations and nationalities, such as Germans and Poles, together to share and interrogate their stories and assumptions (Dausien, 2007).

Oral history and feminism

Oral history has a long tradition in feminism, in making women's lives and experiences known in history. For Gluck, 'women's oral history ... is a feminist encounter, even if the interviewee is not herself a feminist' (1979: 5). In America, for example, feminist historians have used oral history to explore the experiences of nineteenth-century marginalised groups of women, such as blacks in domestic labour (Tucker, 1988) and native American Indians (Perdue, 1980) or pre-Stonewall lesbians (Kennedy, 2006). Inga Elqvist-Salzman (1993), a Swedish feminist, has used oral history, as have others, to study the professional and personal lives of female teachers.

Women's oral history has become well established in the classroom as a discovery/connective tool. The research terrain is rich, covering the women's movement, at various stages, as well as the histories of 'women bound by race, class, gender and sexual orientation' (Armitage and Gluck, 2006: 77). Yet key feminist oral historians, such as Susan H. Armitage and Sherna Berger Gluck, have begun to ask many more questions about what has been achieved; and about the nature of the research process, which turned out, they argue, to be more complex than initially realised (Armitage and Gluck, 2006). The enthusiasm for recovering women's histories remains but there is also a more analytically sophisticated debate. This surrounds, for example, the need to engage in dialogue with narrators rather than simply to rely on the researcher's interpretations, or to interrogate more of the relationship between interviewer and narrator, which cannot simply be captured by notions of 'insiderness'. The insider may, Gluck suggests, be disadvantaged by the assumptions she makes about shared meanings or the interviewer might make about her (Armitage and Gluck, 2006). While there remains a powerful political imperative to recover more and diverse women's stories, the researcher has a duty to 'historicize' and interrogate any account. This includes not only the broader conditions of women's lives, but also the interpersonal, political and social contexts in which narratives are collected. How women may 'perform' their stories has also to be interrogated, since this may be culturally rooted. While shifts in emotional tone might denote special meanings for some women, in certain cultures, among older Palestinian women, for instance, these may reflect cultural prescriptions for telling stories rather than individual states of mind (Armitage and Gluck, 2006).

Oral history has been employed in many other contexts, including by development and aid workers, to 'gain a better understanding of the concerns and priorities, culture and experiences of the people with whom they wish to work. Oral testimony can give those communities more power to set their own agenda for development' (Slim et al., 1993: 1). It provides, once again, space and an audience for the voices of those living in poor and marginalised communities. This is accompanied by major methodological debates around voice, the nature of the interview and memory (see Perks and Thomson (2006) for important contributions on these issues by diverse oral historians). Such concerns lie at the heart of biographical research too.

Enter the Chicago School of sociology

The epic work of William Isaac Thomas and Florian Znaniecki on the experiences of Polish migrants to the United States of America – *The Polish Peasant* – first published 1918–1921, stands as one of the earliest and most important pieces of biographical research. It is now regarded as a classic sociological work, and is historically significant because it inaugurated, alongside the research of Park and Burgess (see below), a movement from positivistic approaches to more constructivist ideas of how the social order was created as well as being open to change. These studies were crucial in the emergence of the Chicago School of sociology.

Thomas and Znaniecki's work was grounded in empirical research and sought to synthesise theory and data, in contrast to other forms of sociology of the time, which were more theoretical. Thomas gathered data largely through documents such as letters written and sent to a Polish newspaper by peasants migrating to America, and through the biography of a young Polish peasant called Wladek Wiszniewski. At the time, the use of letters and biographies was innovative in sociological research, and, as Herbert Blumer points out: 'The life history of Wladek was the first systematically collected sociological life history' (1984: 54). It was also of interest because Wiszniewski was paid for writing his life history, which was 250 pages long.

For Thomas and Znaniecki, personal documents provided the basis for theorising what they termed the disintegration process faced by immigrants. Their focus also encompassed the integration and reintegration of individuals and their families into new lives and cultures (Hammersley, 1998; Sztompka, 1984). The use of personal documents and accounts established a greater understanding of social life through the interactions of the self with groups and the wider society. Autobiographies gave insights into an individual's life process and his/her interaction with others (Bron, 1999). Thomas and Znaniecki argued that: 'We are safe in saying that personal life records, as complete as possible, constitute the perfect type of sociological material' (1958: 1832). Subjectivity and inductivity – allowing narrative material to lead the researcher, rather than simply testing pre-established theory, in the manner of the natural sciences – were brought to the heart of social research.

Case study: An extract from Wladek's autobiography

In the USA: Franciszek came the same evening and almost invited himself to be bridegroom, promising to bring brandy, beer, wine and to pay for the auto. And all would have been quite well if it had not been for another trouble. On January 14th I was dismissed. And the reason was the following: This year the winter was rather hard, so it was very cold in the bakery, for we baked little. Every night I had to wait three or four hours after making the rolls, and having nothing to do I lay upon the table near the oven and fell asleep. It very seldom happened that I over-slept even a little, and I had never spoiled anything and the rolls were always in time. This time I did the same, but I slept perhaps half an hour longer than I needed, and Mr Z. found me sleeping. He got angry, although I should not have spoiled anything even if I slept two hours more ... During this week I did not try to get work, for I had occupation enough at home, preparing for the wedding ...

And with me things went on worse and worse, for after my wedding I remained with $5, while my wife gave $10 to the butcher. I could not find work in spite of my efforts. Brother-in-law could not or would not get work for me; I went from one cousin of my wife to another, asking them to get work for me, but they could not or would not either, although all of them worked in the stockyards ... It would really have been better if I had died long ago, for I have no hope of getting work ... It is awfully difficult to get work without protec-tion, because of the terrible crisis brought by the European war ... I cannot even now take a walk with my wife, for she has not even shoes to put on her feet, but wears my old shoes. And she must bear all this through me, for I brought her to this. (Thomas and Znaniecki, 1958: 2220–1, 2225)

Thomas and Znaniecki, as stated, had considerable influence on the Chicago School of sociology, which emerged around 1920, as did the urban research of Robert Park and Ernest Burgess and their students (Blumer, 1984). Park and Burgess were interested in using the city as a site of study: they wanted to engage with the 'real world'. Howard Becker later recalled what Park considered this to be, as told to him when a student of Park's. Although Park is referring to observation, the account summarises the spirit at work in the School more widely.

Park (please note the dominant use of the male person, characteristic of its time):

You have been told to go grubbing in the library thereby accumulating a mass of notes and a liberal coating of grime. You have been told to choose problems wherever you can find musty stacks of routine records based on trivial sched-ules prepared by tired bureaucrats and filled out by reluctant applicants for aid or fussy do-gooders or indifferent clerks. This is 'called getting your hands dirty in real research'. Those who thus counsel you are wise and honourable; the reasons they offer are of great value. But one thing more is needful; first hand

(Continued)

(Continued)

observation. Go and sit in the lounge of the luxury hotels and on the door-steps of the flophouses; sit on the Gold Coast settees and on the slum shakedowns; sit in Orchestra Hall and in the Star and Garter Burlesk. In short, gentlemen, go get the seat of your pants dirty in real research. (McKinney, 1966: 71)

Why do you think that Park feels that 'real research' is the most useful and valuable?

Likewise, the influence of W.I. Thomas and George Herbert Mead in the development of the School, was great. Chicago sociologists and social psychologists (disciplinary divisions were less solidified then) perpetually got the seats of their pants dirty by engaging in intensive fieldwork among immigrants, young criminals, the poor, etc., and in their own environments. They used various methods and obtained quantitative as well as qualitative data. The researchers preferred the case study and thought it the most useful approach in building theoretical understanding forged in the light of lived experience. One way of building case studies was via participant observation but personal documents such as autobiographical writing were also used.

The Jack Roller

Working in the tradition pioneered by Thomas and Znaniecki and the Chicago School of sociology, Clifford R. Shaw published *The Jack Roller* in 1930 (republished in 1966). This is a monumental and classic life history of a teenage delinquent called Stanley. It is a study in criminology providing an understanding of delinquency from the viewpoint and story of the delinquent. Ken Plummer in his book *Documents of Life* stresses the historical significance of the study for biographical research:

I think it is the most famous case study in criminology, and one of the most frequently discussed in sociology. It has – rightly or wrongly – an almost 'canonical' status amongst life histories (second only, perhaps, to Wladek). (2001: 106)

The Jack Roller involves 'Stanley' and his career in delinquency (although Shaw also researched other delinquents in the study). Stanley was 14 when Shaw first met him. He had been in custody with the police several times for truanting from school, shoplifting and pickpocketing, following an unhappy childhood in which he was brought up by a stepmother (whom he disliked), in a poor area of Chicago. For Shaw, the boy's story formed the central element of his research,

as a device for ascertaining the personal attitudes, feelings and interests of the child; in other words, it shows how he conceives his role in relation to other persons and the interpretations which he makes of the situations in which he lives. It is in the personal document that the child reveals his feelings of inferiority and superiority, his fears and worries, his ideals and philosophy of life, his antagonisms and mental conflicts, his prejudices and rationalizations. (1966: 3–4)

Interestingly, and there are echoes of this in feminist research decades later, Shaw struck up a close relationship with Stanley. The latter said, many years later, that 'the Shaws were my real parents' (in Snodgrass, 1982: 171) and that Shaw was the only person who had any influence over him. Shaw, through Stanley's biography, illustrates how crime is learned, the impact of life in a city and the role of labelling theory in shaping a career of crime.

Case study

Stanley tells his story in his own words and begins by reflecting on his family life:

As far back as I can remember my life was filled with sorrow and misery. The cause was my stepmother, who nagged me, beat me, insulted me, and drove me out of my own home. My mother died when I was four years old, so I never knew a real mother's affection.

My father remarried when I was five years of age. The stepmother who was to take the place of my real mother was a raw-boned woman, devoid of features as well as emotions … The woman he married had seven children, and a bad lot they were, and there were eight in our family, making 15 in all. We all tried to live together in five rooms. It wasn't long before trouble started. My stepmother started to raise hell. She favoured her children in every way. She blamed us for everything that happened, and gave them the best of the food … The stepmother done with us just what she pleased. We were well abused and continuously …

So I grew old enough to go out on the street. The life in the streets and alleys became fascinating and enticing. I had two companions that I looked up to with childish admiration and awe … One was William my stepbrother. They were close friends four years older than me and well versed in the art of stealing …

One day my stepmother told William to take me to the railroad yard to break into box-cars. William always led the way and made the plans. He would open the cars, and I would crawl in and hand out the merchandise. We filled our cart, which we had made for this purpose, and proceeded towards home. After we arrived home with our ill-gotten goods, my stepmother would meet us and pat me on the back and say that I was a good boy and that I would be rewarded. Rewarded, bah! Rewarded with kicks and cuffs. (Shaw, 1966: 47, 50, 52, 200)

The study highlights the principles of symbolic interactionism in focusing on the subjectivity of the social world and in deriving understanding from the experience and interpretations of subjects themselves. For Shaw and other symbolic interactionists, biographies revealed the interplay of the social and psychological in intimate and personal aspects of life (a viewpoint shared by later feminist researchers), which tended to be missed altogether or considered inconsequential in other forms of research. Becker wrote an introduction, in the second edition of Shaw's book, extolling the value and merits of the 'life history' method, and how it was essential in the development of theoretical insight into the processes by which the social order is constructed: 'The life history, more than any other technique except perhaps participant observation, can give meaning to the overworked notion of process' (Becker, 1966: xiii).

He went on to describe the distinguishing features of this method compared to other approaches:

> As opposed to these more imaginative and humanistic forms, the life history is more down to earth, more devoted to our purposes than those of the author, less concerned with artistic values than with a faithful rendering of the subject's experience and interpretation of the world he lives in. The sociologist who gathers a life history takes steps to ensure that it covers everything we want to know, that no important fact or event is slighted. That what purports to be factual squares with other available evidence and that the subject's interpretations are honestly given. The sociologist keeps the subjects oriented to the questions sociology is interested in, asks him about events that require amplification, tries to make the story told jibe with matters of official record and with material furnished by others familiar with the person, event or place being described. He keeps the game honest for us. In so doing he pursues the job from his own perspective, a perspective which emphasizes the value of the person's 'own story'. (Becker, 1966: vi)

Shaw and others in Chicago continued to produce research using the biographical method until the 1960s. Some, like Ernest Burgess, combined life history with statistical methods and saw no contradiction in doing so while also insisting that case studies were more than the equal, methodologically, of statistical approaches. In a discussion at the end of the 1966 edition of *The Jack Roller*, Burgess highlighted the contribution of personal documents:

> To many readers the chief value of this document will not consist in its contribution to an understanding of the personality of Stanley and other delinquents or of the methods of treatment of similar cases. To them its far-reaching significance will inhere in the illumination it throws on the causation, under conditions of modern city life, of criminal careers and upon the social psychology of the new type of criminal youth. (Burgess, 1966: 196)

Other sociologists in Chicago continued to use the case study method from the 1940s onwards. Many focused on deviancy, such as William Foote Whyte (1943) and his well-known work, *Street Corner Society*. There was also Becker's (1963) study *Outsiders* and David Matza's (1969) research, *Becoming Deviant*. Some of this work drew on participant observation but there were many parallels and similarities between this and biographical approaches.

A decline, but keeping the spirit alive

Yet by the 1960s the application of biographical methods outside the Chicago School of sociology had declined. For people like Becker, who lauded the approach, this was surprising, 'given the variety of scientific uses to which the life history may be put, one must wonder at the relative neglect into which it has fallen' (Becker, 1966: xvi). Becker suggested some reasons for this. Sociologists had become obsessed with abstract theory rather than the lives of people. Moreover, as social psychology separated into its own field, sociologists became preoccupied with the structural aspects of social life. Becker argued that, by the mid-1960s, sociology had become overly 'rigid' and 'professionalised' as research moved to being more 'scientific'. Positivism and quantitative research assumed a dominant position in an obsession for more 'scientific approaches' and the search for objective 'truth', via the work, among others, of Talcott Parsons.

However, sociologists such as C. Wright Mills (1970) and Peter Berger (1966) kept the older spirit alive. They sought to maintain a humanistic set of values in sociology, including the desire to create a more socially just world. C. Wright Mills (1970, originally published in 1959), in his seminal book *The Sociological Imagination*, discussed the fundamental issues of sociology by stressing that biography represents a meeting point of history, social structures and the individual agent. The social world is forged in such an interaction, and biography is the site in which struggles to build lives and to create better worlds – however problematic and contested – are played out. The 'sociological imagination', C. Wright Mills stated:

> enables us to grasp history and biography and the relations between the two within society … No social study that does not come back to the problems of biography, of history and of their intersections within a society has completed its intellectual journey. (1970: 12)

His advice to social scientists was to think about the premises underlying their assumptions about how people and society worked:

> Always keep your eyes open to the image of man – the generic notion of … human nature – which by your work you are assuming and implying; and also to the image of history – your notion of how history is being made. In a word, continually work out and revise your views of the problems of history, the problems of biography, and the problems of a social structure in which biography and history intersect. Keep your eyes open to the varieties of individuality, and to the modes of epochal change. Use what you see and what you imagine as the clues to your study of the human variety … know that many personal troubles cannot be solved merely as troubles, but must be understood in terms of public issues – and in terms of the problems of history making. Know that the human meaning of public issues must be revealed by relating them to personal troubles and to the problems of individual life. Know that the problems of social science, when adequately formulated, must include both troubles and issues, both biography and history, and the range of their intricate relations. Within that range the life of the individual and the making of society occur; and that within that range the sociological imagination has its chance to make a difference in the quality of human life in our time. (Wright Mills, 1970: 247–8)

C. Wright Mills implied, in this, a commitment to an interdisciplinary understanding of how macro-level forces and social structure find expression in the inner world and the interplay between them. Such a commitment continues to inspire researchers, including the present authors.

More recent times – and some questions

The Chicago School tradition continued, if on the margins, in the 1960s and 1970s, in the work of researchers such as Becker, Goffman, Downes, Rock, Matza and Lemert. They undertook sociological studies at the micro level, from the perspectives of phenomenology and ethnomethodology, mostly focusing, as stated, on the concepts of career, labelling and deviance. Like the work of previous generations at Chicago, they pursued a naturalistic approach: understanding behaviour in 'real' social and cultural contexts, from the perspectives of the actors. They also continued the older tradition of highlighting the plight of the powerless – the underdog – giving voice and illuminating the injustices of power. The position was neatly summarised by Becker (1967) when he argued that researchers should constantly ask themselves: 'whose side are you on'?

Norman Denzin, however, considered that there was a danger of the stories of individuals becoming a kind of narrative heroic fiction and that Stanley was simply 'a sociological version of a screen hero' (1992: 41). He continued:

> Shaw and Burgess conflated the flesh and blood subjects (the real Stanley) with the empirical subject (the youth who was interviewed) and turned him into an analytic, ideal type, the classic inner city delinquent. He then became a complex first and second order textual production. Stanley and Clifford Shaw … cannot be uncoupled, for to take Shaw (and Burgess) out of the picture is to leave only an empty story of Stanley. There is no Stanley without the investigative tale told by these two sociological experts. The natural history, life history method permitted the illusion to be sustained: that the real Stanley, and the real Stanley's experiences, had been captured. (Denzin, 1992: 41)

There are glimpses here of contemporary debates, echoing those in oral history, surrounding 'auto/biography' and the need to bring the researcher, and issues of power as well as of the complexities of representation, into an understanding of the construction of biographical accounts. A simplistic 'realism' was increasingly challenged. But Denzin was no enemy of biographical research either and from the 1970s became a prolific writer on qualitative research, interpretativism and biography. He explained that:

> The biographical method rests on subjective and intersubjectively gained knowledge and understandings of the life experiences of individuals, including one's own life. Such understandings rest on an interpretative process that leads one to enter into the emotional life of another. Interpretation, the act of interpreting and making sense out of something, creates the conditions for understanding, which involves being able to grasp the meanings of an interpreted experience for another individual. Understanding is an intersubjective, emotional experience. Its goal is to build sharable understandings of the life experiences of another. (Denzin, 1989b: 28)

Denzin elaborated, in this context, on the importance of 'turning point moments' or 'epiphanies' in life histories. He defined 'the biographical method as the studied use and collection of life documents that describe turning-point moments' (1989b: 69).

Epiphanies are 'interactional moments and experiences which leave marks on people's lives. In them, personal character is manifested. They are often moments of crisis which alter the fundamental meaning and structures in a person's life. Their effects may be positive or negative' (1989b: 70). The notion and place of epiphanies in learners' lives has a strong contemporary resonance in research on adult students in higher education (Merrill, 1999; West, 1996).

Enter feminism

By the late 1960s, second wave feminism was proving influential in the academy, particularly in the United Kingdom and North America but also in the French-speaking world (see Ollagnier, 2007). Feminism looked back to the Chicago School but also to the later work of C. Wright Mills (1970). It was concerned with the pervasive influence of gender in people's lives, its positioning and constructing subjects in particular ways, and how this tended to marginalise the lived experiences of women. Feminism and feminist research methods derived from the commitment to giving voice to women previously hidden in social science research or his-story. Social science departments in universities were dominated by male academics and the research topics reflected this in the choice of male factory workers, youth cultures and boys, as well as male pupils in schools.

Feminist academics sought to redress the imbalance. Biographical approaches were deemed highly appropriate to the task: 'Biographical work has always been an important part of the women's movement because it draws women out of obscurity, repairs the historical record, and provides an opportunity for the woman reader and writer to identify with the subject' (Reinharz, 1992: 126). In the UK, Anna Pollert's (1981) sociological study of working-class women working at a cigarette factory in Bristol, and Angela McRobbie and Jenny Garber's (1976) of girls and youth cultures were early biographical studies which sought to bring particular women out of invisibility.

Feminism encompassed a critical perspective that challenged some of the ideas of conventional research, as patriarchal and phallocentric: for treating interviewees as subordinates and for promoting relationships characterised by hierarchy. In contrast, feminist researchers sought to build equal relationships between interviewers and interviewees. Ann Oakley (1981) argued that a biographical interview should be a two-way process – a conversation – in which the interviewer also answers questions asked by the interviewee about the self. The process of interviewing became central to the method, as we explore further in Chapter 7.

Feminists developed the principle that research and interviewing should not exploit the interviewee but seek to empower her. Likewise, the process was a self-learning experience for the interviewer, as Shulamit Reinharz asserted: 'Once the project begins, a circular process ensues: the woman doing the study learns about herself as well as about the woman she is studying' (1992: 127). Both American (Reinharz) and UK feminists (for example, Oakley, Stanley) have been influential in the establishment of biographical methodology. Women's stories highlighted their oppression in society but also provided a means to transform women's lives, illustrating how individual problems are also collective ones (Skeggs, 1997). Like C. Wright Mills, feminists argued that the 'personal is political'. For Liz Stanley and Sue Wise, 'a feminist social science should begin with the recognition that "the personal", direct experience, underlies all behaviours and action' (1993: 164). The influence of these ideas was to find expression in research with other and diverse marginalised groups (Plummer, 2001).

Feminist biographical research often revealed not only issues of gender inequality and oppression but also their interaction with other forms of inequality, such as class and race. Amrit Wilson's moving book (*Finding a Voice*, 1978) on Asian women was an early British example, highlighting how black women's lives were not only racialised but also gendered and classed. At the end of her book, Wilson reflected on her work and why she wrote it:

> Because I felt that Asian women had so much to tell, I wanted to write a book in which they could express their opinions and feelings. There have been things written about Asian women which show them always as a group who can't speak for themselves. They were just treated as objects – nothing more. That they have any feelings about their own lives or that they can analyse their own lives never comes up. I wanted to show how Asian women are capable of speaking for themselves. (Wilson, 1978: 166)

In the USA, bell hooks and other black feminists were influential in criticising the feminism of white feminists, arguing that their theories and writings did not recognise the experiences and voices of being black and female. Another important American group of feminists in the late 1980s was the Personal Narratives Group. Using an interpretative approach, they saw an important aim of research was to gain enhanced understanding from stories. This was seen as a complex process in which women may get confused, even lie and get things wrong. Yet this was also a kind of truth and the task of the interpreter was to understand why this might be so and to what purpose, within the social and personal landscapes of women's lives, past and present. The group sought to discuss the complex meaning of truth in their study *Interpreting Women's Lives* (Personal Narratives Group, 1989).

Research, under the influence of feminism, became increasingly presented and celebrated as a participatory enterprise, not least in the practices of collective biography. The focus could be on processes of subjectivation in women's lives, including in educational contexts, and how people may learn to separate mind from body as well as how other aspects of an external order are imposed. But this can be resisted too, via story telling, written and spoken, producing collective webs of experience to challenge subjectivication. Some of this collective biography draws on the theoretical work of Judith Butler concerning the discursive construction of subjectivity through the dominant narratives of a culture and resistance to them (Butler, 1997; Davies and Gannon, 2006). The assumptions we make about the subject, and subjectivity, in biographical research, remains a major issue.

A participatory ethos, shaped by feminism, has also characterised the use of biographical research in the study of adult and lifelong learning (Armstrong, 1998). Much European work (Bron, Edwards, Merrill) initially focused on women's experience – especially working-class women – of studying in higher education. The research placed the subjects of enquiry as central to the research process, arguing for their voices to be taken into account in relation to policy decisions and adult education. Both Arlene McClaren (1985) and Rosalind Edwards (1993), as ex-mature students themselves, drew on their biographies and included the researcher's self in their studies of mature women students in universities. Their work explored how women students manage in juggling different life roles, with Edwards' study focusing on the relationship between family and education. Merrill (1999), as noted, was interested in women and class, using biographies to illustrate the inter-relationship between private and public lives, the dialectics of agency and structure and the linking of individual biographies to the collective.

Auto/biography

Feminists in the 1980s argued that researchers persistently refuse to interrogate how they generate their stories, echoing arguments in oral history. There was a presumption, as in the natural sciences, that theories and methods neutralise personal and political influences. Conventional detachment and distance were described as a 'fetish', a 'God trick … that mode of seeing that pretends to offer a vision that is from everywhere and nowhere, equally and fully' (Haraway, 1988: 584). Such tricks presented fictions of the 'truth' while denying the interests, privilege and power of the researcher. Michelle Fine (1992) argued for the reflexive and self-reflexive potential of experience, in which the knower is part of the matrix of what is known, and where the researcher needs to ask her/himself in what way has s/he grown in, and shaped the processes of research. The term 'auto/biography' was coined to draw attention to the inter-relationship between the constructions of one's own life though autobiography and the construction of the life of another through biography. The implication is that we cannot write stories about ourselves without making reference to and hence constructing others' lives and selves, and those constructions we make of others in writing their life histories contain and reflect our own histories and social and cultural locations as well as psychologies. A rich seam of explicitly auto/biographical work has emerged over the last two decades (Miller, 2007; Stanley, 1992; Steedman, 1986; West, 1996).

Critical theory and post-structuralism

There have been other influences in the development of biographical research. Critical theory has played a role in biographical approaches within sociology, decades after its establishment at the University of Frankfurt during the 1920s. Some key players have been Theodor Adorno, Max Horkheimer and Herbert Marcuse who drew on earlier critical theorists such as Karl Marx, G.W.F. Hegel and Immanuel Kant, but rejected, for example, the idea of economic determinism. A key purpose of research for critical theorists was to use it to highlight inequalities and oppression and, through agency, transform society. Research was seen as a political act: 'Thus critical researchers enter into an investigation with their assumptions on the table, so no one is confused concerning the epistemological and political baggage they bring with them to the research site' (Kincheloe and McLaren, 2003: 453). As Lincoln and Denzin explain:

> The critique and concern of the critical theorists has been an effort to design a pedagogy of resistance within communities of difference. The pedagogy of resistance, of taking back 'voice', of reclaiming narrative for one's own rather than adapting to the narratives of a dominant majority, was most explicitly laid out by Paulo Freire in his work with adults in Brazil. (2003: 625–6)

The Centre for Contemporary Cultural Studies at the University of Birmingham in England, during the 1970s and 1980s, undertook ethnographic/biographical research from a critical perspective. Paul Willis' classic study, *Learning to Labour: How Working Class Kids get Working Class Jobs* (1977), epitomised the orientation of the Centre. In Denmark, in recent years, biographical methods have been used in the study of working life and learning, using critical theory, alongside social psychology and psychoanalysis (Salling Olesen, 2007a, 2007b; Weber, 2007).

Post-structuralism's prime focus has been on language and discourse and how these serve to position people and to construct who they are and how they think about themselves. We perceive the world, and ourselves, through the eye of language, which is far from neutral. Post-structuralists, including many feminists, have encouraged an interrogation of the role of language, illustrated in the work of Patti Lather (1991), David Jackson (1990) and the feminist Liz Stanley (1992) as well as Judith Butler (1997). Reality and meaning are always linked to other texts and meaning. 'Social science is no longer a straightforward description of reality out there; instead, the terms used become discussed, elaborated upon and contested' (Plummer, 2001: 198).

Yet, as Plummer has noted (2001), there can be a bleakness and pessimism at the heart of some post-structuralist perceptions of biographical approaches and humanistic aspirations. Michel Foucault could be depressingly cynical about the value of human stories: lives, in his perspective, are shaped by power/knowledge formations about which the people involved may have little understanding. Yet Plummer asserts – and this is a view we share – if language and symbolic communication are central to being human, we also have the capacity for reflexivity – for learning – and greater self-awareness, including how power/knowledge, mediated through language, can shape us to the core (2001: 262). A humanistic project – in the sense of taking human beings and their experiences as a base line – remains possible, however fractured and problematic this might be.

Psychology

Psychology, at least in its mainstream guises, has sometimes inoculated itself against this kind of philosophical turmoil by positioning the discipline as more of a natural science. Psychologists, as Louis Smith (1998) noted, in consequence, have had difficulty with biography as a research method. Yet there has always been a subsidiary strand influenced by psychoanalysis and feminism and the need for more humanistic and critical perspectives. Freud of course used case study biographies – as with Little Hans and 'Dora' – to develop his theories on the role of the dynamic unconscious (of what cannot be thought or said and its place in human action) and of sexual repression in human life and its consequences (Freud, 1977). Moreover, Freud used the biographical form to compose biographies of important creative and historical figures such as Leonardo De Vinci (Freud, 1910/1963). Leon Edel (1985) also employed psychoanalytic perspectives for probing issues of interpretation and meaning in a number of biographies.

There have been some psychologists who sought a middle ground. Gordon Allport (1937) produced a series of works on the use of personal documents in psychology. He undertook a study of Jenny (Allport, 1964), via a collection of letters she wrote to her son and daughter-in-law. These provide 'vivid, troubling, introspective accounts of both her life as a working woman and her mental states', as a basis for considering a number of competing theories to interpret the letters (Smith, 1994: 297). An 'eclectic' emphasis on biology, family and social circumstances alongside biography appears, Smith notes, from time to time in psychology, at least on its margins. Eric Erickson (1959, 1963a, 1963b) used life writing as a way of exploring developmental stages in human beings, and other psychologists have used biography to clarify their hypotheses, as in the work of Hudson (1966). The desire to use biographical and narrative material to build a more humanistic form of psychology has never entirely disappeared (Smith, 1994).

Feminist psychologists, especially, have sought to ensure that the discipline remembered the whole people, and social contexts, easily neglected in the predilection for experimental methods. For many mainstream psychologists, the experimental laboratory was celebrated because it was 'sterile, neutral, and fully appropriate for eliciting "objective" phenomena while holding the "noise" of social context and background variables silent' (Fine and Gordon, 1992: 11). Gender could be represented as 'noise' in many social psychology studies. Yet, feminist psychologists argued, women were noisy because their data did not neatly conform to the male patterns (or universal laws) that tended to dominate the mainstream. Such work was often built on a lack of trust, longevity and connection in research: female subjects, so the argument proceeded, were turned into the objects of the experimenter. An alternative critical set of feminist voices found space, and there was great sympathy for narrative and biographical approaches. These alternative traditions are represented, for instance, by Carol Gilligan's (1982) *In a Different Voice,* Mary Field Belenky et al.'s (1997) *Women's Ways of Knowing* and various studies of Hispanic, black and lesbian women (Fine, 1992). Subjects, and the meanings they gave to experience, were placed more at the centre of this kind of psychology, in opposition to the mainstream (or 'male-stream') tendency to flatten, de-gender and depoliticise understanding.

Some feminist psychologists contributed to the alternative collective biographical movement by exploring the body and sexuality, calling on members of a group to write down memories of past events that focus on this physical area. Stories can then be discussed, reassessed and reworked on a group basis. Frigga Haug and colleagues (1987), for example, in Germany, were interested in the therapeutic outcomes of their work by building a greater capacity to resist oppressive and often masculinist versions of femininity and the body.

Education and the study of adult learning

Biographical methodologies have secured a place in the study of education, albeit on the margins. There is a tradition of using life history and biography in the study of the subjective experiences of being a teacher in the United Kingdom (Goodson, 1992; Goodson and Sykes, 2001; Woods, 1993). Ivor Goodson (1994) has argued that teachers' life experience and careers shape their vision of teaching and how this is to be approached, complementing those methods that are mainly concerned with the analysis of interactions in the classroom. The lifeworld and life history of the teacher, away from school, have a direct impact on teaching and what s/he seeks to achieve. In this perspective, teachers are agents in the building of knowledge and the development of a repertoire of responses, however prescribed.

Biographical researchers have also worked among marginalised groups in educational settings, for instance, among those with learning disabilities. This is partly about challenging the negative labelling of people and seeking to give them a voice. Jan Walmsley (2006) has mapped some of this work but also its difficulties, not least when researching with those who may lack basic literacy and whose standpoints have been so neglected in the research literature that orientation is difficult, such as using one's own knowledge to generate questions. The introductory letter, the return of the transcript for correction, the provision of a finished account are all rendered problematic. Yet Walmsley, among others, has described how such difficulties can be negotiated, although the problem of voice, and whose voice is represented, has been an issue.

The study of adult learning and education was long dominated by quantitative surveys (for example, Woodley et al., 1987). One challenge to this came from feminist work on women's experiences of higher education (e.g. Edwards, 1993; McClaren, 1985). Both McClaren and Edwards, as noted above, had been mature women students and brought the personal directly into their texts. By the early 1990s, the proportion of papers at SCUTREA (the Standing Conference of University Teachers and Researchers in the Education of Adults, which is Britain's pre-eminent professional network for researchers in the field of adult and lifelong learning) concerned with life stories, narratives, transformations of selves and struggles over identity, located in socio-cultural contexts, was increasing. In 1988, only two papers had used life history – broadly defined – as an alternative method (Armstrong, 1998), but this was to become a mainstream preoccupation in the 1990s. It was not just a British phenomenon, either, as evidenced in the number of papers devoted to life history and auto/biography in meetings such as the North American Adult Education Research Conference (AERC) (see e.g. Sork et al., 2000). The trend has continued (see West et al., 2001).

The use of biographical approaches in the study of adult learning in France has a well-established history, shaped by the work of Pierre Dominicé (Switzerland), Guy Villers (Belgium) and Gaston Pineau (a Canadian living in France): 'Through their dialogue, respective life trajectories and fields of interest they created and lent solidarity to a body of thought which has become a reference in the matter of life history in adult education' (Ollagnier, 2002: 274). Adult education and life histories became a strong movement and in 1990 a French research network was established: the Association Internationale des Histoires de Vie en Formation (ASIHVIF) (International Association for Life History in Education). In Germany, there is a strong tradition of biographical research in sociology and education, although it is outside the sociological mainstream (Apitzsch and Inowlocki, 2000). Interestingly, there have been major debates in Germany, because of the Nazi era, which include concern about overly naive readings of biographical accounts. Biographies and story telling need always to be critically examined in the light of tendencies towards evasion, silence, and even lies, in people's stories, especially in relation to difficult times (Fischer-Rosenthal, 1995; Rosenthal, 1993).

Within adult education, the work of Peter Alheit has been prominent and influential among adult education researchers across Europe. He has explored how the individualisation of society has resulted in a new paradigm of learning, centred on the necessity of composing biographies. Yet this has to be accomplished in circumstances where people may feel what happens to them is often outside their control, whatever the rhetoric to the contrary (Alheit, 1993; Alheit and Dausien, 2007). The work of Ulrich Oevermann has likewise been important in bringing therapeutic insights to education and life histories in social conditions of flux, unpredictability and emotional strain (see Alheit and Dausien, 2007). The German tradition in life histories has tended, however, towards a more 'scientific' and less subjectivist stance, influenced by 19th-century German philosophers and more recently the work of Fritz Schutze (1992) and Gabriele Rosenthal (2004). Feminism has tended to be more marginal.

Looking forward

In the next chapter, we map more of the contemporary field of biographical research, which has increased in scope and complexity since the early days of oral history or the Chicago School. In Chapter 4, we return to some philosophical and theoretical issues touched on in the present chapter. If chronicling lived experience, however problematic, matters to biographical researchers, theory matters greatly too.

Key points

- Story telling has been important for centuries as a means of communicating intra- and intergenerationally.
- Oral historians have used stories as a means of giving voice to marginalised groups, as part of a broader, egalitarian social purpose. There is nowadays a more sophisticated debate about the problems of doing this.
- The Chicago School of sociology has been important in the development of biographical methods, not least in seeking to ground an understanding of social processes in the experiences of the people at their heart.

(Continued)

(Continued)

- Feminism has had a major influence in terms of both the focus on and in developing and interrogating the processes of biographical research.
- Biographical methods have been more marginal in psychology and education, but there have been strong subsidiary strands.

FURTHER READING

Bulmer, M. (1984) *The Chicago School of Sociology: Institutionalisation, Diversity and the Rise of Sociological Research*. Chicago: University of Chicago Press.

Chamberlayne, P., Bornat, J. and Wengraf, T. (2000) (eds) *The Turn to Biographical Methods in Social Science*. London: Routledge.

Fine, M. (1992) *Disruptive Voices. The Possibilities of Feminist Research*. Michigan: Michigan University Press.

Perks, R. and Thomson, A. (2006) (eds) *Oral History Reader* (2nd edn). London: Routledge.

DISCUSSION QUESTIONS

1. To what extent do you think oral testimony, oral history and biography should be considered a political project?

2. To what degree do you think ethnographic studies like Shaw's *The Jack Roller* transform life histories into fiction, as Denzin (1992) states, making them a 'sociological version of a screen hero'?

ACTIVITIES

1. Talk to someone from an older generation – a relative, parent, etc. – and ask them about their past life and any historical events which they can remember.
2. Reflect on your life history – how has history played out in your time/life, for example, war, fundamentalism, etc.?
3. Consider Thomas and Znaniecki: *The Polish Peasant in Europe and America*. Read the extract below taken from the conclusion of their book, consisting of their analysis of Wladek's biography, and consider the questions posed at the end.

(Continued)

(Continued)

We have determined analytically in the notes the most important facts in Wladek's personal evolution, and we add at this point a brief synthesis of this evolution.

In so far as his temperamental background is concerned, Wladek is perfectly normal, in the sense that there is neither a striking lack nor a striking excess of any temperamental attitude. His organism is healthy without being particularly powerful, and he shows great physical endurance. His sexual impulses are rather intense but never overwhelming, and are subordinated without difficulty to the demands of practical life. Like the average members of his class he uses alcohol freely, but no permanently disorganizing biological effects are noticeable in his behaviour. And we find in his temperament neither any exceptional buoyancy which would push him to search continually for new experiences in any one line nor any exceptional depression that would lead to a too great stability ... His intellectual abilities are above the average, as is shown by the facility with which he learns in school and in the army and by the clever way in which he handles the superficial notions about the world and life which he gained from his unsystematic reading and occasional intercourse with more instructed people, and by his ability to work out general ideas about social conditions on the ground of his experiences and observations. His intellectual limitations are simply due to the lack of systematic training in theoretic thinking, not to insufficient inborn capacity ...

Certain social conditions being given, Wladek's evolution would depend on his attitudes toward the social values constituting these conditions, and vice versa, given certain attitudes toward social values, the social conditions in which he found himself would determine his evolution. The relative importance of different personal attitudes on the one hand, and of different social values on the other hand, may vary within wide limits, and in trying to reconstruct synthetically his personality we must determine first of all the attitudes and conditions which played the greatest part in his evolution, and characterize his type in terms of these...

The most important attitude – or rather, set of attitudes – by which Wladek's evolution is conditioned is the 'social instinct'. He is always completely and exclusively dependent upon society. Even if at moments he isolates himself voluntarily, it is either only a temporary reaction to some rebuke or the desire to attract attention by withdrawing to the background. (1958: 2227–9)

- How might biographical interpretation and analysis have changed since this early biographical work? (Read an extract from a recent text.)
- What did you think about the language in this extract?

3
Mapping the Contemporary Uses of Biographical Research

Anyone who has ever felt left out, ignored, or powerless has the beginnings of an understanding of the feminist and minority perspectives that have arisen in recent decades with great vigour and anger in the field of biography and autobiography. (Louis Smith, 1998: 210)

Overview

In this chapter:

- We highlight that mapping the field is complex, encompassing as it does many disciplines and topics.
- We consider how biographies are sites of conflict between different versions of lives, shaped by ideological climates, cultures, available discourses, but also resistance.
- We see how biographical researchers often work with marginalised groups in ways that can challenge dominant stories in what has been called the 'democratisation of society'.
- We examine the ways in which biographical research encourages interdisciplinarity.

All biographers now

Biography has greatly increased in popularity as a research method in the academy, as noted in the first two chapters. Some use the method, as Louis Smith (1998) suggests, vigorously, and even angrily, as part of a quasi-political project. Others are more content or methodologically driven. Biography and autobiography appear as a key frame through which we wrestle with diverse issues of meaning, power and politics, and try to understand history and selfhood. While Chapter 2 looked at the history of biographical methods, this chapter moves on to map its uses today, which includes how the past continues to shape present research. The influence of the Chicago School and feminism remains strong. Debates on the nature of truth, whose voice and story is being heard, the role of dominant stories and ideology in shaping individual narratives, and the relationship between immediacy and memory, all noted in the last chapter, continue energetically.

Moving to particulars

Biographical research remains a site of struggle over what it is to know and represent subjects – and the status of their stories – and any map of the territory has to encompass diverse epistemological and representational issues (Andrews, 2007). Biographical statements can be seen to emanate from an interaction between the subject and author of a biography, and an audience and the ideological environment they inhabit, including the narrative resources available. Julia Swindells (1995) notes that this perspective helps demystify the notion of biography and autobiography as stand-alone testimonies of individuals, separate from their relationship to the social world and its ideological disputes. We move instead to the idea of biography as interplay between culture, power and available narrative resources, on the one hand, and individual lives and struggles for voice and story, on the other. The feminist movement is a pre-eminent example of how women insisted on the significance of gender in human relationships and challenged the naive conflation of male subjectivity and human identity. Women resisted assignment by others, seeking, instead, to be subjects in discourse rather than objects positioned by it (Smith, 1987). Implicit here is the notion that we rarely make biographies in conditions of our own choosing (Chamberlayne et al., 2000).

Mapping the territory

How best then to map a diverse and extensive terrain, and in sufficient breadth as well as depth, given that the development of biographical methods encompasses many disciplines and topics? These methods have been adopted or rediscovered in diverse disciplines, finding especially fertile ground in gender studies and in researching the experiences of marginalised peoples. They are there too, if more marginal, in disciplines like medicine or psychology, encompassing research on doctors, patients and the stories they tell (Greenhalgh and Hurwitz, 1998; West, 2001).

Obviously, there is insufficient space to map everything, but, like a decent guidebook, we seek to offer glimpses of a rich, vibrant and changing terrain. We draw on the work of internationally known researchers and in certain places (including Chapter 5), use our own work. We have been selective and have chosen research to exemplify a number of different characteristics of the field and how, if biography is the product of a constantly changing, post- or late modern culture, researchers themselves often focus on change processes, including migration and political upheaval. There is concern too with caring and carers, families and family life, professionals and their work and learning, as well as with auto/biography. We exploit our membership of various research communities: education and lifelong learning; health care and medicine; psychotherapy; sociology; and gender studies. Our contrasting academic biographies – sociology, history and education, in Barbara's case; history, education, psychology and psychotherapy, in Linden's – are helpful in the mapping – as is collaboration with colleagues in international sociological and educational research networks (including the International Sociological Association Biography Network and the European Society for Research on the Education of Adults (ESREA) Life History and Biography Network). Examples are drawn from sociology, social policy, health studies, education and research into the professions. We pay relatively little attention to literary perspectives or narrative theory in research but here too lies vibrant territory (Baena, 2007; Swindells, 1995).

Biographical research in sociology and social policy

Biographical research in sociology and social policy is applied to diverse social institutions and change processes, in various countries and cultural contexts. Some studies take a broad comparative sweep, investigating concepts such as individuation, risk and reflexivity, and responses to economic change across different social groups. There have been a number of major collaborative European research projects to this end. Prue Chamberlayne, Antonella Spanò and colleagues have chronicled and analysed responses to economic change across a number of different categories of people, such as unqualified youth, unemployed graduates, ex-traditional workers, the early retired, single parents and ethnic minority groups (Chamberlayne and Spanò, 2000). Their work illuminates the importance of cultural location in shaping people's experiences and the stories they tell. There can be a strong relationship between the cultures in which individuals are embedded and their responses, for instance, to social, political and economic dislocation. Biographical research places people in context.

'Rita' serves as a detailed case study. She comes from Naples and inhabits a world where aspects of a 'pre-modern' culture continue to hold sway and there is a lack of rigid separation between public and private spheres, alongside a persistence of traditional kinship and friendship networks. This makes it easier, as the researchers document, for her to adjust to economic change and 'the end of industrial life' (Chamberlayne and Spanò, 2000: 333). 'Tony', on the other hand, from East London, finds processes of adaptation more difficult. Factors such as a separation between 'work' and family, as well as the 'individualisation' of responsibility in English culture, become obstacles to accommodating to economic deregulation. The researchers weave threads between the detail of lives – including their gendered aspects – and the wider social, cultural and economic context.

> **Case study**
>
> Rita's identification with 'her' factory appears very clearly in her lived life. The central axis in her life is work, but not in the sense of the contemporary 'career' woman who sacrifices family in the name of work … While she devotes herself body and soul to the factory, the fruits of being 'a good worker' are dedicated to the family … [For Tony] it is the loss of the meaning of work which is most painful and which he constantly associated with his illness … what was
>
> *(Continued)*

(Continued)

the point of being conscientious and hard-working when, at the end of the day, all you could see was the possibility of losing your job? ...

For both Tony and Rita, the key problem has been their incapacity to tolerate 'modernised' and impersonal contexts at work ... for Rita with modern managerialism, for Tony with deregulation. While they both present themselves as betrayed and angry, there are great differences in their responses. For Rita, who has in fact made a happy transition into the postmodern world, her portrayal of herself as betrayed serves to hide her own betrayal to the firm, her own metamorphosis from a 'good worker' to happy mother and worker outside the firm. Tony ... is still involved in the painful experience of severance ... re-orientation is easier for Rita ... between 'old' and 'new' lifeworlds. (Chamberlayne and Spanò, 2000: 330–2)

Research like this illustrates the importance of detail in understanding lives and the interplay of the macro and micro in change processes. A dialectic of history and individuality, location and response, is strong in contrast to that of individuality in isolation. The detail matters but generalisation can be difficult when viewed through such a biographical lens. The personal and cultural resources available to Rita, for instance, cannot simply be applied to the whole of southern Italy, since there are 'more fully industrialised settings', which evoke different responses to change processes. Tony too is shaped by a specific culture – a local 'social democratic collectivism' – which may not apply equally across the diversity of East London. Questions of how we move from the particular to the general are, as noted, central to biographical and other forms of qualitative enquiry. This is an issue we take up later in the book.

Eastern Europe

Other studies have documented and theorised the impact and meaning of large-scale political change, in specific social and cultural contexts, across diverse biographies. This includes research on the upheavals in Eastern Europe at the end of the last century. The research raises many questions about the nature and function of memory and can challenge the simplistic idea of dramatic change evoking memory's liberation (Andrews, 2000). It can also highlight the recurring issue of how the researcher's biography and values can shape the construction of a text (Andrews, 2007).

Researchers have noted, for example, using a collection of life stories from East Germany, how people were 'scrambling to construct new and acceptable identities for themselves, ones which will be compatible with the changed world in which they live' (Andrews, 2000: 181). But this is no simple matter of whether people remember their past, but rather which past to remember. The present can, in fact, render people speechless about the past, mirroring, in a paradoxical, troubling way, features of the Communist period.

> **Case study**
>
> Ruth Reinecke is an actress at the Maxim Gorki Repertoire Theatre in Berlin and had been an activist in the movement to bring the wall down. But she describes this time of her life as difficult to analyse. The opening of the wall would have massive implications for the GDR but also her own sense of identity:
>
> > 'When the wall was opened, suddenly another world existed, which I did not know, which I would have to live in, whether I wanted to or not. There was of course a great curiosity to explore the world, this still exists. On the other hand, I had the fear somehow whether I would be capable of making this new world ... my own ... Maybe there was also some fear that I could not stay anymore the same person I had been so far'. (Andrews, 2000: 182)

Questions of 'which past to remember and what story to tell?' indicate how change processes can replace 'one form of speechlessness with another' (Andrews, 2000: 192). And of how triumphalist accounts of liberation from oppression can be disturbingly partial as well as ideologically driven (Andrews, 2007). Past and memory are shaped by the present, the present by the past, while new situations bring their own struggles for voice. Telling stories can be a profoundly political yet troubling act, without a final end.

Molly Andrews has returned to her earlier work on Eastern Europe, and elsewhere, to interrogate her role in constructing the lives of others (Andrews, 2007).

> When I look back on the early stages of this research, I see that in some ways I was trying to save, if not socialism as it was practised, then at least its founding principles. This is not surprising given my preoccupations of the previous years and my own political leanings. I found solace in terms like 'really existing socialism' which, from my perspective, mediated the blows for the principles of socialism. Following the events of 1989, Frida, who I had originally met through my project on lifetime socialist activists in Britain, wrote to me:
>
> Can you imagine turning your back on the Ninth Symphony just because it has been badly performed? Well, I can't! What is great and good and beautiful does not turn out to be paltry and rotten because the wrong people got hold of it and misinterpreted it. (Andrews, 2007: 123)

Andrews graphically writes of how biographical research and interrogating stories is always and inevitably an incomplete, provisional process and of the need to consider, constantly, how our own positioning, needs and trajectory affect what we hear and report. Self-awareness, she insists, has to be at the heart of our work.

Truth and reconciliation

Andrews' research has also encompassed the work of the Truth and Reconciliation Commission (TRC) in South Africa (Andrews, 2007). She poses a series of questions about using biographies in a context that is seen, at least in the eyes of the outside world, as a pre-eminent example of reconciliation and healing. She poses questions of how the agenda of giving birth to a new South Africa affected the stories told, as well as the problematic relationship between telling and healing. Is, she asks, the process of restorying always and inevitably a psychological liberation? In a similar vein, she questions the methodology used in the TRC in some detail. She describes how the research instrument – the statement protocol – could be a blunt instrument and how peoples' stories could be very guided: 'the contours of the stories selected for public testimony were heavily influenced by what the TRC considered relevant' (Andrews, 2007: 158). She documents the ambivalent feelings of some narrators towards the process: how giving testimony might exacerbate broken and devastating feelings, physical and psychological, while at the same time providing some strength and a means to regain personal dignity. Andrews reveals how 'giving voice', which bio-graphical researchers frequently use to justify their work, can be a complicated process, not least ethically, when individual voices are aggregated with diverse others in ways that might leave individuals feeling dispossessed. Andrews concludes by reference to what we as researchers need to do:

> It seems that as researchers we must re-train ourselves; how can we improve our ability to really listen, to entertain the idea that there is, just possibly, a story that we haven't anticipated, maybe one that contradicts our expectations? Our work demands that we develop greater sensitivity to the presence of our own voice. This requires a self-awareness, even humility at times, which we might not always have. (Andrews, 2007: 169)

Andrews' work raises, once more, important questions about truth, representation and memory as well as regarding the role of the researcher. Her writing also exem-plifies the interdisciplinary imperative within biographical research: her first degree was in political science and her PhD in psychology and she draws on his-tory and sociology in her work. She writes that biographical research allows her to explore the common ground between disciplines, because 'personal stories know no disciplinary boundaries' (Andrews, 2007: 10). Such a perspective, as will be illustrated, informs the work of many biographical researchers. We return to inter-disciplinarity below.

Caring, carers and families

Carers and 'cultures of care' have also been a topic for biographical research (Chamberlayne et al., 2000, 2004). A study of two groups of carers in North and East London used 24 interviews to encourage a sample of carers to talk about caring experiences and the support received from various agencies (Jones and Rupp, 2000). The researchers used the 'biographical interpretative method' (see Chapter 6), not-ing the interplay of cultural, familial and intimate worlds in shaping stories and how these could change over time. Neither the told story nor the interviewees' behaviour as carers can be understood, they suggest, without dynamic and changing biographical knowledge of the people concerned and their evolving relationship to families and cultural contexts. Cultural awareness and an understanding of changing personal circumstances can be essential in biographical research.

'Mrs Rajan' is a case study of a woman brought up in an Indian family following strictly religious and cultural rules. After migration to Britain, she felt the rules were perpetually questioned or dismissed as invalid. She experienced minimal support from agencies outside her minority cultural network, while caring for a disabled son. Revealingly, Mrs Rajan talked of not fulfilling the most important duties of an Indian wife. However, on giving birth to a healthy son, Mrs Rajan felt her duty was done and she was able, more assertively, to reject inappropriate family interference and accept professional help. Her sense of identity and agency shifted. The detail generated in the study, and its sensitive and systematic interpretation, illuminates how actions and meanings are to be understood within a whole, yet changing culturally situated life. Other forms of research can get nowhere near these dynamics.

Case study

Mrs Rajan represents a 'carer type' dominated by the experience of migration and conflicting norms and role expectations. Cultural awareness and sensitivity would have been required by social workers, not least in relation to her feelings, with her first child, that she had not fulfilled the duties of an Indian wife. She had suffered from the absence of family support but was not able to seek help from external agencies.

Mrs Rajan struggled to say anything about the painful experiences before the birth of her second son but was 'now able to narrate fluently: an expansive narrative covering her life *after* the birth of her second son consists of about half the interview text'. By what is termed careful 'thematic field analysis', the researchers are able to show 'a mother imprisoned in the home by alien cultural and family traditions'. They are also able to show how story telling in the present will be affected by transformational experiences, in this case, the birth of a second son (Jones and Rupp, 2000: 280, 281, 286–8).

Families and pearls

Families and changing family structures have been of great interest to biographical researchers. Some have explored what they term different 'mentalities' – ways of thinking about and experiencing the world – among what seem to be similar family groups involved in processes of migration. Daniel Bertaux and Catherine Delcroix (2000) offer one example of sociologically informed biographical research on 'mentalities', across several generations of immigrant families in France. They are interested in people belonging to 'common formations' – a sub-society or a migration flow – within which individual histories are embedded. Families are perceived as microcosms – small worlds – yet potentially containing a 'sociological pearl', which can illuminate a thousand cases (Bertaux and Delcroix, 2000: 83). Such a perspective illustrates what can be differing emphases in biographical research, shaped by disciplinary backgrounds. Sociologists, for example, more so than psychologists, may focus on building social types, rather than individual cases (Plummer, 2001).

Bertaux and Delcroix (2000) concentrate on immigrant families in Toulouse, France and how they cope with the precarious conditions of life in a deprived urban area. Thirty families – mostly immigrant families from the Maghreb – provide case histories of living in a low-rent housing estate. Practically all the fathers had been workers in construction or similar industries and many were still employed in those trades. What struck the researchers were differences between households in styles of educating children. The urban environment of the project was rough: some parents were anxious to keep their children indoors when out of school; others allowed their children to participate in a range of activities organised by schools and other associations.

The differences in family sub-cultures, and associated mentalities, were thought, at first, to result from different value systems, but on closer inspection income seemed to make a difference between 'closed' or more 'open' responses to the estate. These issues were discussed with the families concerned – in dialogue – and families reported that they changed as income improved. Biographical methods allow for testing and retesting hypotheses, over time, and for thinking about these with the people concerned.

There is research too on the impact of changing family structures on older family members (Bornat et al., 2000). How do older people talk about and make use of family break-up and 'reconstitution'? Joanna Bornat and colleagues make clear how people can account for their personal feelings and experience by reference to public debate and moralising on the state of the family. We see once more how the wider culture and its discourses intrude into individual narratives. Many older people experience feelings of shame and personal failure in the light of ideological climates: where responsibility for family breakdown is considered a consequence of individual failure or moral deficiency, rather than economic or socio-cultural change. We cannot understand the stories of family members without reference to the ideological climate and how people interact with this, in the light of their experience.

Family myths and even pathology can find expression across the generations. John Byng-Hall (1990), a psychotherapist who uses biographical perspectives, describes how family legends can perpetually shape a family's image of itself. He illustrates this by reference to a family that came to him because of concern over a child's sexual identity. In fact, concerns over sexual identity were a major intergenerational theme: on one side of the family, a grandmother had been the eldest child, followed by two younger brothers. All the same, her parents were so disappointed in her for being a girl that they disinherited her and cut her off. This affected her daughter and the latter's interactions with her children, in turn. Terrible events and tragedies may be re-enacted by children, across the generations. Ruth Finnegan (2006) has written of how all families have myths: for instance, around courtship and love at first sight ('just like her mother') or around tests between competing suitors (or in Linden's case, the loss of family status, finding expression in the narrative of restoration, via education). The life stories of immigrant groups can be distinct yet draw on classic tales of the rise to fortune or success of migrants (such as Irish stories of emigration to America). Family narratives may be tinged with myth: of one day returning home, having made it good. Finnegan notes how, as researchers, when we look at the products of memories, including interviews, we must be aware 'that they are not limpid empirical data, transmitted by mechanical processes' but rather accounts infused and moulded by family legends, disputes and ideology (Finnegan, 2006: 180).

Sure Start

The state of the family – and the interplay of the wider ideological climate – lies at the heart of recent 'auto/biographical' research into 'family support' programmes in the United Kingdom (West, 2007; West and Carlson, 2006). Linden and a colleague, Andrea Carlson, sought to understand the impact and meaning of programmes through the stories of families as well as staff. Sure Start is one of a myriad of initiatives 'targeted' at families, especially in marginalised communities. It is modelled on the American Head Start initiative with the idea that cycles of deprivation can be broken, children helped to go to school better able to learn, and parents encouraged to enter the labour market and/or participate in adult learning and training programmes. A programme like Sure Start, however, represents contested ideological space: it can be seen as an exercise in social control and moral authoritarianism in relation to poor people. A discourse of moral deficiency can stalk some of the rhetoric (West and Carlson, 2006).

The researchers worked with 100 parents, spending many hours with them in certain cases, over nearly five years, enabling changing experiences and meanings to be considered dynamically and reflexively, with the people concerned. Diverse objectives, values and people shape programmes on the ground and biographical methods can illuminate how understanding can change over time. The researchers noted how parents were initially suspicious of Sure Start – 'is this social workers checking on us?' – yet gradually found some meaningful support for dealing with difficult problems, including depression. Professionals themselves could be critical of the deficit models informing social policy and often practised more collaborative and respectful ways of working. The study illuminates how projects could also create some 'transactional space' for popular involvement in planning and running public services and for challenging dominant myths about poorer families (West and Carlson, 2007).

The Sure Start study is described as 'auto/biographical'. Linden and Andrea write about sitting in a car after particular interviews and sharing aspects of their own family histories in the light of what they heard, which could be very distressing (see Chapter 5).

Case study

We sat in the car quietly after ... interviews and relived the material. We felt a mix of humility and admiration, given their [some of the parents'] resilience, but also concern for them and their future. We mused about how much we had to learn

(Continued)

(Continued)

from them – about coping with distressing personal histories, for instance – and contrasted their resilience with deficit models of families and communities (Ecclestone, 2004). We shared aspects of our own family histories and feelings of failure and inadequacy as parents. Linden had been preoccupied with a public career and there was a corresponding neglect of children and family life.

A painful divorce followed, and the feelings of abandonment came to the surface again, in listening to … stories. Memories of childhood were evoked too, and we decided to record this material in field notes, as a way of embodying the auto/biographical process. Childhood had been difficult – nothing in comparison to [some families] – but difficult nonetheless, for both of us. Relationships between parents were fraught, at times, and we each felt responsible and wanted to make things better. (West and Carlson, 2006: 369)

There could be heart-rending accounts of painful experience alongside heroic survival of abandonment and abuse. Parents could embody in their own accounts dominant ideologies: that they were responsible for their own predicament. Yet the reflexive and longitudinal nature of the study enabled some to interpret their lives in new ways, partly through positive experience in the programme but also because of the research. Curiosity, respect, really listening and reflexivity in researchers can affect how people themselves begin to think about their own lives. They may come to re-evaluate these in a new light given the response of significant others and the sense of greater legitimacy this can instil (West and Carlson, 2006). Research, in these terms, can become a form of learning, for everyone concerned.

Such research can also raise questions about the value of one-off interviews, about the importance of trust in research and, once more, about the researchers' assumptions towards the people they are interviewing. Furthermore, the nature of the work can raise ethical questions as to how far researchers should intrude into the painful detail of family lives (West and Carlson, 2006).

Crime

Biographical researchers study topics such as crime and the fear of crime. Wendy Hollway and Tony Jefferson (2000) note how women's and older people's fear of crime can appear greater than among men and younger people, even though the risk of their being victims is 'objectively' less. This has traditionally been explained by reference to 'irrationality'. Hollway and Jefferson use a biographical approach to analyse the diversity of individuals' narratives, which includes how some men can be more fearful than some women and particular women less fearful than many men. Simply focusing on demographic differences, statistically – such as class, sex, race, age and neighbourhood – in building typologies, only takes us so far. Differences between the sexes may not be that startling when the statistics are scrutinised more closely, while there can be as many similarities as differences between men and women. A biographical perspective, they argue, is urgently required to interrogate this, including how people in similar 'objective' situations can respond in quite different ways.

The researchers document how discourses of crime in the media shape the stories people tell but also how people respond differently, in biographically informed ways (the term discourse is used to emphasise the organised way that meanings can cohere around an assumed central proposition, which gives them their value and significance (Hollway and Jefferson, 2000)). Hollway and Jefferson interview 'Roger', for example, and consider why his particular crime narrative is invested with nostalgia for a golden age of traditional, patriarchal authority in which, so his story proceeds, crime and disrespect for adults were less pervasive. In researching biographically, they detail Roger's mixed feelings about his father – there was violence in the family – but also how Roger talks of his childhood as a time when patriarchal authority actually worked, unlike now – given a disabling accident and depression – and the fact that he feels disrespected by his own family and on the wider estate. The nostalgic narrative is partly explained by reference to present impotence. The past becomes configured as an idealised place and biographical methods help us understand why.

A study like this raises many questions of why people tell particular stories and their potential role in protecting vulnerable, anxious parts of themselves. Hollway and Jefferson draw on psychoanalytic ideas – around the defended subject and how we may split experience into good and bad – as a way of dealing with present anxieties. Thus, for Roger, the investment in a discourse of a good and golden age of respect for authority is in contrast to a bad and intolerable present, of disability and disrespect from others. The researchers provide insights that would have remained unchartered without a biographical but also psychosocial imagination.

Biography, health studies and health care professionals

Brian Roberts (2002) notes how interest in biographical methods has grown in health care, social work and related practices, including studies of professionals. This includes how individuals themselves understand their health problems, in the context of backgrounds, personal and family adjustments as well as specific experience of health and social welfare agencies. There can be a questioning edge to this research.

There is, for example, growing interest in the experience of patients in health care systems as well as in the importance of story telling, or narrativity, in health and healing. Narrative methods are being applied in general practice and reminiscence work with older people (Greenhalgh and Hurwitz, 1998; Launer, 2002; Viney, 1993). Biography and autobiography are employed in studies of doctors and their subjective experiences (Salling Olesen, 2007a, 2007b; West, 2001; Widgery, 1993). A seminal biographical study of a doctor is John Berger and Jean Mohr's *A Fortunate Man* (Berger and Mohr, 1967). Dr John Sassall worked as a General Practitioner (GP) in a poor, deprived rural community in the UK. The researchers spent time with the doctor, encouraging him to talk and reflect on his work and its meaning, and his interactions with particular patients.

Berger and Mohr focused on cultural norms and expectations that shaped the interactions between a doctor and his patients. They wanted to understand more of a doctor's responses to particular patients and their suffering and what might be triggered in Sassall's own imagination by specific encounters. They explored how he coped with feelings of frustration, ignorance, uncertainty and impotence in his work. In so doing, Berger and Mohr captured some of the inadequacy and futility, which can haunt a doctor. They laid bare some of the complex biographical topography often hidden behind professional curtains. John Sassall eventually committed suicide.

Linden West's (2001) research among 25 GPs working in deprived urban environments echoes similar themes. The focus of the study – working in contexts of considerable material poverty and powerlessness – touched on related issues although the research was located in the inner city. The study illuminates the psychological and emotional struggles of particular doctors to cope with the material problems and emotional disturbance of patients and the resources doctors draw on in trying to manage and learn from experience. It shows how struggles in the surgery can be rooted in a doctor's own biography as well as shaped by the professional cultures they inhabit. Various researchers have noted how medical culture can neglect the emotional, psychological and socio-cultural aspects of being a doctor, given the continuing dominance of the bio-medical model (Sinclair, 1997).

Case study

There is a continuing tendency, a number of authors note, in medical education, to disparage the emotional aspects of learning, alongside sociological and critical insights, as matters of anecdote and opinion rather than harder and more 'robust' 'scientific' evidence. The gaze of a positivistic natural science paradigm and objectivism remains strong. Despite, as noted, the mushrooming of sociological, psychological, communication and reflective practice modules in medical training, emotional learning and critical perspectives, including struggles for self-knowledge, remain firmly on the edge.

There was, Dr Daniel Cohen, a GP, said, continuing suspicion of subjective and emotional learning within medical culture, or, for that matter, of critical perspectives in what was a practically orientated profession. Yet such understanding was at the core of becoming a better, more authentic, doctor in which the science could be connected with other ways of knowing. He told a story of a Somali woman refugee who came to his surgery:

' ... A mother and five children, father may have been killed in the war there ... Children with a huge range of problems from asthma to epilepsy ... the mother ... brought me a present for Christmas ... I was immensely moved because it was a really strong symbol that we were providing ... a secure base ... and that she identified me as one white British person in authority who she can trust ... we ended up having the most extraordinary conversation about Darwinian evolution in relation to why were her children getting asthma and eczema here when children didn't get it in Somalia ...'

(Continued)

(Continued)

He realised, in telling the story, that this was part of his patient feeling human again, rather than being labelled a problem, and that he was also connecting his own family history with the patient's. A GP, in his family narrative, had provided a secure, supportive space for his parents and other relatives fleeing from persecution.

'... I think it is in a way always coming back to the business of a personal search, actually trying to find out what life is about and what you should be making of it and having others there who listen and encourage'. This was a form of auto/biographical lifelong learning that transcended the dualities of the personal and professional, self and other, thinking and feeling, culture and interiority. (West, 2001: 85–7)

Henning Salling Olesen (2007a) has ploughed similar terrain in studying GPs and the formation of professional subjectivities in Danish contexts. Doctors are shaped by their involvement in professional practice, by belonging to and identifying with, to greater or lesser degrees, the profession, but also by their wider life histories. The subjective aspects of medical practice have to do with how doctors relate to the knowledge base and cultures of the profession as well as how they may respond to interactions with patients. In-depth biographical interviews were undertaken with various GPs – some very painful – and the results of these fed back. Salling Olesen concludes that there are basic struggles over professional identities and asks how GPs can sustain their position between an increasingly industrialised and technical health system and the messy needs of individual patients.

Nurses and nursing

Nurses and processes of nursing are similarly the subject of a growing body of biographical research. There can be a critical edge to the work as the nursing profession has struggled with the dominance of an objectivist paradigm in medical research. The randomised control trial and large data sets, based on statistical forms of evidence, have constituted the gold standard for research and the meaning of valid 'evidence'. Statistical approaches, however, do not fit at all well, it has been suggested, when seeking to understand the lived experience of nursing, or of being nursed. Qualitative approaches have gradually found greater space and acceptance, as has radical questioning of what nursing and health care are there to do and on whose terms (Banks-Wallace, 1998; Falk Rafael, 1997; Gramling and Carr, 2004; Kirby, 1998).

Falk Rafael (1997), from a Canadian perspective, argues for a reinstatement of social activism in nursing practice and suggests that narrative oral history, from a feminist and postmodern perspective, offers a mode of research with the potential and power to transform political and social realities. She quotes a study of public health nurses who experienced significant distress in their work through the reduction and redirection of their practices (there are similar examples of this in various countries, including the United Kingdom (Howatson-Jones, 2009)). Story telling gives space to naming what is oppressive but also to what may be missing in dominant constructions of nursing or of what is involved, biographically, in learning to be a nurse.

Rafael suggests that research can assist nursing to return to a wider, less instrumental purpose of building a healthier society, not least by exposing forces that serve to silence the voices of the 'disadvantaged'. In a similar spirit, nursing researchers are using what is termed a lifelines approach – visual descriptions of an individual's life events in chronological order. This includes interpretations of the events depicted – alongside 'reflexive interviews' – to record the coping strategies of women using, as one example, crack cocaine. Similarly, nursing researchers investigate the psychosocial development and coping strategies of young women in general (Gramling and Carr, 2004). There is currently a Royal College of Nursing oral history project, supported by the Wellcome Trust in the United Kingdom, which provides a means to chronicle the history of nursing in the wider context of health, social policy and women's history.

Other biographical researchers question health care policy. Wendy Rickard has researched various marginalised groups such as prostitutes and people suffering from HIV and AIDS (Rickard, 2004). Her motivation is fuelled by various factors: a growing criticism of biomedicine and its neglect of the patient and the lived experience of health and health care, and changing power relations between health professionals and the recipients of health care. Biographical methods have become important in promoting participatory and inclusive approaches to health research and can contribute to the development of more sensitive policies in caring at all levels.

Biographical research, teachers and lifelong learning

Biographical methods are used in researching social work and even managers and entrepreneurs in different contexts and countries (Chamberlayne et al., 2004). Teachers have their biographers too, and the work of Ivor Goodson and Peter Woods has already been noted in the last chapter. They continue to influence the application of biographical approaches to understanding teacher identity and professional practice. This includes, once again, the interplay of powerful ideologies, the cultures and sub-cultures of schools, and resistance to these, fuelled by teachers' own experiences of learning (Woods, 1993).

We have noted the emergence of biographical approaches in the study of adult and lifelong learning, in Europe and beyond, and how this has grown apace in recent years (West et al., 2007). Biographical methods are used for examining informal and non-formal learning in family, community, therapeutic and professional settings but also as a pedagogic tool in the education of diverse professionals, in both the Francophone and Anglophone worlds, including, recently, educational and career guidance workers in the United Kingdom (Dominicé, 2000; Reid and West, 2008).

There has been a shift from adult education to lifelong learning in policy discourse and the boundaries between learning and personal experience have become increasingly blurred. Learning is now recognised as taking place in a variety of domestic, social and work-based settings. Biographical approaches are well equipped to explore these different dimensions and to understand the synergies, or lack of them, between varying forms of learning, including informal, non-formal and formal (Edwards, 1997; Hodkinson et al., 2004; West, 2001, 2007). Learning in the workplace represents a specific and evolving area of research (Andersen and Trojaborg, 2007; Eraut, 2004).

Danish research illustrates some of the benefits of what is termed a life history perspective in understanding learning in organisations such as the office (Andersen and Trojaberg, 2007). Anders Siig Andersen and Rebecca Trojaberg use life history case studies to illuminate how responses to education in work-based settings can be deeply influenced by negative biographical experience, and people, as a result, may feel nervous and unsure of themselves as learners at work.

People, in consequence, can develop a preference for routinised work assignments and the absence of courses with exam-like situations as well as for safe social climates where there is little or no competition. They may prefer clearly defined roles within the organisation and even a top-down management approach rooted in experiences of family life. In some working environments, particular staff may act as loyal, diligent and conscientious employees and like what this brings by way of approval from superiors. Different staff, with different biographies, may react against hierarchical cultures and thrive on fluidity and flatter management structures. Biographies provide a key to understanding these differing responses.

Biographical methods continue to be used to chronicle and theorise the experiences of adult entrants into further and higher education in the United Kingdom, employing and developing well-established concepts such as the learning career (Crossan et al., 2003). Adult learners can have broken or limited patterns of participation in education. Learning careers, when viewed biographically, may be contradictory and volatile while learners have to find the resources to manage and reconcile different aspects of their identity, including being and feeling working class, a mother and a learner in higher education, at one and the same time (Merrill, 1999). (See Chapter 5.)

Radical territory

The commitment to marginalised peoples continues in the work of a number of biographical researchers. Some of this was forged, as explained in the previous chapter, in the feminist movement and in the desire to make room for her-story. Many classics of feminism began with a personal narrative and many women's lives have been told in these terms. But research and writing have increasingly moved away from some kind of essential women's experience to highlighting difference, encompassing ethnicity, class, disability, age, health and sexuality (Armitage and Gluck, 2006; Plummer, 2001).

Biographical researchers continue to work with varied groups to chronicle and challenge dominant stories. Certain principles of choice, equality and individuality have become more widespread, it has been suggested, as a result of doing biographies. Working-class people, in these terms, may be challenging middle-class accounts of their lives which presume to know their needs and to speak on their behalf. The holocaust survivor, lesbian and gay coming-out stories and the narratives of indigenous peoples have also claimed greater space (Plummer, 2001) although, as Andrews (2007) reminds us, complicated questions of voice and whose story is heard remain.

The desire to engage with diverse voices remains strong, notwithstanding. Daymond and others (2003) have recently produced *Women Writing Africa*, for example, which provides a comprehensive history of Southern Africa's women's complex lives and experiences. This followed a similar collection, edited by Susie Tharu and K. Lalita on *Women Writing in India* (1991). There is also Fiona Ross' *Bearing Witness: Women and the Truth and Reconciliation Struggle in South Africa* (2003) as well as Tanya Lyon's *Guns and Guerrilla Girls: Women in the Zimbabwean Liberation Struggle* (2004), which provide space for narratives riddled with the painful experience of violence, loss and suffering.

Researchers may explicitly seek to work 'with' people rather than 'on' them, 'in dialogue' (Flecha and Gómez, 2006). Dialogue, radical biographical researchers claim, is a critical ingredient in helping define lives (whether in the context of family and personal relations, or the crisis of many traditional organisations, and/or in the search for new and more direct ways of participation) or in struggles for the international implementation of human rights. In Spain, for example, there are studies among Romany peoples (Gitanos) of educational participation, grounded in what the researchers call 'egalitarian dialogue and consensus'. The methods used involve building daily life stories and communicative observation (in which researchers and participants share interpretations), as well as 'communicative discussion groups' based on trust and creating comfortable forms of exchange, in which listening is cherished (Flecha and Gómez, 2006: 137–8). This provides another form of collective biography (Davies and Gannon, 2006).

Biographies and community development

Biographies from and on the margins take many contemporary forms. In their book *Listening for a Change*, Hugo Slim and Paul Thompson point to the value and power of such methods in community projects in 'developing' countries or among marginalised peoples. The approach ensures, they insist, that the voices of ordinary people are listened to, to improve lives in democratic and empowering ways. Researchers use visual biographies among North American indigenous or First Nation peoples: a visual biography traces the life of a particular phenomenon such as a famine or a crop or diet. Maps and historical transects are also utilised (such transects represent changing conditions through time and can be compiled by walking through an area with older inhabitants and recording their recollections of various conditions at key moments) (Slim et al., 1993).

Life histories help in understanding how people cope with recurrent disasters such as drought, famine, flood and displacement, which may affect many millions. In such situations, people often make decisions based on precedent. Many communities, for whom such disasters are a frequent occurrence, have a kind of shared crisis history, which is transmitted from generation to generation and is taken account of in decision-making. People coping with drought or famine will utilise strategies for procuring food or grazing which have proved effective in the past. An understanding of a crisis history becomes important for relief, if programmes are to be supportive of people's own coping strategies. Conducting interviews is one way of building such histories. Another source is oral artistry: times of disaster become part of the collective memory and gather around them songs, stories, legends and proverbs. These, too, can be drawn on to understand events and piece together precedent (Slim et al., 1993: 27).

Interdisciplinarity

If biographical research is found in challenging spaces and can question dominant ideologies, it also transgresses overly rigid academic boundaries. Biographies, in their nature, appear to evoke an interdisciplinary spirit, partly because lives transcend academic categories, as Andrews (2007) observed. Various sociologists have embraced forms of psychology that help explain the unpredictability of subjective behaviour as well as its development, in a social context. Hollway and Jefferson (2000) use the label 'psychosocial' to describe this approach. Salling Olesen (2007a) and Kirsten Weber (2007) make use of psychoanalytic ideas, alongside critical theory, in their work on doctors as well as on gender and caring. West (2005, 2007) notes that the idea of adult learning as a vehicle for building greater agency among marginalised peoples is old but that a detailed focus on the interplay of outer and inner worlds, on intrasubjective and intersubjective dynamics, has emerged in recent years. Biographical research is generating new kinds of interdisciplinarity.

There is interdisciplinary movement among some psychologists too, concerned with more socially and culturally aware forms of analysis. A recent study by Stephen Frosh and colleagues (2005) of 11–14-year-old boys chronicled experiences of masculinity and interpreted these in interdisciplinary ways. They note a greater social awareness in psychoanalytic theorising, alongside social psychology's willingness to engage with 'meaning' and to explore how subjects are positioned by powerful cultural and interpretative repertoires. But the response of individuals to their positioning requires, they insist, in-depth psychological understanding too. Some boys may question their positioning while others do not, for example. The researchers use biographical interviews of 'a clinical style' to encourage an exploration of openness, contradiction and emotionally marked material. They examine the processes involved in boys succumbing to or resisting homophobia: where resistance can be forged through identification with significant others. In one young man's narrative, there is strong identification with a mother, in the context of a violent father. In the interview – conducted by a man – a process of identification and splitting is discerned in which the 'bad' actual father is contrasted with the 'good' interviewer. The researchers conclude that the social discourses around being gay and of what constitutes a good father should not simply be seen as templates to be passively drawn on. Rather, there are more dynamic internal forces 'constructing and policing certain modes of masculinity and inhibiting others' (Frosh et al., 2005: 53). The capacity for agency and reflexivity means that discourses do not hold absolute sway and can be resisted and commented upon. The development of selfhood involves a struggle to build an authentic identity and self-narrative within confusing and often coercive ideological structures, using available but also potentially diverse narrative resources. We move now, in the next chapter, to consider some key theoretical perspectives that are used in biographical research of this kind, including feminism and psychoanalysis. We pay especial attention to theories that have shaped and inspired our own work.

Key points

- Biographical methods are used by diverse researchers, drawing on different academic disciplines.
- They are applied in studies of managing macro-level change and migration processes as well as of political upheaval. Biographical understanding requires cultural knowledge as well as an understanding of how subjects are shaped by but also shape their cultural worlds.
- Biographical methods enable researchers to chronicle changes in how people conceptualise their past in new ways, in the light of changing presents.
- The stories people tell are sites of competing ideological influences.
- A commitment to the marginalised and to giving voice remains an important, if not exclusive, aspiration in biographical research.
- The interdisciplinary imperative is currently strong.

FURTHER READING

Chamberlayne, P., Bornat, J. and Apitzsch, U. (eds) (2004) *Biographical Methods and Professional Practice: An International Perspective.* Bristol: Policy Press.

Chamberlayne, P., Bornat, J. and Wengraf, T. (eds) (2000) *The Turn to Biographical Methods in the Social Sciences.* London: Routledge.

Hollway, W. and Jefferson, T. (2000) *Doing Qualitative Research Differently: Free Association, Narrative and the Interview Method.* London: Sage.

Plummer, K. (2001) *Documents of Life 2.* London: Sage.

West, L., Alheit, P., Andersen, A.S. and Merrill, B. (eds) (2007) *Using Biographical and Life History Approaches in the Study of Adult and Lifelong Learning: European Perspectives.* Frankfurt: Peter Lang.

DISCUSSION QUESTIONS

1. Think of your own biography: in what ways might interpreting it require inter-disciplinary perspectives? Think of when you were born and the historical, social, cultural but also family influences at work in shaping your life.

2. What do you assume about people's capacity to know, to remember and to tell stories, more or less openly, about themselves and their lives?

3. In what ways could biographical methods be used in your community, region or country as a vehicle for community development?

4
Identifying Some Theoretical Issues

Theories are simply ways of piecing the world together; though they can come in many forms ... and have many purposes (explanatory, sensitizing, connecting). But always they work to provide a link between the very specific and particular and the more abstract and general. Life stories are nearly always geared to the more specific and particular and theory gives them a bridge to wider concerns. It can help the story find a place in the wider world. (Ken Plummer, 2001: 159)

Overview

In this chapter:

- We examine some different theoretical perspectives underpinning biographical research.
- We discuss the theoretical perspectives which have influenced us, including feminism and psychoanalysis.
- We consider how biographical researchers use theory to varying degrees but strive to ground their theoretical understanding in lived experience.
- We note that theory is essential in moving beyond description, as important as the latter is.
- We develop a schema for categorising and positioning different theoretical perspectives.

Introduction

Some theoretical perspective underpins all research, as theory and method are intertwined and inter-related: we cannot make sense of the world without having ideas of how the world works or of what it is to be human. We cannot interpret the detail generated in our research without having some framework to piece together, however provisionally, the fragments of stories to enable them to find a place in the world. Although many social researchers are using biographical methods, they are not homogeneous in their choice of theory (or methodology) and draw on a wide range of ideas under the diverse if often overlapping labels of psychoanalysis, feminism, interpretivism, hermeneutics, symbolic interactionism, critical theory, post-structuralism and postmodernism. In this chapter, we pay particular attention to those theoretical perspectives that have enabled us to build bridges to wider worlds.

Barbara, as noted, has drawn, in the main, on sociological theory and Linden on more psychosocial perspectives while feminism is a shared influence. We explain how and why these theoretical orientations help us to weave connections between individual subjects and the bigger picture. While we cannot cover all the available theoretical perspectives associated with biographical/ life history research (and are conscious of differences between mainland Europe, the Francophone and the Anglo-Saxon worlds (West et al., 2007)), we nonetheless introduce a provisional schema for categorising various theoretical orientations. We hope this will help you to think about how you might position yourself.

Theory is also used to differing degrees and with varying emphasis by biographical researchers. Some may give greater primacy to theory and tend to use stories as a means to test particular hypotheses. Others seek to generate theory more inductively and pragmatically from their material – as in 'grounded theory' (see Chapter 7) – while many biographical researchers are cautious about the possibility of producing overarching explanations. They stress, instead, the situated, contextual and localised nature of explanation.

Definition

A social theory is a set of interrelated abstract propositions about human affairs and the social world that explain their regularities and properties. Theoretical statements differ from descriptive statements in that they are abstract propositions that go beyond description by attempting to explain some feature of society. Theoretical statements may, or may not, form part of a fully fledged social theory. Theories can be distinguished by their level of generality. General theories offer abstract propositions about social action or society as a whole, while theories of the middle range either make propositions about more limited aspects of human and social affairs or the propositions are less abstract. (Brewer, 2002: 148)

The theoretical roots of biographical research, for many, lie in symbolic interactionism, as described in Chapter 2. Nowadays, there is a wider range of theory in use in biographical research, while the values, attitudes and biographies of the researcher can shape, as with us, the choice of theoretical frameworks. We tend towards ideas that make sense to us biographically as well as intellectually. Choosing a theory is not a neutral process, as positivists maintain, but rather a subjective and social one in which the subjectivity of the researcher – in interaction with cultural and intellectual structures, power, language, experience and unconscious processes – has an important role.

There are, we emphasise, important theoretical differences in the biographical research family – around the status of narratives, for example. Some see them as representing the 'reality' of lives (the realist position); others believe they offer a more qualified and partial 'truth', shaped by the workings of language, power and the interaction between researcher and researched (a critical realist position). There are differences that stem from contrasting assumptions about the nature of human subjectivity and the status and transparency of narratives. Stories may be considered the cornerstone of our identity while others regard them as potential covers for deeper and often disturbing psychological processes. In this view, stories take on a defensive role, representing, often unconsciously, how we want to appear to an audience or researcher (Sclater, 2004). There is also tension between notions of voice and letting particular people speak for themselves – especially the marginalised and oppressed – and those who consider this to be naive. Stories should never simply be accepted at face value.

Barbara's approach

Barbara draws on three theoretical perspectives in her work: symbolic interactionism, feminism and critical theory. Like Linden, Barbara adheres to theories which encompass humanistic and subjectivist concerns. At first sight, Barbara's choice of symbolic interactionism with feminism and critical theory may appear to be oppositional, as symbolic interactionism focuses on the individual while feminism and critical theory stress more collective influences in people's lives, including repressive social norms. However, the three theoretical perspectives share similarities and can be seen to complement each other.

Symbolic interactionism interests me, writes Barbara, precisely because it is grounded in humanistic understanding and the potential of people as agents. A key purpose of the Chicago School was to define a different way of researching from the then dominant positivist or determinist perspectives. Symbolic interactionists view social reality from the perspectives of the social actor(s). Knowledge of the social world is found through engaging with concrete situations and with how people interact with others, and construe, symbolically, the problems they face. Theory is grounded in an awareness of the complex details of daily life, based on what is termed a pragmatic philosophical position. Construing the world is a practical, situated activity – rather than an abstract one – for subjects and researchers alike.

By interacting with others, self and society are made through a process of negotiation and interpretation. Meaning is symbolically created through language, developed in interaction with others. The scaffolding of symbolic interactionism was derived from these ideas and also formalism. Society, in this latter perspective, involves some regularised structure, in which repetition of patterns of interaction, or forms, helps account for the coherence and reproduction of a social world. But the Chicago School thought of humans as dynamically living and organising what they did in the light of situations they encountered (Barley, 1989). The following description of symbolic interactionism by Bernard Meltzer et al. is useful.

Definition

[Symbolic interactionism] … refers to the fact that social interaction rests upon a taking of oneself (self-objectification) and others (taking the role of the other) into account …

Society is to be understood in terms of the individuals making it up, and individuals are to be understood in terms of the societies of which they are members. (Meltzer et al., 1975: 1, 2)

Symbolic interactionism also focuses on the development of the self and asserts the self-reflective nature of the inner world and human behaviour. Herbert Blumer remarks that there is no one definition of symbolic interactionism but three under-pinning premises:

1. Human beings act towards things on the basis of the meanings that the things have for them. Such things include everything that the human being may note in his world – physical objects, such as trees and chairs; other human beings ... institutions ... guiding ideals ... activities of others ... and such situations as an individual encounters in his daily life.
2. The meaning of such things is derived from, or arises out of, the social interaction that one has with one's fellows.
3. These meanings are handled in, and modified through, an interpretative process used by the person in dealing with the things he encounters. (1986: 2)

Although focusing on the individual, symbolic interactionists stress that individual behaviour has to be understood in the context of interaction. It is also interesting that the Chicago School encompassed a diverse group of people, including those who would have perceived themselves as social psychologists, such as George Herbert Mead.

George Herbert Mead

Mead was an important influence in the Chicago School, and for both of us. His work is useful for thinking about the dynamics of inner and outer life. Mead thought that human beings should be researched in their natural surroundings and that individuals are not static, but rather the self, or society, is in a process of development and change as well as continuity. His naturalistic approach to understanding human behaviour stemmed from his adherence to pragmatist philosophy. His theory of self is explained in his well-known work, *Mind, Self and Society* (1934/1972). Mead asserts that the self is developed through participation in social acts and the attitudes that the generalised other (the person(s) who the self interacts with, which can include a whole society) has towards the self in situations of social interaction. For Mead, 'the individual is always dependent on the group for his self' (1982: 163). The self, therefore, takes on the role and attitudes of others. Such a self has to understand how s/he is seen and to respond to this within a shared set of meanings. In the process, the individual becomes an object to him/her self:

> The individual experiences himself as such, not directly, but only indirectly, from the particular standpoints of other individual members of the same social group, or from the generalized standpoint of the social group as a whole to which he belongs. For he enters his own experience as a self or individual, not directly or immediately, not by becoming a subject to himself, but only in so far as he first becomes an object to himself just as other individuals are objects to him or in his experience; and he becomes an object to himself only by taking the attitudes of other individuals towards himself within a social environment or context of experience and behaviour in which both he and they are involved. (Mead, 1934/1972: 138)

The self, according to Mead, comprises the 'I' and 'me'. The 'I' is the organic self while the 'me' is the self constructed through interaction with the generalised other(s): it is an externally prescribed self:

> The 'I' is the response of the organism to the attitudes of the others; the 'me' is the organized set of attitudes of others which one himself assumes. The attitudes of the others constitute the organized 'me', and then one reacts toward that as an 'I'. (Mead, 1934/1972: 175)

Mead's self is intersubjective and reflexive. His work is helpful for biographical research because it enables us to think about how 'we deal with constructing and reconstructing or making and remaking selves through interactions and language learning, as well as adjustment and readjustment to culture, subcultures and their symbols, all in the process of social interaction and within a range of institutions' (Bron, 2007: 218–19). Agnieszka Bron (2002, 2007) draws on Mead's theory of intersubjectivity and language in understanding how adult immigrants to Sweden cope with transition, learning and identity. Mead's work has been helpful to Barbara in thinking about how working-class adult students survive in university and wrestle with questions of how others may see them, and how they may come to see themselves.

Moving on

Barbara found the work of later symbolic interactionists – in the 1960s and 1970s – particularly relevant. They used life histories, as well as participant observation, to focus on the micro level and the subjectivities of lives. Past and present lives were studied in order to understand the individual in relation to the group and society. Many studies, as outlined in Chapter 2, centred on aspects of crime and deviance such as Clifford Shaw's (1966) *The Jack Roller*, David Matza's (1969) *Becoming Deviant* and Howard Becker's (1963) *Outsiders: Studies in the Sociology of Deviance*. In contrast to positivist perspectives on crime and deviance (which tend to focus on the pathology of crime and to theorising causes at a very general level, and measuring, statistically, the power of particular 'variables', such as class and poverty, to induce pathological behaviour), symbolic interactionists examine the processes of how an individual becomes a criminal or a deviant, through social construction, labelling and agency, which leads to the notion of 'career' being applied in, what at first sight, may seem surprising contexts.

Mead (and social interactionists) was interested in the role of agency, or the I, in shaping lives. The construction of an agentic self had to do with individuals taking some control, and finding resources, for potentially radical questioning of how they may have been labelled or constrained. Several working-class adult students that Barbara interviewed found educational resources – and thus agency – to overcome structural inequalities in their lives. This often stemmed from a critical incident. In a Scottish study on participation and non-participation in further education, a woman called 'Mary' took the initial steps into learning (and later completed a degree) after the death of a grandfather, which left a gap in her life. Initially, notions of agency were remote:

I was so busy I didn't really think about it. My days were pretty chaotic I suppose so I just got on with it but then grandpa died and there was just this big hole in my days and I thought I have got to do something. I found the house quite isolating I suppose you would say. My husband went to work and came home but I had nothing to talk about my day. None of the other folks I knew had babies by then ... I saw an advert in the paper for cooking classes here and I thought I'd give that a go. It said that there would be a crèche for the wee one. So I thought that would be good for him too. I couldn't even find it at first. I was quite nervous about it all. I suppose at that time I really didn't have a lot of confidence. But I thought it would be good for both of us. When I got to the class it was all old age pensioners. Nothing against them but I suppose I had hoped it would be people my age to talk to and meet. And it turned out that (her son) was the only one in the crèche. But we kept coming. I must have liked it I suppose.

The concept of agency is important in understanding how adult students develop, or not, a learning identity and career. Symbolic interactionists did not use career in the traditional sense of linear progression associated with employment. Rather, in writing about 'dope fiends' (Becker, 1963), mental patients (Goffman, 1961/1968), deviants (Parker, 1974; Shaw, 1966) and nudists (Weinberg, 1966), they explored how a past and present life history, and actions, as well as cultural and social processes, shaped the development of careers in diverse contexts.

> **Paul Armstrong discusses the meaning of life career**
>
> A person's life history or biography can be seen as a network of inter-relating careers. But this is still inadequate unless we move to Everitt Hughes's idea of 'life career' as a dynamic perspective in which people see their life as a whole, a totality, and interpret the meaning of various attributes, actions and events which happen to them, and thereby using the concept in a broad sense to incorporate personal circumstances, decisions, incidents and coincidence, which occur within a highly structured situation with a limited number of cultural options available. Like career, biography is sequential: no one point in time can be understood without looking at what went before. (Armstrong, 1982: 7)

Barbara first used the concept of career in her PhD, examining the experiences of working-class women students at university. At that time, she was influenced by Howard Becker and Erving Goffman's approach to career. Goffman belonged to what was termed the ethnomethodological branch of symbolic interactionism. Ethnomethodologists focus on the way in which behaviour, shared meanings and social order come to be taken for granted, as normal, within a cultural setting. It is a naturalistic and humanistic approach, which, for Martyn Hammersley and Paul Atkinson, means that 'as far as possible, the social world should be studied in its "natural" state, undisturbed by the researcher' (1992: 6).

The social order is maintained through everyday social interaction and in explaining how social activity occurs, ethnomethodologists emphasise the importance of understanding the commonplace or everyday taken-for-granted activity. Ethnomethodology also stresses that the sociologist is a social actor who has her/his own perception of social reality. Both actors and sociologists are 'theorisers' of their social world. Everyone, in short, is a sociologist as well as a theorist to an extent. Ethnomethodology emphasises the importance of understanding how people themselves theorise their life rather than seeing the researcher as the sole source of 'theory'.

Goffman's definition of career, used in studies of what he terms 'total' institutions, such as asylums (distinguished by closure, rationalisation of everyday living and disciplinary control), has been helpful in Barbara's work on women students. Although representing very different social contexts, she drew an analogy between Goffman's inmates in his study *Asylums* (1961/1968) and working-class women at university. Like Goffman, she was interested in how the women coped in the context of an 'elite' university, and how they changed and developed as persons:

> [M]ature students, like inmates, are entering a new institution in an unknown social context. Although less extreme and committing than a total institution, university life does have a profound effect upon the lives of students. They leave changed persons. Goffman's concept of mortification of the self is applicable in a modified and less extreme form. The self of mature students is partially stripped on entry to a university and their identity rebuilt as they progress through their student career. The process and outcome of mortification is a liberating one for mature students. (Merrill, 1999: 128)

Barbara went further in developing the concept of learning career with a number of colleagues, using biographies of adult students from the Scottish research. Learning career was 'a concept that facilitates an understanding of the biographical processes experienced by adult learners in returning to learn and their subsequent engagement in learning over a period of time' (Merrill, 2001: 1). Subsequent to this, in research with Rennie Johnston, she began to consider, in greater depth, its non-linear dimensions. To do this, we used the term 'learning identity' as a way of acknowledging the irregular and complex interrelationship of learning and identity and the fact that, particularly for non-traditional adult students, 'learning identities co-exist with and influence, and are in turn influenced by, other adult identities' (Johnston and Merrill, 2004: 154).

David Matza's notion of 'drift', which was originally applied to delinquency, was drawn on in the Scottish study. Again, the context was different but the theoretical approach helped to explain the dispositions and learning careers of marginalised students in further education. For Matza:

> Drift is a gradual process of movement, unperceived by the actor, in which the first stage may be accidental or unpredictable from the point of view of any theoretic frame of reference, and deflection from the delinquent path may be similarly accidental or unpredictable. (1964: 29)

Barbara and colleagues noted that the stories of some participants indicated senses of drifting in and out of learning, for example, at particular moments in the life course. Periods of participation could reflect and reinforce experiences of agency in biographies while periods of non-participation reflected times when, for various reasons, structural factors dominated. Lisa, in the Scottish study, opted for a Youth Training Scheme (funded by the Government for young unemployed people) in hairdressing. She did not complete this because she got pregnant at the age of 17; by the age of 28 she had two more children and was a single parent. This was something she regretted:

> I wish I had never had any weans [children]. I wish I could have been a hairdresser or a dancer, and stayed on at one of those things that I liked and never had any weans. That I had my own place and had my life, do you know what I mean, because it is hard.

Lisa was later involved in informal learning and community activities. Through a youth project, she enrolled on a parenting course with the Open University. She was using and experiencing agency to make up for what she saw as her failure at school: 'Because I wasn't very clever at school and I know that if I put my mind to it I can do it. It was for my own benefit'. She drifted into a hairdressing course too but did not complete it because of personal, structural and institutional barriers. The reasons were partly financial but at a personal level she was living with a violent, non-supportive partner who did not take kindly to her attending college. He was aggressive towards her:

> It was jealousy as I was out meeting a lot of folk. It was like 'who was I meeting, who was I talking to?' ... all that kind of stuff ... But I wasn't caring what he thought ... At the end of the day I was out for me and I had gone to college. I always use to try and go but eventually I couldn't keep going.

During this time, two of the children were taken into care. Part of the problem was her uncertainty about herself as a learner – there was no well-defined learning identity:

> It was good and I liked it and I picked up a lot ... but I felt a bit worried that I couldn't keep up with it. That was another thing. I was worried in case I wasn't doing well enough.

Feminism

If the work of the symbolic interactionists provided one leg of a conceptual triangle, feminism offered another. As observed in Chapter 2, second wave feminism stimulated the development of feminist theory and methodology in academia. Maria Mies (1991) has argued that the feminist critique of traditional research originated not only in universities but also in feminist social movements. Dorothy Smith asserted that: 'The women's movement has given us a sense of our right to have women's interests represented in sociology, rather than just receiving as authoritative the interests traditionally represented in a sociology put together by men' (1987: 85). bell hooks (1984), the black feminist, similarly observed that academic knowledge was dominated by 'a white male canon'. Feminists raised the question of who has the power to construct knowledge and criticised 'male sociology', or the 'malestream', for ignoring and dismissing the role and lives of women and for focusing research on the public world of men. Feminist researchers highlighted the importance of researching the personal lives of ordinary women in the home as well as their public lives in the workplace and elsewhere. In researching the private, everyday lives of women, they emphasised how 'the personal is political', as in the gendered distribution of emotional labour.

Feminist research can be socially critical and highly political although there are different feminisms (for example, liberal, radical feminist, socialist feminist (Marxist), post-structuralist, postmodernist) reflecting a range of ideological and epistemological positions. All feminist researchers, however, share a common aim of challenging gender inequalities in society and transforming the lives of women. For Maggie Humm:

> Feminism is a social force ... [and] depends on the understanding that, [in] all societies which divide the sexes in differing cultural, economic or political spheres, women are less valued than men. Feminism also depends on the premise that women can consciously and collectively change their social place ... a belief in sexual equality combined with a commitment to eradicate sexist domination and to transform society. (1992: 1)

Barbara locates herself still – even though this may be viewed as unfashionable or out-of-date – as a socialist feminist. Socialist feminism argues that women's oppression is rooted in the capitalist system and its inherent practice of private property. This is in contrast to radical feminism which views men as the oppressors of women. Rather, gender relations are constructed through the power relationships and class structures which shape a capitalist society. In this sense, both women and men are oppressed and alienated by their roles and need to be liberated from this state of being.

Feminist approaches to research stress the need for subjective engagement and for forms of relationship which challenge the power nexus between the researcher and the researched. Interviews, and, in particular, biographical and auto/biographical approaches, became a favoured means of doing research. For Natalee Popadiuk: 'the feminist biographical method is a powerful tool. It engages in research from a unique perspective that provides depth, meaning and context to the participants' lived experiences in light of the larger cultural matrix in which they live' (2004: 395).

Barbara continues to find a Marxist theoretical framework relevant, too, for understanding biographies. Marxist or socialist feminism focuses on women's oppression and exploitation in the family and the workplace and as a reserve army of labour. There is a hard political and material base to people's lives, beyond language and how this may position us. A political and conflict standpoint is required to challenge the way in which dominant power structures intrude and shape biographies and the expectations, as well as the selves, within them. Postmodernism focuses on difference and the multiple representations of women, even questioning the category of woman itself. It can be seen as a kind of retreat from the reality of class and material oppression or even from the notion of a reality at all as 'interpretation feeds upon interpretation in a swirl of language and symbols' (Roberts, 2002: 7). However, it needs to be stated that aspects of postmodernism favour the biographical approach in a world where there can be increased sensitivities to diversity, difference and dialect. Ethnic, sexual, religious, cultural or aesthetic minorities are more able to speak for themselves in a celebration of a plurality of perspectives, and local and contextual studies find more space as notions of a single grand human truth have been challenged (Stones, 1996).

Nonetheless, there is a downside to this, as feminism, in recent years, has become more dominated by postmodernism in universities:

[T]he emergence and stronghold of postmodernism and the decline of Marxist feminism in the academy has established a discourse which is far removed from the material reality of working class women. Academic feminism is becoming elitist, excluding 'other women' through its language and content. (Merrill and Puigvert, 2001: 308)

Beverly Skeggs is scathing of such academic feminists in her study of working-class women learning in a further education college in the UK:

Often, the more theoretically sophisticated feminist analysis becomes in the academy, the less likely it is able to speak to women outside of it. The debates that rage between postmodern and materialist feminism occupy a completely different space to that occupied by the women of this research. Feminist knowledge has been produced but it has only been distributed selectively. (Skeggs, 1997: 141)

The recent interest in postmodernism has also coincided with a retreat from a concern with social class among sociologists in the United Kingdom. Once central to sociological theory, class can be viewed as irrelevant and an out-of-date concept for categorising people's lives (Pahl, 1989). Yet there are signs that some sociologists are re-engaging and re-asserting the importance of class (Crompton, 2008; Devine et al., 2005; Savage, 2000). As Skeggs asserts: 'To abandon class as a theoretical tool does not mean that it does not exist any more; only that some theorists do not value it … Retreatists either ignore class or argue that class is "an increasingly redundant issue"' (1997: 6, 7).

The stories told by the women and men in Barbara's work have highlighted how social class is still alive and continues to structure people's everyday lives through inequalities of material wealth and access to resources. Class also, as Andrew Sayer reminds us, 'affects how others value us and respond to us, which in turn affects our sense of self-worth' (2005: 1).

In adult education, the tradition of academic women working and researching with working-class women in democratic ways has continued, across Europe and beyond. Dialogical feminism is a perspective that listens attentively to and values the voices of other women and their experiences (Puigvert and Valls, 2002). It draws on the ideas of Paulo Freire (1972a, 1972b, 1976) and Jürgen Habermas (1972) in promoting notions of authentic dialogue in which everyone contributes on an equal level, with the belief that transformation can occur through dialogical relationships.

Critical theory

The third arm of Barbara's triangle is critical theory. The application of critical theory to biographical research is strongly associated with feminism (although its roots are male dominated as much sociology is) and Danish life history research on lifelong learning and working lives. Critical theory, as observed, was developed by the Frankfurt School of sociology. The School derived its influences from many sources such as Marxism (humanist Marxism not determinist Marxism), philosophy, psychoanalysis, theology and romanticism. Craig Calhoun states that:

> Critical theory was the name chosen by the founders of the Frankfurt School in the period between world wars to symbolize their attempt to achieve a unity of theory and practice, including a unity of theory with empirical research and both with an historically grounded awareness of the social, political, and cultural problems of the age. (1995: 13)

Barbara favours humanist Marxism rather than determinist/classical Marxism. The former starts with the individual and recognises that a person is not simply a product of social forces and structure: a person has the capacity to use their subjectivity in their interactions in society. Marx outlined this clearly in his *Theses on Feuerbach* (1845). The struggle becomes one of moving from states of alienation to situations whereby women and men fulfil themselves and find their human essence. Marx inter-relates structure and agency in discussing the dialectical relationship between the individual and society whereby men and women 'make their own history, but not ... under conditions they have chosen for themselves; rather on terms immediately given and handed down to them' (Marx, 1852/1973: 287). Social class is objective and subjective at one and the same time as well as central to Marx's analysis of capitalism. A person's class is defined by ownership or non-ownership of the means of production (although this can be seen, by Marxists, in much more complex ways). Marxism links social theory to political action. Through the process of class consciousness, class struggle and collective action, people can use their agency to overcome oppression and transform society. Marx's definition of class is now viewed, by some, as being inadequate and too narrow a definition for the postmodern world. This issue is being addressed by the 'new' analytical Marxists in their re-workings of Marx's theory of capitalism and class (Cohen, 1988; Postone, 1993; Wright, 1985, 1997).

Critical theory has sought to challenge and critique dominant ideologies and power structures which attempt to represent the existing social order as natural and right, as part of stifling potential dissent. The approach strove to expose inequalities and injustices in society, perpetuated by ruling elites or classes. The term was an attempt, as Horkheimer (1982) stressed, to distinguish it from 'traditional sociology'.

Critical theorists have also challenged what they perceive to be an unreflexive instrumentalism, where research is constructed as a technical matter, with clearly delineated sets of problems, and the aim is to establish and measure causal links between key variables, without reference to social justice or human values. Habermas (1972) was concerned about how social science was increasingly led by the language of prediction and control, alongside an objectification of social processes. The Enlightenment, he noted, had spawned the hegemony of a detached, allegedly neutral instrumental reason as a way of orientating the researcher, and this brought with it a neglect of, or even blindness towards, the oppressive nature of social realties. A critical orientation has to do with struggles to emancipate people from relations of dependence shaped by powerful ideologies that persuade them that the social order – around processes of production or reproduction – is 'normal' (Crotty, 1998).

Critical theory has found vibrant expression in biographical research and educational practice, through the influence of Paulo Freire, Paul Willis and Henry Giroux. The following example is of the use of critical theory by colleagues in Barcelona.

An example

The Centre for Research in the Education of Adults (CREA) at the University of Barcelona has developed a critical theoretical perspective to their research and practice of adult education through the notion of dialogic learning. They draw on Habermas' theory of communicative action and Freire's concept of egalitarian dialogue to develop the literacy skills of adults through literary circles (a learning situation which entails adult learners and a tutor meeting to discuss a novel). Ramon Flecha (2000) outlines the principles in his book *Sharing Words*. Participants in the literary group form a research group to look at participation and non-participation using life histories as a form of dialogic research.

Critical theory offers a means of using individual stories and whole biographies to understand and explain how uninterrogated yet oppressive scripts, alongside harsh material realities, can shape what people say and do. The social order may be taken for granted or challenged. Critical theory helps us to understand that, although biographies are individual, they are redolent with the collective: people from similar socio-economic backgrounds, such as white working-class women, share common experiences of class and gender inequalities. Rather like the snowflakes quoted at the beginning of the book, however, each is distinct too. It depends on our focus. Critical theory, combined with feminism and symbolic interactionism, can help identify and explain the workings of structural inequalities (what is in-built and replicated), and their oppressive dimensions, but not in overly determinist or flatly uniform ways.

Linden's approach

Connecting inner and outer worlds

Linden has drawn on psychology, sociology and cultural theory in his work on learning, change processes and motivation. He has made use of the sociological concept of marginality in his work on learners and learning. Marginality refers to situations in which people may not be full members of a potential group and stand on the margins between differing social spaces, wondering, at some level, where they belong. A marginal person can be in transition between worlds whose norms and values may conflict, which can induce status confusion and vulnerability but also freedom to innovate and a capacity to be critical of a predominant social order (Hopper and Osborn, 1975; West, 1996).

Such a social perspective developed out of concern that the psychology of human motivation and learning, dominated as it has been by American psychologists, could be profoundly asocial and ahistoric. Sean Courtney (1992) noted how learning was frequently constructed as an isolated, unsituated, cognitive, knowledge- and skill-orientated activity, which failed to locate it, and patterns of social participation more generally, in a lifewide, lifelong and cultural context. The adult learner, he suggested, could be more of a life spacer, someone more likely to try out new things and who was open to life's possibilities and challenges, but this was shaped by new forms of interaction with others. Courtney brought the wider social context into the equation, including constant change, which was also central to American ideology. Courtney wove a theory of learning as an encounter with change and of learners wrestling with issues of selfhood and agency: at least in profounder forms of experience.

His notion of learning involved something deeper than skills acquisition: people were often seeking to effect and change the lives of others as well as of the self. But this provoked a further question: why do some people, more than others, even in oppressive circumstances, become life spacers? Why are they relatively open to engaging with experience, in all its diversity – to pain, joy, suffering and injustice, as well as transcendental possibilities? Even if this was largely social in origin, Linden turned to psychoanalytic ideas to explain how changes in social relationships might evoke changes in the inner world – why, in short, some people retreat into paranoia and fundamentalisms of various kinds, in the face of difficult experience, while others become more creative and open to new ways of seeing and being (Frosh, 1991). Linden turned to object relations theory and the role of significant others, as well as of narrative repertoires, in theorising life spacing.

The work of Melanie Klein (1998) also helped him understand the ambivalence and anxiety that can lie at the heart of encounters with change. Anxiety, in her perspective, reaches back to earliest experience and our utter dependence on others: even confident people can feel helpless and overwhelmed in new and demanding situations, such as entering a course in higher or adult education. There is a linking back, unconsciously, to early feelings of dependence and inadequacy, as past and present elide. Klein termed this 'memory in feeling', expressed in bodily and emotional states, rather than conscious thought. Embodied memory can be especially intense for those 'taught', from earliest times, that they are of little consequence, or inadequate or that authority is not to be trusted. A range of psychological defences may come into play, including withdrawal, denial of needs (that something may be important or desirable), omnipotence or omniscience.

Biographical research provided one way to chronicle and theorise such processes among adult learners. There are constant glimpses of anxiety and defensiveness in narratives: early experience is never simply transcended and past and present constantly intertwine (West, 2004b, 2007). Linden has drawn on other psychoanalytic theorists, too, such as Donald Winnicott (1971), to explore the resources people use to manage transitional processes. As suggested, these include significant others and new and creative forms of story telling – a work of art or integrating a new narrative, like feminism – to symbolise new biographical possibilities. People and symbols, like a new idea, can be seen as 'objects', which are internalised and become part of a psychological dynamic. The self and subjectivity in this object relations perspective are conceived as dynamic, a never complete product of relationship with actual people and diverse objects, including the symbolic (Hunt and West, 2009; West, 1996, 2001, 2007). The 'truth' of such theory is pragmatic, tested on the basis of its utility in clinical as well as biographical research. This is middle-range theory that cannot be proved in any absolute sense.

The self at the heart of such theory is not a given but deeply contingent, constructed and developmental. Contingent, in its fundamental reliance on others; constructed, because we are forged in our interactions with others and whole cultures, including oppressive social and educational forces; developmental, in that the self is open to change and can challenge subjectification and transform itself in the process in creative and courageous acts (Butler, 1997; Frosh, 1991). This is a self that is emotional, embodied, relational, socio-cultural, discursive and potentially agentic at the same time.

It is also a self whose capacity for thinking, at least of any significant kind, is vitally embedded in feeling rather than detached from it. Linden and a colleague, Celia Hunt, have drawn on the neurophysiological work of Antonio Damasio (2000) in exploring this idea. He argues that a pre-linguistic, bodily core self, experienced through feelings, gives rise to our memory- and language-based autobiographical self. There is a challenge here to the idea of self as solely a product of language, society and culture. Bodily experience and neurological patterning, shaped by our relationships, join self-reflexivity and story telling, and the imprints and oppressions of culture and structuring processes, in this more holistic, interdisciplinary perspective (Hunt and West, 2009).

Things shared

Barbara and Linden share some theoretical influences derived from psychology, for example, Mead, and the distinction between I and me, in the making of selves. The 'I', as noted, is characterised by a capacity for immediacy in the present, for spontaneity, creativity and challenge while the 'me' can represent the constraints of the past, of tradition, culture and institutional contexts. There are echoes here of a classic psychoanalytic typology: of the self as a source of conflicting imperatives between the id (emotional, spontaneous, libidinal) and the superego, which we can think of in terms of the imperatives of the established order. The ego, or more conscious self, has a mediating role in this conflict, and the making of selves can be interpreted as a dynamic engagement with conflicting imperatives out of which the more agentic self emerges or is made.

However, in object relations perspectives, there is a more explicit interrogation of how the social is internalised through the medium of relationships. People, and patterns, 'out there', via processes of projection and introjection (in which others imbue us with meaning and we imbue them, in turn, often unconsciously, with a range of characteristics) become part of us, like characters in a play. Some characters may represent unhealthy or even abusive constraints. Others encourage feelings of legitimacy, spontaneity, creativity, questioning and agency: like a good teacher, therapist or even a researcher. We carry such people in us, as objects, and they can provide internal symbolic and emotional resources in our struggles to be and to compose a life on slightly more of our own terms (Sayers, 1995; West, 1996, 2001).

Transitional processes

Linden has used other psychoanalytic ideas to think about transitional and change processes. Carl Gustav Jung (1933), for instance, was interested in stages of psychological development and in using biographies to explore these. He developed his theory of psychological individuation, change and growth, drawing on biographies and clinical experience. Among other interests, he noted how in midlife men may struggle with the contrasexual opposite (what has been repressed), or succeed in integrating the repressed, more feminine sides of themselves, into a more balanced psychic whole, or what he called individuation.

Jung influenced the work of Daniel Levinson (1978), who used intensive biographical interviews to generate in-depth data from a sample of 40 men in four diverse occupational groups. His focus was the midlife crises, beginning roughly at the age of 40. There is a shift in time perspective, he suggested, at this stage, in relation to the years left to live and there can be a felt disparity between what has been accomplished and what one might really want. Midlife was conceived as a time to build some greater equilibrium between the polarities of young–old, masculine–feminine and attachment–separateness.

These ideas have found expression in Linden's work on gender, with reference to doctors, in which cultures and sub-cultures, as well as people, can be thought of in gendered terms. Doctors may struggle to find in themselves what may be culturally other, such as hitherto repressed and 'feminine' potentialities, including the ability to relate meaningfully to others (West, 2001). It should be noted, however, that Jung and Levinson have been criticised for ahistorical, asocial tendencies in conflating male experience and development in specific cultures, with human development as a whole, across all cultures (Gilligan, 1982; Sayers, 1995). Moreover, the evidence of increasingly unpredictable biographical trajectories in late- or post-modernity may problematise overly rigid notions of developmental stages.

Gendered subjectivities

Carol Gilligan (1982) has used biographies to construct a different theory of psychological development: while men and women may face the same dilemma of reconciling conflicts between separation and attachment, they can approach this from a different direction. If male development can be premised on the importance of separation and increasing autonomy (because of the need to separate and be distinct from the mother), women tend to start from a more comfortable relationship with same-sex intimacy, gradually exploring ways of managing and tolerating separation. The interplay between the social, cultural and psychological is a major issue in much of this writing.

Recent biographical research has illuminated some of these theoretical issues. Kirsten Weber (2007), whose work has been noted, uses critical theory, alongside psychoanalysis and feminism, to explore the idea of the workplace as a gendered battlefield. She mines biographies to examine how her subjects' basic orientations to learning may manifest themselves along deeply gendered lines. These processes are partly theorised with reference to the classic psychoanalytic insights into male struggles with intimacy. But this is not to neglect culture, language or material conditions. Gender is inherent, in her view, in social structures, stemming from historic divisions of labour and is reproduced or changed within the scope of the accessible choices that people make. Yet in understanding reproduction and change processes, Weber observes that girls tend to identify with and separate from a model of their own gender while boys' paths to autonomy involve separation from a first intimacy. These patterns of early interaction are reinforced by language, as symbolic representation, all of which serves to define what she calls 'gendered subjectivity'. (Weber, building on the work of others, distinguishes gender subjectivity – the processes by which a person becomes a psychological subject – and gender identity, which refers to sexuality and cultural conceptions of gender.) Gendered subjectivity may find expression in the differing responses of men and women to new kinds of training opportunities in which 'learning' to care for others is required.

Men, mirroring earlier patterns, may seek competency by first demonstrating degrees of autonomy, in a predominantly feminised cultural space. They can strive to progress in more individualistic ways while women tend to look for intimacy as a prerequisite of achieving greater confidence and competence in what they do. Psychological dynamics, in such studies, represent a kind of embodied, internalised culture. There is a synthesis of theoretical elements from Marxism (social and historical factors) with psychoanalysis (in an embodied and symbolic sense, characterised by contradictions and tensions). The psychic processes – in which social conflicts are played out – are not fully transparent and conscious; rather they are more often unconscious or preconscious. Henning Salling Olesen (2007b) regards the notion of the unconscious to be the fundamental contribution of psychoanalysis to social science and biographical research.

Carolyn Steedman (1986) similarly integrates feminism, elements of Marxism and psychoanalysis in her work. Her starting point is the specifics of place, politics and class, which, she insists, need to be at the core of analysis. But a psychological frame of understanding, she argues, is required, around the nature of desire. Steedman condemns a great deal of sociological biography as stolid, with a psychological sameness in characterising representations of working-class life (as in the work of Richard Hoggart (1957) or Jeremy Seabrook (1982)). Steedman engages with what she terms 'the subterranean culture of longing' (in her mother's life, for example) for what one can never have. She takes issue with the way in which biographers have attributed, under the influence of Marxism, a psychological simplicity to working-class people:

But if we do allow an unconscious life to working class children, then we can perhaps see the first loss, the earliest exclusion (known most familiarly to us as the Oedipal crisis) brought forward later, and articulated through an adult experience of class and class relations. (Steedman, 1986: 14)

Her mother wanted 'a New Look skirt, a timbered country cottage, to marry a prince' (1986: 9) because she was cut off from things she desired. Steedman's work resonated deeply with Linden's own biography, and the need to capture the complexity and psychological subtlety, as well as fantasies, of family life, including the workings of desire, within a classed and gendered social order (West, 1996).

Doctors' biographies

Both feminism and psychoanalysis have shaped Linden's understanding of the working and learning lives of doctors (West, 2001). Dr Aidene Croft, for example, was a 'foreigner' and a lesbian, who was working in a difficult, demanding and impoverished part of London's East End. She mentioned her sexual identity and how this fitted uneasily into the 'male' and predominantly heterosexual culture of medics and training. She was glad to be a representative, in the study, she said, of women and men like her, against the presumption of many doctors that they are all, or should be, straight, have a heterosexual partner and '2.4 children' at private school. Aidene's experience of being an outsider, as well as emotionally vulnerable, was pivotal to her story. She felt herself to be alienated from 'malestream' medicine and was especially critical of initial training and the wider masculine culture of the profession. Aidene used psychotherapy, as well as new relationships, to achieve greater levels of self-insight, understanding and confidence, and to better connect with many of her marginalised, emotionally struggling patients.

It is important to emphasise that psychoanalytic theory raises fundamental questions about subjectivity and the stories at the heart of biographical research. The 'psychosocial' actors, as we can term them, may not be conscious of what they do: their actions – and narratives – may be rooted in desire, or its frustration, that requires psychological as well as a sociological explanation. This applies too in the actual processes of doing research, as Michael Roper (2003) has observed. Research is a relationship in which unconscious processes are also at work. Our narrators may attribute to us, as researchers, characteristics from significant past relationships. They may wish to appease, or to please, in telling stories (West, 1996, 2007). Psychoanalytic theory has a significant contribution to make in understanding lives but also processes of biographical research: not least, once more, in challenging the conventional distinctions between immediacy and memory, past and present, self and other.

A critical note

It is important to mention that some of the ideas at the core of this chapter, including feminism, have been subject to major criticism. Martyn Hammersley

(1995, 2000, 2002), for example, takes issue with the idea of research as emancipatory. Molly Andrews (2007) also warns us about only hearing what we want to hear or what fits in with our current needs and preoccupations as well as our ideological predilections. Our collaborators may be induced to tell stories in particular ways, according to what we might represent to them, whether consciously or not. Hammersley is also concerned about potential bias in what we hear and report. He similarly questions the idea of research as a tool against simplistic notions of oppression, which he rightly argues is a more complex notion than the oppressor–oppressed model of the world. White feminists, as black feminists have stated, often neglect racism and can be oppressive in their ignorance. The world is not easily or appropriately divided between oppressor and the oppressed, the powerful and powerless. Foucault or, for that matter, psychoanalysis have challenged these binaries. We can be active agents in our own oppression and complicit in the oppression of others while being oppressed ourselves.

Hammersley also asserts that research may be judged in other ways than its emancipatory potential: understanding complexity is a worthwhile goal in its own right. We agree, as we do with his suggestion that some of the values and theoretical influences associated with feminism are not exclusively feminist. However, where we differ has to do with the potential of research and research relationships to be empowering, to encourage questioning and reflexivity in and towards experience as well as concerning the processes of research. We have noted how the social order – and its dominant discourses – can pervade the stories people tell, but that people can reflect on these in the light of new experience. Research, in these terms, especially of a longitudinal and dialogical kind, can provide transitional space for really reflexive and critical learning.

Developing a categorisation

The different theoretical frames shaping biographical research are important and we have developed a simple schema for categorising some of the differences. They can be represented on a continuum: at one end, there is the highly 'scientistic' and objectivist orientation. The emphasis here can be on the importance of building overarching theory and on minimising the presence of the researcher rather than on intersubjective processes or more situated and partial understanding. At the other end, emphasis is given to engaging with subjectivity and intersubjectivity, focusing on immediate relationships. This includes the importance attached to building dialogue and reciprocity in research itself:

Conclusion

The theoretical bases of biographical research overlap but vary too. Symbolic interactionism has an important place as have the Frankfurt School and feminism

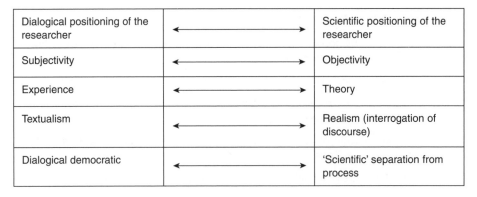

Dialogical positioning of the researcher	←——————————→	Scientific positioning of the researcher
Subjectivity	←——————————→	Objectivity
Experience	←——————————→	Theory
Textualism	←——————————→	Realism (interrogation of discourse)
Dialogical democratic	←——————————→	'Scientific' separation from process

Figure 4.1   Positioning within biographical research

in identifying repressive social norms and how these come to seem natural. Postmodernism has contributed, if in contested ways. Psychoanalytic perspectives provide insights into the dynamic and relational quality of subjectivity as well as of the working of desire and resistance. These are being integrated with socio-cultural and historic understanding as well as the neurological and embodied in thinking about the selves at the heart of biography. As researchers, we may draw on different theories or syntheses: there is, to an extent, a distinct Anglo-American research stream and a predominantly Continental European one, although there is overlap too. Feminism and subjectivism appear stronger in the former, alongside symbolic interactionism. Moreover, doing biographical research – as stated from the outset – can propel us towards interdisciplinarity as we wrestle to make sense of and represent the diverse dimensions of lives.

Key points

- Biographical researchers draw on a wide range of theoretical and epistemological perspectives.
- Theory, in the biographical perspective, tends to be middle range and/or pragmatic rather than overly abstract, although this can vary.
- Research is always and necessarily underpinned by particular theoretical perspectives, even if these may be obscure.
- Barbara makes use of feminism, symbolic interactionism and critical theory in her work, while Linden has drawn on psychology, sociology, feminism and psychoanalysis.
- Theoretical and methodological perspectives can be represented on a continuum from scientistic, more objectivist approaches to a more humanistic, subjective emphasis.

FURTHER READING

Blumer, H. (1983) *Symbolic Interactionism: Perspective and Method.* Berkeley: University of California Press.

Calhoun, C. (1995) *Critical Social Theory.* Cambridge, MA: Blackwell Publishers.

Crotty, M. (1998) *The Foundations of Social Research: Meaning and Perspective in the Research Process.* London: Sage.

Denzin, N.K. and Lincoln, Y. (eds) (2003) *The Landscape of Qualitative Research.* Thousand Oaks, CA: Sage.

Hammersley, M. (1995) *The Politics of Social Research.* London: Sage.

DISCUSSION QUESTIONS

1. Which of the theoretical perspective(s) discussed interest you and why?

2. Is there a particular biographical moment in your life – a transition or epiphany – to which a particular theoretical perspective may speak?

ACTIVITIES

1. A fieldwork activity: choose a social situation in which you are undertaking an activity with a friend or friends. At the end of the activity, ask each person in turn how he or she perceived the situation, and might interpret what went on, using some of the ideas in this chapter.
2. Think about your life career as a learner and chart it out on a timeline. Would you tend to think of yourself, at various times, as a defended subject?

5
Illustrating Good Practice

Case Studies

I know there are connections in life and there are ... narratives ... woven together in ways that we ... don't always understand when you are in them and if that means what I think it does [it is] a hugely beneficial thing to do to draw people's biographies together, because understanding the way that things are woven together and the connectedness of it ... can help enormously in the drawing together of programmes for individuals and coping with things that aren't working very well at the time ... it is a brilliant process, a brilliant thing to do. (A participant in a teacher education programme called Teach First, based in 'challenging' London schools.) (Linden West, 2006: 1; and 2009, in press)

Overview

In this chapter:

- We use four case studies from our own work to illustrate the potential of biographical research in greater detail.
- We look at structuring processes such as class, gender and ethnicity in biographical research.
- We examine how biographical research can enable complex 'psychosocial' connections to be woven across time and disparate experience.
- We consider how metaphors can be crucial in building understanding in research.
- Some ethical issues are introduced when engaging with painful aspects of biographies.

We offer, in this chapter, a number of in-depth case studies from our own work, designed to illustrate, further, how we use biographical methods and the role of theory in the interpretation of the processes and outcomes of research. The cases provide the backcloth to the next set of chapters, which are designed to help you to get started on selecting topics, doing interviews and interpreting material. We illustrate the extraordinary potential of such research to get to parts that many other forms of enquiry fail to and how narrative material enables us to weave connections between apparently disparate aspects of lives. The case studies encompass: research among families in marginalised communities, introduced in Chapter 3; work on gender and ethnicity in the learning lives of doctors (also introduced); and recent research on trainee teachers placed in difficult London schools. An example is also drawn from Barbara's work on adult learners in higher education, wrestling with the complexities of class, gender, ethnicity and identity in their lives. The cases illuminate our key interests in transitional processes and the interplay of structure and agency.

Families and their interactions with agencies

The research among families focused on whether particular 'family support' programmes were supportive or intrusive (West, 2005, 2007, 2008a, 2008b; West and Carlson, 2006, 2007). We wanted to chronicle and interpret the meaning and significance of interventions through the narratives of the families themselves, in the context of whole lifeworlds and histories. Sure Start, one of the programmes in the research, is, as indicated, a major, multi-agency initiative in the United Kingdom. It involves diverse professionals working collaboratively to support 'vulnerable' families with young children under the age of five, living in over 600 areas identified as having high levels of deprivation. The project is modelled on the American Head Start initiative (it is also similar to Best Start in Australia) and seeks to break cycles of deprivation and enable children to go to school better able to learn, while parents are encouraged to enter the labour market and/or participate in adult learning and training programmes (West and Carlson, 2006).

New Labour

Sure Start can be regarded as quintessentially New Labour, combining top-down approaches – target setting, highly conditional short-term funding and regular audit – with efforts to involve local people in the development of public services. Rhetoric of community empowerment co-exists with an emphasis on getting parents into the labour market as a means to tackle poverty. Like many such initiatives, Sure Start is deeply contested: these projects have been labelled overly intrusive and patronising – even morally authoritarian – towards marginalised families and are seen as derived from deficit models of people and communities (Coffield, 1999; Ecclestone, 2004). Parents rather than poverty, or the breakdown of adult solidarities in a more individualised culture, are blamed for diverse social ills.

According to the large-scale national evaluation of Sure Start (using survey methods, a range of measures over time and interviews with large randomised samples of parents), the programme appears to have had only minimal impact on families. Researchers, for example, have failed to find any discernable developmental, behavioural or language differences between children living in Sure Start areas and those living outside, although there is recent evidence that this may be beginning to change (NESS, 2005, 2008). It should be added, however, that the families in the national samples were not necessarily participating in programmes, which might be a major methodological weakness. And the design of the national evaluation did not allow for any dynamic, sustained and in-depth exploration of the meanings of experience for parents and children, over time.

The research questions shaping the auto/biographical study focused on the extent to which deficit models might drive programmes or whether the situation on the ground was more complex, with professionals and even parents shaping what was done. Does Sure Start represent a form of social control and discipline, we asked, getting people to think and feel in the 'right' way, rather than encouraging them to think for themselves and even to question dominant agendas? Might competing agendas be in play over what Sure Start represents? Might some parents, in particular programmes, be encouraged to question service providers and provision, and become more active citizens in the process rather than simply 'consumers' of services? Moreover, we wanted to explore ways of organising support that might best enable vulnerable families to seek and find appropriate help in the first place, given evidence of suspicion and resistance to public agencies, professionals and their agendas in many poorer communities (Ranson and Rutledge, 2005).

The method

We worked with opportunistic and purposive samples (see Chapters 3 and 6): 'opportunistic' sampling means more or less what is suggested. Researchers engage with those willing to participate, or who are interested or can be persuaded to be so, as we visited the project and asked for contacts from the staff. People could also have a particular experience they really wanted to share. A 'purposive' sample is designed to interrogate specific theoretical interests, for instance, the role of men in the project or in emotional labour in families, given how particular forms of male employment have diminished in marginalised communities (West, 2008b). We spent many hours with individual families (as well as staff), over five years, in up to seven research cycles. We visited a range of courses and meetings – formal and informal – over that time. We began by asking parents to share, in concrete terms, specific experiences of the programme – of encounters with particular services, courses or individuals and how helpful or otherwise these had been. People were asked to describe personal histories as well as experiences of living in the area, and any changing relationships in families, with children or a partner, as a result of specific interventions. As the research evolved, and relationships strengthened, these issues were revisited in what became a dynamic, iterative process, generating, testing and retesting hypotheses over time. Some participants became more confident and increasingly curious about their own lives: it was unusual, they said, for anyone to be interested and to listen, respectfully.

Interviews were taped and fully transcribed, using oral history conventions (see Chapter 7 for a discussion of these). Themes were developed inductively and parents asked to read transcripts, identify issues themselves and reflect on the process, including how easy it was to talk to us. A proforma was devised for analysing individual cases (see Chapter 8). This included transference and counter-transference issues in the research. (Transference refers to how researchers may come to represent, often unconsciously, significant people from a person's past – such as a parent or similar authority figure – while counter-transference concerns what this might evoke in researchers). Each proforma contained standard biographical data and emerging themes as well as references to reading or emerging ideas. Field notes and diary material were incorporated too while each of us as researchers separately completed a proforma for every participant and then compared notes and integrated the material.

Sure Start: a sustaining space?

Various themes crystallised around the metaphor of space. (We all make use of metaphors in research and writing: the spatial metaphor, in this instance, ranged from thinking about inner psychological space and mental health issues, to the quality of spaces between families and professionals, as well as the nature of the public space that was created in the project.) The programme might represent, for instance, 'sustaining space' for hard-pressed families struggling with poverty, family breakdown and/or mental health problems, or a transitional space, in which people might come to think and feel about themselves in new ways.

Heidi, a young mother with a partner and two young children, offers a case of finding sustaining space. She got involved in the Sure Start project by attending parent support sessions, a playgroup (with the children) and adult education classes. She also received specialist psychological support for a difficult mental health problem. She, and her partner Joe, were approached by a community worker and asked to participate in the study. They were cautious about seeing us, although agreeing to do so. We explained that Sure Start had commissioned the study because they wanted to understand the project from the perspectives of parents like themselves. We talked of wishing to explore family interactions with particular staff and services and to understand the significance and meaning of these within whole lives.

Joe said, early on, in a first interview:

> It's what happened to us as kids and it is difficult for those who have felt pain, to let others in, as people have got scars and that is one thing which they won't get rid of. It takes a long time to build confidence up … I was put in care when I was 14; I went to a children's home and then went to foster parents into a bed-sit. The bed-sit didn't go down very well. So, basically I ended up on the streets sleeping rough.

Heidi shared similar experiences:

> My dad didn't want me; he only wanted my sister and my brother, not me. So they left me in hospital and I've been with my aunt and uncle when I was three. Then I've been in another children's home then foster homes, then I stayed at my godmother's house and then in other people's homes and I said 'that's it, when I'm old I am going to settle down and have kids of my own, I don't want them to go the same way, what I've been through' … It is hard to explain to someone about what happened to me when I was a baby. Because I still haven't got over it, why my parents left me …

The material poured out as Heidi described being moved from one step-family to another, like Joe. She cried and we asked if she wanted to stop the interview but she insisted on continuing. She had never been able to talk to anyone about her life history before, she said. It was hard to explain, and she did 'not really understand myself why the things that had happened had happened, and not knowing how or where to start'.

She recently began a new parenting course: '[this] gave me more confidence to know what to do with my two children. At the end of it all I got this certificate. So I was really happy and pleased about it … '.

But her troubles, she said, were 'big', and she struggled with them all the time:

[B]asically we haven't got no family to help us, we're just basically on our own and that's it. At least we've done something good for a change. At least no one can slag us down at the end of the day … I don't want them [the children] to go the same way, what I've been through.

Sure Start appeared threatening at first, they said. They were afraid that people might be 'checking' on them and 'that was going through our heads all the time'. They were frightened of the children being put in care, of patterns being repeated, over time. Heidi said that they had to:

make sure we're looking after them properly, feeding them properly, things like that … To see if they are well looked after, washed and cleaned with clean clothes on their backs every day of the week. Making sure we've got food in the cupboards and food in the freezers … basically, it's what happened to us as kids. That's what most of the problems are, people have got scars and that is one thing which they won't get rid of.

Heidi talked of learning, gradually, to trust her community worker and other Sure Start staff as well as some of the other mothers she met:

They are more like mums to me. Like I've never had in my life. It feels more a part of my family as well as a friend … they feel like I am part of their family as well. Because I go to family group … and I meet with other mothers there.

Heidi began to have psychotherapy, which would have been unavailable without Sure Start. Her relationship to the project shifted, however contingently – as did the research relationship – from suspicion to greater trust. We arranged a second interview six months later. Heidi, especially, seemed pleased to see us. There had been positive feedback from the community worker about the first interview and Heidi remarked on how easy it had been to talk. Both Joe and Heidi read the transcript and 'liked having it all down'. They had thought further on their life histories. Heidi mentioned her 'psychological issues', which prevented her from cooking, among other things. There were too many 'unpleasant memories' in which her confidence 'had been destroyed'. Joe did the cooking and was helping to make certain dishes: 'eventually I will get there, one day'. Joe insisted, forcefully, that Sure Start was 'mainly for women there you see, so I wouldn't really get involved in that ... I can cope with near enough anything personally. I can deal with almost anything'. He was more distant, at times, in the interview, suspicious even, although contributing too. Heidi finished by telling us that she felt happier with the children because she had 'started putting my foot down on them, saying "right, you have got to listen to me, not me listening to you" ... I am more relieved that they are starting to listen to me now'.

She elaborated further on the importance of contact with other mothers and workers as well as her feelings of achievement in a number of the adult classes. Joe and Heidi were not alone in saying this. The meaning of Sure Start changed for many such parents, especially women, from an uncertain, even threatening space, to more of a sustaining one. Parents had been very suspicious: 'was this social workers checking up on us?' Yet most of the sample came to see the project as a resource, although some parents continued to resist involvement.

Tom Schuller et al. (2007), in researching the wider benefits of learning, and using biographical interviews, have noted the 'sustaining' effect of participation in parenting programmes and adult learning for many mothers. They observed how taking part in educational programmes enabled parents to maintain a sense of personal identity whilst bringing up small children. There was physical relief at getting out of the house, at having a temporal structure to the week, and having access to adult conversations. These processes were not to be judged simply in individualistic terms: time and again, understanding that other parents had difficulties with breastfeeding, or controlling their children, or with their own irritation and anger, provided a sense of relief and helped build self-confidence as well as mutual support. In small, but significant, ways the social fabric was strengthened and the lives of specific families improved.

More surprisingly, perhaps, the Sure Start project (like other particular family learning projects (West, 2007)) created what we termed 'transitional' and 'transactional' space. Transitional space is a concept originally developed by the psychoanalyst, Donald Winnicott, to denote and theorise changes in relationships between people. He was interested in the infant's struggle to separate from a prime caregiver and what made this possible, in psychologically healthy ways. He was to apply the idea to processes of separation and self-negotiation in adult life too, exploring what enabled people to move from dependency and defensiveness towards greater openness to experience and creative forms of endeavour; from relatively insecure to more confident forms of attachment (Winnicott, 1971). Spaces might take many and varied forms, such as an adult learning group or therapy. Significant others, and their responses, were seen to be important in re-evaluating self and possibility. A person could come to think and feel differently towards self, 'reality' and future possibilities because of the capacity of significant others (like a teacher or other respected professional) to contain anxiety, to encourage and challenge but also to respond to what was being attempted in ways that legitimised risk taking.

'Transactional space' can be considered a quasi-political concept: if parents are initially invited into a project on others' terms, how much might they be encouraged to question and shape agendas, which include those of local public services? There is a relational model of citizenship here, in which we learn our place as citizens in everyday encounters, and in the stories we hear, rather than simply through formal instruction in educational settings. Our sense of selves as potential political agents, in alliance with others, can shift, given the availability of space, in which to learn new ways of thinking, feeling and being (Biesta, 2006).

A young mother called 'Margaret' provides a case in point. She became an activist in a Sure Start programme, if reluctantly. She was fighting depression and struggling in an abusive relationship when she first engaged with the project. Going to Sure Start meetings was a major step. She was surprised to find that 'you did have an input and I felt involved, so … I just felt safe and relaxed'. Her growing trust of particular staff was central in her story in enabling her to take risks. She felt 'cared for and understood' and better about herself in the process.

Margaret joined the management board and more parents got involved. It was, at first, as she put it, 'completely alien'. The parents huddled together in a corner, trying to understand the language and rituals of professionals and local politicians. Representatives from public bodies would change at every meeting, making it difficult to build relationships and trust. Moreover, 'the suits', as the parents put it, seemed intent on pursuing their own agendas:

> For the first couple of times I was really nervous, but now it doesn't faze me, at first I used to sit in the background … it actually made a big difference that I knew they could trust me to do something and I wasn't going to make a big cock up of it.

Margaret described challenging certain professionals in a meeting over child protection policies and the treatment of local families (which, along with domestic violence, was a major issue on the local estate):

> I was very nervous about saying it; I got it out the way and thought it wasn't too bad … It was about the child protection … I knew I wanted to say it but would it come out properly, and it did so I was happy. It was a big step for me …

Most in the room would not have understood the biographical significance of her comments. For Margaret, in the totality of her life, it represented movement in a transitional space, a step towards embracing a new, more complex identity from simply 'being a mum, stuck at home'. She had claimed space for herself, in both transitional and transactional terms, and overcame, at least for a while, a potentially crippling anxiety. Such processes are small scale, barely discernable and easily missed yet biographically important. Auto/biographical research can illuminate such micro-level, dynamic shifts, in fine-grained detail, in ways that other methods may miss.

Research like this can, however, raise ethical questions: around the role of researchers, or the boundaries between research and therapy, and the need for a duty of care when working as a researcher. Research can represent a kind of seductive imperialism, claiming to empower yet exploiting people primarily in the interests of researchers and their careers (Hey, 1999). We return to some of these issues in Chapter 10 but it is important to consider the ethics of biographical methods (or other forms of research) from the outset. Questions are also posed about how to represent biographical material and around what is required by way of anonymising sensitive material, which we consider in Chapter 9.

Working and learning in the inner city

The second case comes from the auto/biographical study of the working and learning lives of family doctors or General Practitioners (GPs) located in difficult, demanding inner-city communities (West, 2001, 2004a). There was a particular interest in illuminating and theorising the emotional experience of being a doctor when faced, for instance, with depression or hopelessness in patients, which can result from poverty or poor housing: things not easily resolved by medical interventions alone.

The fragmented, neglected condition of the inner city, and its mounting crisis of social exclusion, escalating problems of mental health (in which one in three families is estimated to have someone suffering from mental illness (LSE, 2006)), will impact on a doctor and her work. Alienation, growing inequalities in health care and life chances as well as tensions in and between communities can play their part too. There are higher levels of unplanned pregnancies and substance abuse, as well as mortality rates, relative to national averages, in such areas. Two-thirds of asylum seekers and refugees in England and Wales arrive and settle in London. There are large numbers of people sleeping rough, squatters and hostel dwellers, while inner London has been the focus of a national HIV epidemic (West, 2001). Doctors can come to feel 'on the edge' themselves (another metaphor!) when working in these contexts. Their morale can be poor and incidences of stress, alcoholism and mental health problems, and even suicide, may be increasing (Burton and Launer, 2003; Salinsky and Sackin, 2000; West, 2001). There could also be – under the pressure to perform and meet targets to provide new services as well as to avoid blame and litigation – a disincentive for doctors to be open and honest about failure and difficulty in their work; or towards what they do not know or cannot handle.

Certainly, the morale of many doctors has, for a time, seemed shaky and there is resistance to greater prescription by government and its agencies. The pressure for improvement and accountability as well as 'efficiency', set alongside the low trust of policy makers – 'Dr Harold Shipman replacing Dr Kildare in the popular imagination' (Smith, 2001) – can find expression in ubiquitous clinical protocols, the monitoring of performance, compulsory reaccreditation and a drive for evidence-based practice. There is also a history of neglect, within medical culture, of the emotional and social dimensions of being a doctor (Burton and Launer, 2003; Sinclair, 1997). Despite the introduction of sociological, psychological and, to an extent, narrative forms of understanding in the professional curriculum, critical and emotional forms of learning – including locating professional practice in a broader culturally and socially aware critique – may continue to be marginal in medical culture with its no-nonsense, practical ethos (Burton and Launer, 2003; Sinclair, 1997).

The study involved an opportunistic and purposive sample of 25 GPs and lasted four years with up to six cycles of in-depth biographical interviews. Transcripts and tapes were used to establish themes and consider their meaning and significance, collaboratively and dynamically, over time. The study became, in certain instances, a profoundly 'auto/biographical' and dialogical process with reference to gender, masculinity and the nature of emotional labour, as Linden was wrestling with similar issues in his own life and professional practice, not least in training as a psychotherapist (West, 2001, 2004a).

Crisis and an epiphany

Dr Daniel Cohen, a participant in the study (whom we met in Chapter 3), felt like an outsider in medicine:

> I don't believe in what the mainstream believes in … I am … often appalled by the discourse … the whole set of assumptions about the nature of reality, about … the doctor's power and … sexist and racist … ideas and … the collusion around that … I feel profoundly alienated … Like mining a seam of gold called the medical fact … from a pile of shit … the patient's … life … a way of talking about patients as if the patient isn't there …

Daniel had experienced a crisis of career eight years previously. He was unhappy at work, he said, while vocational education, of whatever kind, seemed incapable of meeting his needs. Being a doctor forced him to ask basic questions of himself, he said, at many levels, as he engaged with patients who were frequently asking questions, sometimes profound, of themselves. There was no neat distinction between the patients' questions – 'who am I?' or 'why do I have the kind of problems that I have?' or even 'what is good and decent?' – and those faced by a doctor. There was a seamless web, he insisted, connecting their struggles to his.

Daniel used psychotherapy and experiential groups to consider issues in his personal and professional life as well as revisiting his family history. He was the child of refugees from Nazism, which led him, like many others, into the caring professions. The desire to heal, he thought, was primarily directed at self. He was brought up with the experience of Nazism and fleeing persecution, but the emotional dimensions of this were rarely talked about in his family. He was driven by a need to succeed and never to complain or rebel. What 'right' had he to complain about anything given what his family had been through? He described himself as having been outwardly successful but inwardly distressed.

There was, he said, continuing neglect of the subjective and emotional dimensions of being a doctor, or, for that matter, of critical social perspectives in what was a practically orientated profession. Yet such understanding might lie at the core of being a more authentic doctor: the science had to be integrated with other ways of knowing, social critique with empathic understanding and technical know-how.

Daniel placed new relationships, and self-awareness, at the heart of a kind of epiphany in his life: a moment of significant change and transition (Denzin, 1997). He came to feel better about himself as a doctor and more able to manage different aspects of the work. Two colleagues, a therapist, a new partner and their young children, alongside a supportive, 'learning' sub-culture in the practice where he worked, helped him towards engaging more openly and eclectically with patients. GPs' working lives, Daniel concluded, were situated between the truth discourse of the mainstream and the uncertainties and messiness of whole people and whole problems. A subversive synthesis was required, taking what was essential from the medical model but locating this within a person- and narrative-centred approach, as well as cultural and self-awareness.

Learning to be a teacher

The third case derives from research into teacher education, this time involving a group of would-be professionals, working and learning in difficult and 'challenging' London schools (West, 2006, 2008a). Participants in the research were part of a new teacher education programme called 'Teach First'. This recruits from among 'the brightest and best' graduates from 'elite' universities. Participants have a six-week induction programme provided by a university and then work towards Qualified Teacher Status (QTS) in the first year, completing a portfolio as evidence of reaching a range of standards, with the support of university tutors and schools-based mentors. Participants take a probationary second year and a management leadership course run by a Business School. They can then choose to stay in teaching or opt for a different career: a potentially alluring prospect given the top companies endorsing the project and providing mentors (Hutchings, 2007).

The efforts of particular trainees to become teachers and to work in authentic ways – in situations often evoking difficult feelings – echoed aspects of Daniel's story. The trainees were engaged in significant transitional processes in their own lives – from university into a possible career – and feelings of vulnerability and uncertainty could surface despite their educational success. This related to the need to better know the self in working contexts and to understand how best to engage with pupils and their difficulties; or to the role of schools in multicultural communities; or how to manage feeling cynical, at times, not least in relation to achieving Qualified Teacher Status (QTS) ('jumping, sometimes cynically, through hoops', as one participant put it). There could be troubling concerns over the lack of any clear, structured relationship between their experiences in schools – with pupils and teachers, or issues of racism and sexuality – and the formal aspects of training.

It should be noted, by way of ideological context, that a discourse of leadership from 'gifted and talented' people – bringing leadership to bear on the problems of the many – infused the programme, reflecting the increasing influence of private-sector rhetoric in education. This is in marked contrast to earlier discourses of educational improvement, which were often predicated on recruiting more people into teaching from marginalised groups. Teach First was seen as a vehicle to challenge, change and modernise teacher education as a whole and the trainees were often encouraged to perceive themselves as a new kind of elite (Hutchings, 2007) – all of which could be seductive yet might add to the pressure to succeed.

Rupal

Rupal, for example, was placed in a mixed secondary school with a high level of students eligible for free school meals (over 40%). Educational attainment was poor. One thing that attracted Rupal to the school, she said, was the diversity of cultures among pupils, who often needed support with English as an additional language. She felt ethnic minority pupils would benefit from the presence of an Asian teacher, acting as a role model. She initially embraced the Teach First project because it projected enthusiasm and a chance to 'offer a ray of hope'. Rhetoric of leadership, however, did bring pressure, including the fear of not living up to high expectations, which echoed themes across her life. 'I've always tried to do everything that I can, I always pile on too much and then like drown under everything'.

Rupal worked hard with particular pupils:

> There's so much I want to give to them … I am an Asian girl and I am getting some-where … There's … a couple of really bad kids … but most of them are really nice people just looking for attention, they've all got problems … and they just want someone to care for them … It's very difficult … one black guy he's just a nightmare, he's got so much attitude … My Year 10 … just hell … just taking the piss … they are really pushing me as hard as they can … A lot of time I end up … just going round sorting out behaviour problems … Discussions … I couldn't do that because they don't respect me and it's learning how to do that.

Her anxiety increased as the placement progressed, intensified by problems in her private life. She talked of 'leading a double life' and the 'challenge' of being part of an ethnic minority culture while also embracing London and its hedonistic side. She reflected on a difficult family history, of losing a sister to terminal illness, and being an anchor to her parents, one of whom had a severe disability. She had been forced to grow up early and had needed to earn money while doing her degree. She said, 'I still value my religion and the rest of my culture but I still have fun like the rest of them'. The challenge was to reconcile different parts of her life and to feel better as a teacher. She was aware that teaching asked a lot of her and that 'I work hard and play hard'. She knew her public self had to appear competent even if built on a fragile base. But it was hard to keep up appearances and she turned to coun-selling for help.

She began, in her first year, to articulate what she saw as the weakness of teacher education. She talked of the meaninglessness of 'standards' when there was little or no space to explore and interrogate what they might mean in the specific context of her classroom:

> [M]aybe we should be responsible for our own learning and progress, but when we are doing a full teaching load you do tend to forget the training stuff … in some ways it is pointless, going through, doing all this portfolio stuff, making sure you have met each standard to me is nothing.

She became disenchanted with doing assignments and craved, sometimes desper-ately, forms of knowledge that could be applied in the classroom:

> It is having some knowledge and applying it, but you don't necessarily have to learn knowledge from reading books … You make learning a lot more active and in the same way that in the classroom students are learning, I am learning, I learn every lesson. And that is where the learning is valuable, because I read a paper and I will forget it. I can't remember what I read in that journal in a week's time. It means nothing to me.

She perceived the school as difficult and riddled with tensions between the staff as much as pupils. Her departmental head was helpful but had other participants to look after and Rupal sometimes felt abandoned, echoing earlier life experience. Disruptive classrooms, including racism, dug deeply into her. She could empathise with young Asian pupils, and they with her, she remarked, but felt undermined by racist behaviour from particular white and black boys. She thought there was insufficient support or time to think about this or about the role of schools in multicultural environments. Ironically, the process of the research provided a more structured and supportive space, she felt, for considering her working life and training:

> [I]t was good to see them [the transcripts] ... I think there are times before that we have spoken and I remember coming out feeling as if I had managed to reflect and actually think something new, because I spent quite a lot of time in the last two months ... reflecting on what I am doing here ... the whole point of it ... I think that the Teach Firsters who haven't had this opportunity ... have probably missed out in the sense that if I hadn't [had] this then I would have just been stuck in the school not having anyone else to discuss anything with ...

Biographical research can illuminate the complexities of learning and transitional processes, beyond a potentially reductive, one-dimensional rhetoric of people as 'leaders' and change agents, which may characterise contemporary educational discourse. We are given access, instead, to narratives of resilience but also of difficult emotional experience, when working in troubling contexts. Ironically, academic high flyers can struggle in such situations, and may need to learn, among other things, about their own vulnerabilities as a way of better understanding their pupils (West, 2008a).

Class, gender, ethnicity and learning in higher education

The final study – of adult learners in higher education and the place of class, gender and ethnicity in managing identities – employed a more explicitly sociological frame of analysis (Merrill, 1999, 2003, 2007). Lifelong learning and widening participation policies in the UK have opened up educational opportunities in higher education for more working-class adults. However, achieving a higher education qualification is not always easy because of gendered, classed and raced inequalities, as well as having to negotiate movement across different cultural spaces. Biographies of women adult learners, particularly working-class women, consistently reveal the struggles and the determination of women to transform their lives through education, and yet how difficult this can be (McClaren, 1985; Merrill, 1999; Skeggs, 1997; J. Thompson, 2000).

Working-class adult students bring with them into higher education their life experiences and biographical and cultural baggage; or, to draw on Bourdieu's work, a particular habitus or set of dispositions which incline them to react in certain ways. During their university career, adult students develop and (re)construct a learning identity. However, the integration of adult students into a university culture can be far from straightforward:

[T]he reality of accessing education and staying in further and higher education, particularly for working class women, remains difficult for institutional, structural and cultural reasons. These are further underpinned by gender and class factors. Although there are now large numbers of adults in both further and higher education sectors, in the UK, institutions continue to be largely structured around the needs of young people rather than, for example, women who have multiple roles in the private and public spheres. Women's lives and participation in education also expose the inter-connectedness of gender and class in shaping identities. (Merrill, 2003: 134)

Gender, class and biographical approaches

We have observed how feminist researchers have used biographical methods to give voice to women's oppression. As Jane Thompson explains in relation to working-class women students:

[Biographical methods are] a way of exercising critical consciousness and of producing knowledge from the inside about gender, class and education, deriving from personal, particular and shared experience. Not in the pursuit of ultimate truth but in the search for greater, more nuanced, understanding. (2000: 6)

Feminist biography has highlighted more of the interaction between the personal and political, between public and private lives. Individual biographies reveal that personal experiences at the micro level are often shared, as gender, class and ethnicity are played out in everyday situations. In C. Wright Mills' terms: 'the personal troubles of milieu' are linked to 'the public issues of social structure' (1973: 14). The biographies of the women students Barbara worked with reveal how gender and class, and, for some, race, intersect. Biographical research becomes a rich tool for chronicling these processes:

Biographical research may at first sight appear to be too individualistic an approach for engaging with class (and gender) and adult learning as biographies are largely analysed as an individualistic way of understanding the social world. Yet in constructing a biography a person relates to significant others and social contexts: a biography is, therefore, never fully individual. (Merrill, 2007: 71)

The two student examples below are drawn from a European Commission (EC) funded project entitled 'Learning in Higher Education' (2004–2006), involving seven European countries. The research was undertaken with a colleague, Rennie Johnston.

Paula

Paula is in her late 30s and a mother with two boys. She was interviewed first in her final year of a BSc in Applied Social Sciences at the University of Southampton, New College and then two years later when she was a teacher in a secondary school in a working-class neighbourhood. Paula has a strong working-class identity, at one time referring to herself in her role as teacher as a 'defender of her class'. She feels very strongly about not patronising or making unjustified assumptions about working-class kids.

> I think I will stay in a school that I work in because I can say to them, I do say to them: 'I was the same as you and there is no reason if you want other things you can't get them. Whatever it is doesn't matter, whether you want to be a teacher, whatever it is, you can get there'.

Her class identity is closely connected with a learning identity, one that was initially shaped by her mother's wide reading but also by her own childhood experience at school:

> Yes [I was] well behaved and got on with my work. I just feel that there was a lot of potential that I had that was totally wasted because assumptions were made about me. Too young at the time to know but I do feel it came back to my background and my family and where I lived and that influenced how they treated me and that's why college was never even mentioned.

Although Paula did well at school, she was expected to go out to work. It was only later when she had been working in a bank for some years, and was a mother, that she asserted some agency in response to the prevailing sub-culture of the bank. She began to compare herself with her (predominantly) male colleagues: 'They didn't see things in the same way and I did more work than them'. She began 'questioning the moral issue of the job I was doing and I thought I can't do this for the rest of my life ... I just thought there had to be more to life than this'. This feeling helped Paula to overcome longstanding, negative feelings about undertaking further study: 'Before I felt I hadn't proved my potential, I knew I was capable of more but was always quite scared of getting above my station.'

She was prompted to start borrowing books on sociology and politics from the library and then to apply for an Access course. (An Access course is aimed at adults with the aim of equipping them with the relevant skills to study in higher education.)

> And [the Access course] fired me and oh it's just ... yes I felt I fitted and I thought I made this happen – this is what I want to know about and this is some of [the] things that I have never ... been quite been able to explain. Yes I can see why I am being ... I am what I am.

Paula's belief that people and institutions continually made assumptions about her continued as an adult student at university. While at one level she thrived, through her love of the subject, well-developed reading, a reflective approach and highly developed organisational skills, she still lacked confidence in a university environment, like several of the project participants:

> You never lose that. I don't think you ever lose that – you learn to live with it but you don't ever lose that. You always think I am not worthy of this. That's something

I feel and you still think that you shouldn't be here and you are a con – you know, how did I get here and I slipped through the net and I shouldn't be here.

An important element in her feeling that the university was 'other', in cultural terms, was the use of particular, often obtuse, academic language. Paula thought that:

language is used to exclude particular people and this was a real barrier in the learning environment … This is something that colleges and universities often forget; they assume that their audience have all been educated in a similar way to them. This increases the workload of students from non-traditional backgrounds.

She made a distinction between two different language codes: one for university, one for home. Later, however, she saw this as an advantage in her work as a teacher:

I can communicate with some parents far more effectively than other teachers because I can put things in a way they understand. They do not feel patronised or intimidated when I speak to them, and consequently a good relationship can develop.

Despite periodic bouts of feeling unworthy, Paula was successful at university. She was able to compensate for negative feelings by specifically choosing courses and tutors that enabled and encouraged her to use her life and work experience in her academic studies. She also drew on support from her peers. A key factor in stimulating her learning, and in negotiating a new identity, was the use and acknowledgement of life experience, a common feeling amongst mature students in the study:

I think the key factor was taking into account life experience … using the experiences that mature students have got. The more I go on the more I realise that learning whether it's at a school, a college or a university, they are so narrow in the way that they teach or assess.

Thus, Paula was able to make active and meaningful connections between her experiences and sociological theory. This was very productive for her studies, not least in writing what she saw to be an impressive final dissertation, which focused on children, class and health.

Paula's negotiation of a learning identity was tied into her working-class habitus:

I see myself not as moving between class. I see myself as having achieved something within and saying 'yes' I am working class and this is what I have achieved. But I wouldn't want to think that my roots have changed. I looked at some of the other people I worked with and think, no I am not like you and don't want to be like you.

Paula's structural position was fixed, although she was still able to compose and exercise agency to good effect in higher education. Her agency had been constrained, initially, by class and family assumptions, and only emerged later in her life, partly in reaction to the structural unfairness of a gendered workplace. However, as a working-class mature student, she felt in the minority, alongside mainstream, younger students. Yet Paula was able to build on and translate her experience into an appropriate academic language while making full use of her strategic and organisational skills in pursuing her studies and her ultimate goal of teaching and supporting kids from backgrounds like her own.

Mark

Mark's identity revolved around being working class and black (of Asian Caribbean descent). He used agency successfully as a learner while maintaining his ethnic and class background. Mark studied for what is termed a 2+2 Social Studies degree at the University of Warwick while in his late twenties (a degree aimed at local adults with the first two years being taught at a Further Education college and the last two years at Warwick). He was first interviewed towards the end of his degree programme and then two years later. While at university, he became a successful rap poet. He now works in this field, mostly with schools, doing poetry with children and running cultural identity, tolerance and black history workshops. He also became a poet laureate in a local city. Mark enjoyed learning at school despite having attended several different schools. For him, school and learning was an escape from an unhappy home life. He was the eldest of five (one brother later died). His mother was very young, at 16, when she had him. Domestic violence was part of family life and his father also spent time in prison. Mark lived with foster parents for some of his childhood:

> I always did like going to school. I moved around a few primary schools. I passed my 12+ [an entry test] and went to a grammar school. I think the reason I enjoyed going to school so much was that home life was sort of up in the air and also other issues which made me delve into my schooling and education. My brother went the other way and ended up in a life of crime. I found almost solace in going to school – that's why I enjoyed it. I put the time in and did quite well. Yes it was a positive experience.

Mark could remember key teachers who supported his learning and this still had an impact on him, as past and present merged in the story telling: 'There were two people that … probably took an hour out of their time over a period of years to talk to me one-to-one, how is it going sort of thing and took an interest'.

He went to a grammar school (a state school, as noted, that requires people to pass an entrance test). He was the first person in his family to do so but felt that as a result of family life, he did not do as well as he might have done:

> well I didn't go off the rails, but I think the lack of parental guidance at that time when you are about 12 or 13 makes you try to grow up and tries to make you be a leader or joker of the class … I basically wasted my time. I wasted the opportunity. I know I had the capability and the talent, well not so much talent it was more like a work ethic … I just kind of grew up a little bit too fast at that time.

He left grammar school with three 'O' Levels (exams taken at the age of 16) and went to art college for two years, which he really enjoyed:

I could be an individual at art college and express myself – I didn't excel at it. I did enjoy producing quality work but what I enjoyed more was the environment – freedom … I kind of fitted into that you know youth looking for identity, growing your hair, you know art student.

He continued his education by taking what is called a Higher National Diploma (studying in higher education but at sub-degree level) in advertising, in London, where he was easily distracted from studying by rave culture. Mark left his studies and stopped attending classes. He felt that there was 'nothing really to tie me down. I then kind of drifted into a job and that was the end of my education really'. Returning to the Midlands, he became a chef but lost the job when the hotel closed down. Being unemployed and living on benefits forced him to take positive steps to change his life and career: he had children to support as a single parent. This led to his opting for an Access course at a local college. Learning became important in his life, once more, and this time he was determined to work hard and achieve. Returning to learning offered a means of re-gaining an identity or, as he described it, 'to be myself': he could even grow his dreadlocks again. Completing an Access course made Mark feel confident about learning when he started the 2+2 Social Studies degree:

I felt head and shoulders above the rest because I felt that they were coming in similar to how I was a year ago … I knew the college, I knew the lecturers … So I kind of coasted through which was a bit hard for the group dynamics because I always had an answer.

For many 2+2 students, the transition from college to Warwick is a difficult period. Mark prepared himself for this, as he knew that the culture and language would be different: 'I kind of see it as the analogy of jumping into the swimming pool. Everybody is going to go under for some amount of time – the first few weeks'. He developed a coping strategy:

I came over to Warwick a few times before and checked out the place and got to know it and I got used to the feeling of being the odd one out. You know a lot of the students are younger so there is the age thing … Also I am not the ideal student in the way I look I suppose. I am the working-class dodgy looking geezer and with respect quite a lot of people at Warwick are middle class.

He was aware that his cultural capital was different and that he was marked out by his clothes and speech, but like others in the study, Mark adapted to the student role and 'learnt the ropes' of a new institution and became more of an independent learner:

I wasn't going to sit at every lecture and listen to every single thing because my brain just couldn't take it … so I realised very quickly you had to be selective. So I pushed for essay titles straight away, I pushed for essay deadlines and indications of questions.

At the same time, he decided that there was no point in doing certain essays. In *Boys in White*, Becker et al. (1961/1977) observed a similar pattern of behaviour among the medical students they studied: 'Students reason from their definition of the situation:

if there is more to do than can be done in the time available we can solve the problem by taking short cuts in the way we learn' (Becker et al., 1961/1977: 117). For
Mark, this was linked to an instrumental or what he calls 'a functionalist' approach
to learning and he was very clear that he was doing a degree in order to improve
his job prospects:

> I kind of sussed the game out to start with, which is important, you just can't take
> it as a personal thing – it's a processing of people every year and you've got to play
> the game so it was functional. I was doing it for a reason – the hours were counting
> up and I was looking at added value eventually. That's what kept me going.

In both interviews, he mentioned being working class several times but also stressed
that being black was central to his identity, which stemmed from his childhood:

> My dad instilled a lot of views in me about racism and how it's a bad society and
> how you should be proud to be black and black pride. But he had it a lot harder
> than I had. I don't think it's so in your face as it was as political correctness stops
> people saying some words.

His notion of who he was, ethnically, was challenged by what he learnt on a mod-
ule about migration and identity. He emphasised how 'it changed my life' when he
discovered that he was descended from indentured labourers of Indian origin.
Mark's father had always thought they were of Jamaican, Afro-Caribbean origin:

> At a lecture I was sitting there looking at pictures of what I thought were my family
> members and they were pictures of indentured Caribbean labourers and I was
> really shocked … my identity, physically I was walking around going 'I'm Asian,
> I'm Indian'. My dad had assumed an Afro-Caribbean identity though he was Asian
> looking so that had a massive impact – just that lecture – a personal thing that had
> to do with my identity. I then wrote a poem called 'I am Anglo-Indo-Caribbean' so
> literally those three words affirmed my identity.

Mark's structural position was less fixed and secure than Paula's. Yet by drawing
on a range of personal resources he was able to develop some agency in engaging
productively with university culture. He maintained his working-class and black
identity and superimposed a learning identity upon this. Yet this could also be
problematic: 'Constantly on my shoulders there are two voices. But they are not
good or bad, they are my working-class response and my academic response and I
constantly have to choose which I do'.

The identities of being black, working class and a university graduate still interact and are being worked through in his role as a poet and with children in schools.
At the same time, he is more comfortable with multiple identities:

> I think my outlook mainly has changed – confidence levels, massively, massively
> changed. I think I'm more confident in my identity as a whole, more accepted and
> also more confident if I'm not accepted. Yes I think I am happy with my identity
> now and realise how learning helped me put that into perspective. I have tons of
> poetry about identity that just keep coming. I think words have helped me with my
> identity and that's what learning for me has done.

On reflection, Mark believed that going to university was 'the best thing I ever did really, I can't say enough about it' and he is considering returning at some future date to do a postgraduate course.

In both these instances, learning identities changed as a result of engagement with higher education. Both Paula and Mark were successful in university by adapting to objective requirements for success, but without abandoning who they were in the process. Learner identity is shaped and transformed through the dialectics of structure and agency. The self is an ongoing biographical project, as Shilling stresses: 'The building of a cohesive self is a never ending process precisely because of the individual body's unfinishedness and openness to cultural influences' (1999: 558). Studying in higher education develops and transforms an individual's learning identity and habitus through the interplay of structure and agency, culture and individual lives. Adult students leave as changed persons, yet for some, they continue to identify themselves in recognisable, biographically connected ways. They need not lose their working-class cultural capital, indeed they can build on it, with new forms of intellectual and social capital.

Making connections

The cases in this chapter reveal different approaches to biographical research: by a sociologist and by someone more drawn to psychological interpretations. Yet there is overlap and space for conversation across the boundaries. The socio-cultural lies at the heart of family life and selfhood, as in the experiences of the doctors and teacher-trainees. The psychological is evident in adult learner narratives, around issues of identity, selfhood and struggles for agency. Biographical research constantly raises other questions: about the relationship between past, present and future, or between who a person has been, is and might be, and how change can be theorised. Biographical research gets to parts often neglected in conventional research and helps us begin to weave new empirical and theoretical connections. We now turn to more practical issues to help you get started and to undertake research like this. Yet, as will be observed, the practical issues of sampling and doing interviews raise major questions about validity and the quality of our relationships with the other.

Key points

- Case studies can reveal the power of biographical research in understanding individual lives and subjective experience but in ways connecting to wider social and cultural processes.
- Case studies highlight the interaction and inter-relation between agency and structure in people's lives.
- Both sociological and psychosocial dimensions are important in understanding biographies.
- Case studies may powerfully illuminate how individuals manage change and multiple identities in their lives.

FURTHER READING

Merrill, B. (1999) *Gender, Change and Identity: Mature Women Students in Universities.* Ashgate: Aldershot.

Merrill, B. (2007) 'Recovering Class and the Collective', in L. West, B. Merrill, P. Alheit, A. Bron and A. Siig Andersen (eds) *Using Biographical and Life History Approaches in the Study of Adult and Lifelong Learning.* Frankfurt-am-Main: Peter Lang. pp. 255–78.

West, L. (2001) *Doctors on the Edge.* London: Free Association Books.

West, L. (2007) 'An Auto/Biographical Imagination: The Radical Challenge of Families and their Learning', in L. West, P. Alheit, A. Anderson and B. Merrill (eds) *Using Biographical and Life History Methods in the Study of Adult and Lifelong Learning: European Perspectives.* Hamburg: Peter Lang/ESREA. pp. 221–39.

West, L. and Carlson, A. (2006) 'Claiming and Sustaining Space? Sure Start and the Auto Biographical Imagination', *Auto/Biography,* 14: 359–80.

DISCUSSION QUESTIONS

1. Are there any biographical resonances for you in reading the material in this chapter?

2. What do you think about the boundary between research and therapy in some of this work?

3. Do you tend towards a more sociological or psychological way of understanding lives? If so, why?

4. Are there particular metaphors that attract you in considering aspects of your life history or maybe your biography as a whole? The metaphors of the journey or of 'patchworking' a life are frequently used and might help you think about this.

6
Getting Started in Research

We insist that the presence of the researcher, as an ordinary human being with the usual complement of human attributes, can't be avoided. Because of this we must devise research of a kind which can utilize this presence, rather than pretend that it does not happen. (Liz Stanley and Sue Wise, 1993: 150)

Overview

In this chapter:

- We examine the role of the researcher's self and biography in the choice of a research topic.
- We look at ways of getting started and identifying research questions.
- We introduce different sampling methods.

Introduction

In Chapters 3 and 5, we illustrated the range of work and approaches in the biographical family, which raised issues of truth, of researcher 'bias', of unconscious processes and the workings of power; and of the interdisciplinary imperative. We have also illustrated how biographical methods can illuminate complex dynamics easily neglected by other researchers. In the next three chapters, we move to the specifics of how to do biographical research, which includes interviewing, analysing and representing data. We consider, first, how to select a research topic, which can involve an explicitly autobiographical dimension: it is entirely legitimate – if also requiring some thought – to choose something important in our own life or family. We think further about the role of the researcher and move on to topics such as working alone or as part of a team. We examine choosing samples in research and the differing assumptions and aspirations that shape this. We ask questions our own students raise: 'can you really work with only one person?' or, 'the numbers are very small, and does this really count therefore?' This chapter also considers how best to make contact with people and institutions and the need to be clear about ethical issues (a matter of increasing importance, especially in health-related research). And we introduce the role of critical friend(s), of support groups and of piloting research, and the importance of being realistic yet also passionate about research.

You, our readers, will be at different stages with varying levels of experience. You may be an individual researcher doing a Masters degree, or writing a Doctorate of Education or PhD dissertation; or you may be writing an undergraduate assignment. You might be a researcher working in a research team, addressing a very specific research topic, or you may be a practitioner in a public service wanting to use biographical methods to build better professional understanding. If you are a research student, the most difficult issue to resolve can be 'what should I research?' Whatever your situation, the choice of topic needs to be something you are interested in and motivated to work on, otherwise it will be difficult to keep going through hard times and you might end up dropping out or feeling disillusioned.

The following questions might be helpful in getting started:

- What do I want to research and what do I feel passionate about? You may have more than one idea initially.
- What would I really like to understand?
- What do I want to find out about the topic: what are my research questions?
- Is my topic and are my research questions realistic and possible within the time, resources, and – if a funded project – the funding I have?
- Why does this topic interest me and why do I think it is a good topic to research?
- What theoretical and disciplinary approaches may be of interest and what do I need to read?
- What is the existing literature in the field?
- Why have I chosen a biographical approach and is it the most appropriate?
- Whom do I want to interview, why and how many times?
- What are the ethical considerations?

What to research?

For students and new researchers, it is important to consider where you stand in relation to the differing theoretical and disciplinary influences as well to the varying ways of thinking about the nature of research. The starting point could be to engage in a very small study, perhaps with a relative or friend. It is partly a matter of finding out and learning what is the best approach to biographical research for you; or even whether you want to work in this way at all. At one extreme, you can learn by going out into the field and doing research, albeit with some prior thought and reading. At another, you could immerse yourself in the literature on the theory and practice of biographical research and attend workshops/conferences (these are not mutually exclusive). If you are a research student, you might feel that this could be a lonely business and look for a group of other doctoral students to work with as critical friends. Other researchers may be part of a team, some of whom have experience of biographical research. Being a member of a team can enable you to work collaboratively and discuss the research, its design, problems and potential with colleagues. Biographical research represents a collage of shades, emphases and ways of understanding, rooted in different disciplinary and methodological traditions, although there are, as described, aspects in common too. You need to make choices, however, with a clear rationale.

Whatever approach is taken, research is fundamentally about learning, as mentioned in Chapter 4. The word research derives from the French rechercher, to seek. As researchers we seek, through experience, to understand how others live and make sense of their lives; and our own too. Maybe we are seeking answers inside ourselves and experience can be a source of data and a means to understand and empathise better with the other but also ourselves. Yet there are dangers, as noted, of bias, of only seeing what we want to see or of only hearing material that speaks to present needs, however unconsciously. Nevertheless, the self and subjectivity can be a rich resource in making sense of others' experience and to challenge, in turn, our own assumptions, as in Linden's work on families. Yet working more auto/biographically, and valuing subjectivity and intersubjectivity, can ask a lot of researchers, including self-knowledge. We need others alongside to assist in a task that can be exciting as well as puzzling, liberating as well as sobering, profound as well as messy.

The role of the self in choosing a topic

The choice of a topic may be shaped by a funder's agenda and or by personal or professional concerns (Bertaux, 1981a, 1981b; Clough, 2004): it is not a neutral process (Esterberg, 2002). Corrigan's (1979) study *Schooling the Smash Street Kids* is relevant because, unlike most social researchers, he discusses, from the outset, 'why bother to do research?' He outlines his biography to explain why he chose to research working-class boys' experience of schooling.

> As an 11 year-old boy from a south London working class background I felt that I was lucky when I passed the 11-plus and went to a grammar school. In my first term I was fairly afraid of the institution, worked as best as I could, and managed to come top. During the term, however, we were all asked if we wanted to see the school play, *Othello*. We were told to go home and see if our family wanted to go. My mum and dad had something on that night; I didn't care for Shakespeare and I didn't buy any tickets. I was one of a very small minority, and at the end of the school term was told, not that I had done well, but that I must support the school more.
>
> I didn't understand that very well then; it puzzled me because I thought school was about academic subjects. The rest of my time at school was similarly affected by a whole series of events which I could not fathom. My parents assured me that these didn't matter; but it was as if there were unwritten goals and rules which I did not comprehend. (Corrigan, 1979: 4, 5)

Corrigan's writing is refreshing in that researchers rarely explain how and why they chose a research topic. It appears as a given, as if there are no experiences or puzzles, rooted in biographies, which have led people to engage with a topic. Even in research textbooks on 'how to do it', the initial processes of getting started and identifying a focus are rarely discussed biographically. This may emanate from the historically powerful imperative in the academy to distance self and subjectivity from the academic project in the name of good and impartial science.

We noted, from the outset, how the topics we have pursued are deeply interwoven into the fabric of ourselves and our biographies:

Barbara

I mentioned in Chapter 1, and further illustrated in the last chapter, how issues of gender and class have been central throughout my life and that this is reflected in my research interests. In the preface of my first book, *Gender, Change and Identity: Mature Women Students in Universities*, I wrote:

> I wanted to understand the world of adult education from the viewpoints of the learner, particularly women adult students, within a framework of gender and class relationships.
>
> Gender, class and race inequalities have been central concerns throughout my life. Being female and of working-class origin, I soon came to experience initially class, but later gender discrimination and inequalities in society. Later, as a teacher in a multicultural comprehensive school, I quickly became conscious of the pervasiveness of racism in society through the lives of the black pupils.
>
> Many of the pupils at the school where I taught had been alienated by the white middle-class school system and left school having underachieved. Did the adult students at Warwick share similar life histories? If so, why had they chosen to return to learn, and why at this particular moment in their lives?
>
> My development and research work brought me into contact with mature women students … However, it was gender issues that stimulated my interest and thinking … although I could not ignore the links between gender and class. I was struck by the women's enthusiasm and determination to learn, despite the problems they faced both within and outside the university. (Merrill, 1999: vi–vii)

Linden

As mentioned, I was interested in what motivated people to learn; and at some level was asking questions about my own motivation. In my first book – *Beyond Fragments* (1996) – I wrote of needing to understand motivation in new, interdisciplinary ways. Motivation had partly to be understood in social terms, not least in understanding how history, culture and class, alongside a present social situatedness – for example, social marginality – may shape attitudes towards educational participation. My parents were shaped by the structuring processes of class and gender, and the discourses surrounding them. My mother was born in 1913 and women, on the whole, for her generation, were not encouraged to go to university (West, 1996: 21–3). Senses of the complex psychosociology of my family's life, understood in historical, structural but also psychological terms led me to being interested in other's lives and to building some interdisciplinary understanding of the web of emotional, psychological, relational as well as socio-cultural strands which lie at their heart.

(Continued)

(Continued)

Later, in my research on doctors and their experience of the emotional aspects of their work, I realised I was asking questions of myself, as a man – about dominant discourses of masculinity – and as a professional and a father, and in training as a psychotherapist.

I was interested in concepts of gender and the emotional division of labour in families, in working contexts and across whole cultures. In the book on doctors, I wrote:

> I suggest the personality, background, situation as well as the conceptual frame of the researcher always and inevitably shape the way people tell their stories, and how these are interpreted … I was, during the time of the research, undergoing major changes in my life and renegotiating aspects of my identity. This included continuing to train as a psychotherapist, negotiating difficult transitions in my role at the university, which led me to question the relative weight given to a public as against a private self. I was beginning to establish more of a 'patchworked' lifestyle, in which psychotherapy and intimate life had greater priority. I was reading the psychoanalytic literature and seeing training patients … Gender loomed large in this context. Psychoanalytic history and writing are redolent with gendered assumptions. Freud was the good bourgeois, in patriarchal Vienna and reflected his times. He wrote about the enfranchisement of women, for instance, and thought John Stuart Mill's arguments overlooked domestic 'realities'. A woman's role was to keep a household in order, to superintend and educate the children. He conceded that the day might come when a different educational system would make for new relationships between men and women, but, after all, *'nature'* had destined women, *'through beauty, charm, and sweetness'* for something else (Gay, 1988). But there was another side to the story in Freud's acknowledgment of the fragile construction of gendered identity (Connell, 1995). Further, as Joseph Schwartz (1999) suggests, the historically very male world of psychotherapy has been shaken to the core by feminist perspectives, over the last two decades (West, 2001: 35).

> My struggles to rethink what it meant to be a man and father as well as a therapist – to understand more fully my own emotional experience, and to interrogate the constructed nature of gender, through a psychosocial frame – were at the heart of engaging with others.

Janet Miller (1997) argues that not only does the choice of a topic reflect our own autobiography but so too do our research questions:

> beginning with the story of (my) own interest in the question (I am) asking and planning to research into. From that initial story, (I) may move towards the mapping of (my) developing sense of the question's interest for (me) onto the history of more public kinds of attention to it. This becomes a way of historicising the questions (I am) addressing and of setting (my life) and educational history within contexts more capacious than (my) own. Theory becomes theories; historically contrived to address or explain particular questions; and we are all theorists. (Miller, 1997: 4)

The questions we ask of ourselves, of which we may at first be unclear, can be integral to choosing a research topic and to shaping our engagement with the other.

Identifying research questions and the research process

A frequent mistake, whether writing an undergraduate dissertation or a postgraduate thesis, is to choose too big and broad a topic. For example, unemployment might be of interest but this needs to be narrowed down by looking at some particular aspect, such as:

- Do women and men experience being unemployed differently?
- What impact does class have on unemployment?
- What are the barriers to entering employment when you are unemployed?
- How does being unemployed affect the self in relation to health and social issues?

Studying motivation in learning, 'psychosocially', is another example. It is, potentially, a massive topic and ways have to be found to focus a study, such as engaging with particular kinds of adult students entering higher education (West, 1996). An initial focus might be:

- What factors in a present life affect the decision to enter an Access to higher education course?
- What is the place of class, gender, age and family in the choice, both past and present?
- What is the influence of significant others?
- What is the influence of a learning life history, which includes schooling and other experiences?

Of course, as the researcher finds his or her feet, it may be possible to explore other issues and weave these into interviews and interpretation but this can only come with confidence, wider reading and experience.

We also have to be realistic in terms of time and resources. This means that the research topic and questions need to be focused, at least to an extent, in the interests of manageability. We cannot research or know everything about a topic. If choosing a focus may not be difficult because of an interest generated by our own histories, what might be difficult is transforming the topic into a realistic research project.

It is essential not to construct too many questions. Identifying and formulating research questions is not always easy or clear-cut. Being overly prescriptive and rigid may blind the researcher to what people are saying of their experience and lives. Researchers, however, need some structure alongside flexibility as new questions emerge from the research. Biographical researchers can have differing stances towards this: some insist on more structured questions, to focus a study, while others thrive on open-endedness and uncertainty, using the material itself, inductively, to shape and alter the focus and process of enquiry.

The following are examples of research questions taken from a project on retention of non-traditional students, and its relationship to the development of learner identities in higher education, referred to in the last chapter:

(Continued)

(Continued)

- Why and how do some non-traditional students successfully socialise into a student role and career, completing HE studies while others from similar backgrounds drop out or drop out and re-engage later?
- What processes enable them to become learners in HE, and how is this subjectively understood?
- How and in what ways does (or does not) learner identity develop? And how is this constructed?
- How can biographical methods contribute towards enriching our understanding of the psychosocial dimensions of learner identity and processes of completion and drop-out?
- How do factors such as social class, gender, ethnicity and age impact upon completion and drop-out rates?
- What developments in thinking, in organisation, culture and practice are required to achieve more effective completion rates for non-traditional students in higher education?

Textbooks and the literature on research – as well as published accounts of research – can give the impression that the focus and questions emerge and develop in a clear, linear and ordered manner. In reality, this is rarely the case, as questions change and we can feel muddled and lost as well as struggle to articulate what we want to know or should ask. Accounts of doing research get sanitised, partly because of the need to appear competent and logical in what we do. It is important to remember that in practice it is very unusual for research to go smoothly. Rather, it can be a messy business in which there are setbacks and progress is uneven. Here are some of the problems we have experienced:

- Our questions change and we get confused about what it is that we want to know.
- A delayed start to the project as the funding body is late in giving approval and funding delays the appointment of research assistants.
- Falling behind deadlines as outlined in the research plan, for example, interviews taking longer than planned because participants may not be able to attend for interview in the scheduled timescale.
- An identified case study institution decides not to participate.
- Comparative European research takes longer than planned because of the need to understand different contexts and the need to reach consensus in relation to biographical approaches.
- Arguments about the nature of interviews and the extent to which they should be semi- or un-structured.
- Some participants may not turn up for their interview.
- Some participants may decide to drop out of the research project.
- A research assistant may leave during the project.
- Crises of confidence, including over the focus and questions.
- Too much to handle.
- Trying to get the data and material in order too quickly.
- Not enough focus/too much focus.
- Personal troubles intervene.
- Getting ethical approval takes longer than expected.

Choosing a sample

Once a decision has been made on a topic and possible questions, there is the need to consider who to work with and how many times. Depending on the nature of the study, you may need to select an institution(s) as a case study(ies): such as a university, hospital, community centre, etc. Sampling is the term used for the process of deciding how many institutions and people to work with. Jennifer Mason defines sampling as: 'selecting groups or categories to study on the basis of their relevance to your research questions, your theoretical position ... and most importantly the explanation or account which you are developing' (1996: 93–4). Or, as Ken Plummer puts it, rather graphically: 'Who from the teeming millions of the world population is to be selected for such intensive study and social science immortality?' (2001: 133).

Howard Becker in his book *Tricks of the Trade: How to Think About Your Research While You're Doing It* begins his chapter on sampling by saying: 'Sampling is a major problem for any kind of research. We can't study every case of whatever we're interested in, nor should we want to' (1998: 67). He goes on to criticise the scientific, positivistic approach which assumes that: 'We need the sample to persuade people that we know something about the whole class' (Becker, 1998: 67). Quantitative researchers argue that a large number of people within a given population have to be researched if findings are to be valid, reliable and generalisable (see Chapter 10). Qualitative researchers have responded and justified the use of small samples, even of one or two subjects, including the researcher's self – on different grounds – such as whether lives are information-rich and provide substantial material from which to weave a better understanding of important issues (Burgess, 1984; Glaser and Strauss, 1967; Steedman, 1986). Michael Erben argues:

> What the size of such an interview sample should be will be dictated by the purpose for which the research is being carried out. The exact size of any sample in qualitative research cannot be ascertained through quantitative methods. It is for this reason that it is all the more important that the consciously chosen sample must correspond to the overall aims of the study. (1998: 5)

Generalisability can be an obsession among quantitative researchers but may be less important for some biographers. The latter can be more interested in working with people who have potentially rich experience to share while samples may be constructed with the potential intensity of experience and the possible quality of the insights generated in mind. Yet qualitative researchers, including biographers, can get defensive when other researchers criticise their work for being unrepresentative. They may take steps to ensure that their samples share characteristics with a wider population such as Shaw's study of Stanley in *Jack the Roller* (see Chapter 10).

In Linden's work on doctors, the sample size – 25 – was partly shaped by issues of representativeness (age, gender, ethnicity, working location, etc.) but also by awareness of the dominance of positivistic assumptions in the medical world and a need to appear respectable. This meant generating a huge amount of narrative material (too much, in fact, to handle, given up to five cycles of interviews over the study) and there needed to be more of a focus on a small group with particular and rich experience to share. This may be part of a larger question: whether social researchers are primarily interested in social types and categories or individual lives. There is a potential tension here between orientations informed by the humanities and the social sciences. In the humanities, more importance can be attached to what may be unique and subjective and there is less preoccupation with the general or structural. This tension exists at the heart of biographical enquiry, and our own work, and we return to the issue in Chapter 10 and at the conclusion of the book. We are searching, in the spirit of C. Wright Mills, for perspectives that incorporate social forms and inner worlds, and the dynamics between them, and do justice to what is unique but also representative.

We have also learned not to feel defensive about small samples, or doing individual biographies, which, in fact, have been the norm in psychoanalytic forms of knowledge generation as well as for historians over a long period (Plummer, 2001; Rustin, 2000). Single life histories can provide rich material while the unique and human-centred can be used as a basis for generating highly original forms of interdisciplinary understanding, drawing on historical, social and psychological imaginations (see Chapter 9). Bent Flyvberg has written that:

> For researchers, the closeness of the case study to real-life situations ... is important for the development of a nuanced view of reality, including the view that human behaviour cannot be meaningfully understood as simply the rule-governed acts found at the lowest levels of the learning process, and in much theory. (2004: 422)

Mike Rustin (2000) reminds us that good biographical research, including the individual case study, like good literature, can sensitise us to what is common or representative in human experience. We can recognise in others' lives things we and a range of people share, and good research can help us see others, but also ourselves, in a new light, like Beckett's fictional Godot or Shakespeare's Hamlet. Good biographical research in the main is not about numbers per se but the power of description, analysis, insight and theoretical sophistication. But we have to address questions of representativeness and how we relate the particular to wider human groups, or concerns, even if this is done in more of a literary, humanistic spirit.

Sampling: troubling to students

Nonetheless, we are very aware that the size and nature of samples troubles students. Anxiety may partly stem, as noted, from the literature and from positivistic assumptions about the nature of academic enquiry. Some PhD supervisors, including ourselves, can get anxious about students using small samples because it might be criticised by external examiners, or research colleagues, as 'unscientific' or 'unrepresentative'. Research may involve more than one supervisor and a research panel – a Chair, and a first and second supervisor at Canterbury Christ Church University, for instance – and attitudes about sampling may vary in the group. In situations where students are involved in choosing supervisors and/or examiners, this can be dealt with by opting for people who use biographical or similar methods and understand the issues. The number of participants chosen in funded research may also depend on money available, the length of the study and the number of researchers. But funding bodies can be influenced by the quantitative paradigm too and may rarely fund research based on small numbers.

Biographical researchers themselves vary, as noted, in their attitudes towards sample sizes: it can come down to money or the need to convince policy makers. Some biographical researchers have constructed samples to represent the categories used in large-scale surveys or have correlated their data with findings from such work, to build a stronger case for generalisability. One major United Kingdom study of the wider impact of participation in learning correlated biographical evidence with findings from 'large-scale data sets', including the 1958 and 1970 British Birth Cohort Studies, known as the National Child Development Study (NCDS) and BCS70, respectively. The team drew particularly on NCDS data relating to changes in the lives of adults between ages 33 and 42 (Schuller et al., 2007). In a related way, Hollway and Jefferson (2000) selected 37 people for their biographical work on the fear of crime to reflect differences generated by the British Crime Survey around sex, age and high- or low-crime residential location. Such large-scale surveys often derive from random samples, designed to secure as representative a group as possible from whole populations. Yet, Hollway and Jefferson (2000) proceed to interrogate the idea that large data sets are always and inevitably a source of validity or sound knowledge. Categories such as class and gender, when broken down into sub-sets, and on closer inspection of the original data, reveal a diversity of response, or potential ambiguity and nuance which gets ironed out in the analytic and writing process. A great deal can be lost when researchers are too distant from actual cases. Difference between people in similar situations can be dismissed as irrationality or statistical error. Or as unimportant relative to the need to simplify in order to build statistical links with whole populations, in manageable ways. Biography can challenge some of this to the core and we return to the issue in Chapter 10.

Other biographers, such as Gabriele Rosenthal (1995) in her study of holocaust witnesses, have interviewed large samples, in her case 810 people, but she had a big research team and a substantial grant. Large is not necessarily good: small can be beautiful, sometimes more so. Janice Morse (1994), for instance, advises no more than six people while seminal work by Carolyn Steedman (1986) has been based on two people, a mother and daughter. Rob Evans, in his research on the learning experiences of German university students, discusses some of the problems in very practical ways:

> The number of interviews aimed at from the outset underwent significant changes as feasible workloads crystallized out of the original (over-ambitious) aims ... The aim was to collect in-depth interviews and transcribe as many as possible fully for analysis with electronic language corpus analysis software ... The number of transcripts ultimately transcribed sufficiently in order to be included in the corpus remained at seven in total. It is clear, however, that even with this significantly reduced number of full transcripts (the original aim had been to transcribe at least 20 in full!) there are methodological and practical arguments against even such a number. The simplest argument is the sheer weight of work involved in the transcription process. (Evans, 2004: 69)

The weight of work is an important consideration but so too are qualitative questions about what our subjects have to offer by way of experience, how rich their stories might be, and of what we need to do to enable them to build thick descriptions of lives, as a basis for more sophisticated forms of understanding. We now want to illustrate other kinds of sampling and the terms that are used.

Opportunistic sampling

Opportunistic sampling is when researchers take advantage of situations to interview individuals, through luck, chance, the right word being said, or because people offer themselves (Miles and Huberman, 1994). One person who volunteers willingly to tell their life story can be preferable to any number who are reluctant: better one enthusiast than an army of the press-ganged! Dan Goodley in Goodley et al. (2004) writes about the life story of Gerry, an adult with learning difficulties, and explains that he met Gerry through doing voluntary work:

> He had always intrigued me. Here was a person who boasted a rich and varied life. Unlike many of his peers, Gerry dipped in and out of service settings, professional cultures and institutional practices. While many people with learning difficulties inhabit these contexts from residential home, to day centre, to charity-organised disco on a Tuesday evening, Gerry entered these places only from time to time. His life appeared to say something about existing differently from his welfare-located peers. Maybe he appealed because his ordinary life of family, friends and work seemed so extraordinary in view of many lives of institutional living experienced by so many of his friends. (Goodley, 2004a: 72)

Sociologists frequently claim to have found their participants through opportunistic encounters. W.I. Thomas, for example, met the person for his study with Znaniecki, *The Polish Peasant in Europe and America*, by chance, as was the case with Stanley in Clifford Shaw's (1966) work.

Criterion, theoretical, purposeful/purposive sampling

John Creswell states that criterion sampling 'works well when all individuals studied represent people who have experienced the phenomenon. All individuals meet this criterion' (1998: 118). The researcher selects relevant people for research on the basis of their experience, such as diverse doctors (in terms of gender and ethnicity, for instance) working in difficult parts of London and the Medway Towns (West, 2001). Or, as with Barbara's (Merrill, 1999) research, there is interest in working with a range of mature women students in universities.

Theoretical sampling is often associated with what is termed the grounded theory approach. (Grounded theory refers to a process by which categories or themes are systematically derived from a careful analysis of data, following particular procedures.)

'For a grounded theory study, the investigator chooses participants based on their ability to contribute to an evolving theory' (Creswell, 1998: 118). The term purposeful sampling can be used interchangeably with theoretical sampling. Mason defines theoretical sampling as follows:

> Theoretical sampling means selecting groups or categories to study on the basis of their relevance to your research questions, your theoretical proposition ... and most importantly the explanation or account which you are developing. Theoretical sampling is concerned with constructing a sample ... which is meaningful theoretically, because it builds in certain characteristics or criteria which help to develop and test your theory and explanation. (1996: 93, 94)

Thus, in the study of doctors, gender became conceptually important as a way of thinking about the cultures and sub-cultures of the medical world as well as of individuals and their biographies. The sample was expanded, at a crucial stage, to include more women doctors as a way of chronicling experiences of emotional labour in domestic as well as professional space (West, 2001). Mason stresses that theoretical sampling is not rigid and the sample may change as the research progresses: 'Theoretical or purposeful sampling is a set of procedures where the researcher manipulates their analysis, theory, and sampling activities interactively during the research process, to a much greater extent than in statistical sampling' (1996: 100).

Glaser and Strauss' (1968) study of terminally ill patients dying in hospital is often cited as an example of theoretical sampling. More recently, in the field of adult learning, Tom Schuller et al. (2007) in their work on the wider benefits of learning, referred to above, used purposeful sampling for the biographical parts of the study, on the basis of identifying potentially interesting categories of people gleaned from the large 'data sets'. Different sampling methods can be combined in one study.

Snowball sampling

Snowball sampling involves the researcher asking participants if they know of other people – friends, work colleagues or members of the family – who might be willing to be interviewed. Numbers, in short, can snowball. This type of sampling is useful if the research focuses on 'hard to reach groups' such as the homeless or drug takers. In a study undertaken by Barbara and others on adult participation in further education colleges in Scotland (Gallacher et al., 2000), the team wanted to include non-participants. Some participants in the colleges were asked if they knew of people who had never participated in further education and they suggested various individuals and acted as a link to them.

If you are involved in a mixed methods project, questionnaires provide a good tool for obtaining volunteer interviewees by inviting participants to complete a form (given at the end of the questionnaire), if they are interested and willing to be interviewed. Such an approach enables the researcher to recruit willing participants but this may not provide equal numbers in terms of gender, age, class or ethnicity and not everyone identified for interviewing will be willing to give up his or her time. Which sampling approach to choose depends too, as repeatedly emphasised, on what is appropriate for the particular study and what it aims to do, and this could mean convincing policy makers who may revere numbers more than qualities.

Preparing yourself for undertaking interviews

Once a decision has been taken on how many people should be interviewed and on what terms, there are several preparatory steps to be taken. On the practical side, it is important to involve participants from the start and to be honest and explain clearly and comprehensively what the research is about and what is being expected. Initially, the contact may be by letter, email or phone, inviting people to be interviewed as well as explaining the aims and objectives of the study, including how long an interview may take. All communication should be in clear and intelligible language. There are ethical issues to consider such as confidentiality and that participants can leave at any stage of the research, if they want to. (Ethical issues, as we keep saying, are of profound importance and we return to them in Chapter 10.) Not everyone will respond positively and volunteer to participate, which can be for very good reasons: they may simply have more important priorities. Gerson and Horowitz (2002) have considered some of these issues.

Securing the help of strangers is, in some respects, the most anxiety-provoking task of the interviewer. It takes a strong belief in the value of one's project and a certain amount of chutzpah to ask others to share their most personal, intimate stories for no other reasons than the advancement of knowledge and the possibility of increased personal awareness. Even though most agree to help, the possibility of rejection arises anew each time a new batch of letters is sent and a new set of phone calls made. Convincing others to contribute to a project that must necessarily be a collective endeavour depends on having a strong belief in the value of the study and a warm but persistent approach. If these initial contacts secure a high level of participation, it becomes easier to keep spirits high when the inevitable, if rare, rejection occurs. (Gerson and Horowitz, 2002: 209–10)

If institutions are to be used as case studies, permission will have to be gained at an appropriate level. Enquires have to be made as to who might be the right person to approach. The aims and objectives of the research will need to be explained, as will issues of confidentiality and anonymity, which can relate as much to institutions as individuals.

It may be necessary and important to send out, in advance, notes of guidance for interviewees and a consent form. The one illustrated below is taken from the study of motivation among Access students.

Access student motivation

A study being undertaken by Linden West and Mary Lea in the Unit for the Study of Continuing Education at the University of Kent.
  Notes of guidance for interviewees and conditions of use form

1. This particular research project is concerned to understand the motivation of Access students in depth. The methodology involves conducting a series of interviews over a period of time with a view to understanding participation in learning and motivation more generally, in the total context of a person's life history and current circumstances.
2. We are conducting interviews with thirty students from a number of institutions. The students have been chosen to assure a range of ages, occupations, unemployed and employed people, social and ethnic backgrounds as well as gender balance.
3. Given the potentially sensitive nature of the material, you have an absolute right to refuse to answer any questions asked as well as to withdraw from the research at any stage. We will be careful not to push you in directions you do not wish to go, or to assume the role of the therapist.
4. You have the right to withdraw retrospectively any consent given and to require that your data, including recordings, be destroyed. Obviously, it is important for the researchers to know your position as soon as possible after reading transcripts. Refusal or withdrawal of consent would normally therefore be within two weeks of receiving a copy of the transcript.
5. Confidentiality is a key issue. We will provide each interviewee with a conditions for use form which will allow you to preserve anonymity if you so wish. As a general rule the material is to be used for research purposes only (unless prior permission has been obtained, for example to use tapes in teaching). We will take all steps, if this is what you desire, to preserve your anonymity in the presentation of case studies.
6. Each of you will be given transcripts of your interviews and, if you wish, a copy of your tapes. You may edit the transcript as you see fit and we would like you to return the final form of all transcripts two weeks after the final interview in the stamped, addressed envelope provided. The final edited versions of the transcripts and all the tapes will be kept with the researchers (Linden West and Mary Lea) in the Unit for the Study of Continuing Education. Apart from specified researchers, any other access will be with your permission only. We will also try to arrange at least one event to which all participants in the project are invited, which will provide you with an opportunity to discuss and criticize our findings and analysis of motivation.
7. In general terms these procedures are informed by the British Psychological Society's statement of Ethical Principles.
8. Thank you for all your help in and contribution to our research.

(West, 1996: 219–20)

Some students and researchers new to biographical work become very anxious about conducting a first interview, which is the subject of our next chapter. The telling of life stories and the memories it may evoke can be painful, intimate and deeply emotional for interviewers as well as interviewees; and we need to be aware of this possibility beforehand. Irene Malcolm (2006) has outlined her experiences of undertaking life history interviews for the first time as a research assistant, working on a large funded project on learning life histories. Her experience was highly emotional as her first interviewee, a woman, became upset and cried as she told her life story. She felt, as an interviewer, unprepared for the situation. She argues, as a result, that training, guidance and support should be given to new, inexperienced researchers. Similarly, it is important that students receive support, advice and training from supervisors. Pierre Dominicé (2000) suggests that supervision – as practised in a range of therapeutic, health and educational settings – should be a feature of doing educational biographies. It can also be helpful, even essential, to have a critical friend(s) or a support group (this could be peers) to talk to and who can give feedback on what we are doing, saying and writing, including its emotional and autobiographical dimensions. It may also be helpful, provided an interviewee agrees, to observe a biographical interview done by an experienced researcher.

Conclusion

We have emphasised that you should choose a topic of real interest: you will have to live with this for a long and potentially intense period of time, especially if writing a PhD. A carefully thought-out research proposal and plan will also facilitate the development of research. At the same time, research will not always go as planned. We have to learn to be flexible and reflexive in our use of biographical methods. Research can be a source of surprise and of profound learning.

The researcher's self, as constantly stated, is always present: doing research is a journey for the researcher as much as the researched. Penny Burke states:

> I have written myself into the book as a co-participant of the research. The research process was complicated *and* enhanced by my position as a teacher researching her students, and as a woman juggling paid and unpaid work, trying to negotiate the patriarchal boundaries that separate the private and public realms of social life. I did not experience my research as a separate entity. My life as a mother, wife, grand-daughter, daughter, friend, teacher, student, external moderator and researcher all overlapped, clashed and reinforced each other in ways that are rarely written about or theorised in the academic world ... My research was influenced by my identification as a feminist, my subjectivity and the many other dynamics that determine my perspectives and identities, so I was drawn to the theories that resonate with my own experiences, values and beliefs. I found this in critical research and feminism, both of which politicise research. (Burke, 2002: 4–5)

Doing biographical research can be rewarding and enjoyable but also painful, perplexing and political. Such issues, in the context of doing interviews – which have a central place in biographical research – are explored in the next chapter.

Key points

- The values, attitudes, interests and autobiography of the researcher can be used in choosing a research topic.
- However, the choice of a research topic may be constrained by the priorities of research funding bodies or by available time and resources.
- Quantitative approaches to sampling are, in the main, inappropriate for doing biographical research, although they can be used to select sub-samples.
- Preparation and support are important when undertaking biographical interviews, especially for the first time.

FURTHER READING

Becker, H.S. (1998) *Tricks of the Trade: How to Think About Your Research While You're Doing It.* Chicago: University of Chicago Press.

Esterberg, K.G. (2002) *Qualitative Methods in Social Research.* Boston: McGraw Hill.

Goodley, D. Lawthom, R., Clough, P. and Moore, M. (2004) *Researching Life Stories: Method, Theory, Analyses in a Biographical Age.* London: Routledge Falmer.

DISCUSSION QUESTIONS

1. Why is generalisability not considered to be so vital when using biographical approaches?

2. Why are scientific sampling approaches as used in quantitative research considered, at least to an extent, to be inappropriate or even unhelpful?

3. Why have you chosen to do biographical research?

ACTIVITIES

1. If you are undertaking research, reflect upon why you chose a particular topic and identify in what ways it reflects your interests, experiences, attitudes and autobiography.
2. For each of the sampling approaches outlined in the chapter, suggest a topic of research for which that sampling approach might be appropriate.
3. If you are about to undertake your first biographical/life history interview, note your concerns and anxieties but also what you are looking forward to.
4. If you have undertaken biographical interviews, reflect back to what you were concerned or anxious about.
5. Identify a research topic and write a letter to invite a sample of people to participate in the study.

7

Interviewing and Recording Experience

There was also one aspect of creative process that had turned out to be fundamental ... the aspect of perception of the external world. Observations of problems to do with painting had all led to the idea that awareness of the external world is itself a creative process, an immensely complex, creative interchange between what comes from inside and what comes from outside. (Marion Milner, 1971: 146)

Overview

In this chapter:

- We consider the nature of interviewing and examine different views on this, including those drawing on feminist and psychodynamic ideas.
- We consider different approaches to biographical interviews, including the narrative and interactive interview.
- We provide examples of interviews from our own work and consider the importance of building trust.
- We consider how to transcribe interview material and the conventions which can be used.

We suggested at the end of the last chapter that there is much to think about in relation to interviewing. We now consider more of the theory and practice of biographical interviews and how best to generate what can be called rich description or 'good stories'. By good stories, we mean narrative material that is both rich in detail but also experientially inclusive and reflexive in character. We note, in doing this, that biographical research is an act of interpretation from the outset and the researcher shapes the process and its qualities. At another level, we offer examples of different approaches to interviewing, including an example taken from a collaborative European project in which we are both engaged. We also consider differing approaches to transcribing interviews and the conventions that can be employed.

A creative act

Doing biographical interviews is not simply a matter of good technique, as important as this is: they represent a potentially creative space between people, requiring attention to their emotional qualities as well as conceptual insight. This is partly about using non-threatening and open forms of questions. It is also to do with the research relationship and the 'psychosociology' of the *inter*-view.

Of course the term *inter*-view implies relationship. Traditionally, this has been thought of in negative terms, at least in mainstream research: the researcher, subjectivity and intersubjectivity, have been a problem, a source of 'bias' or distortion. From this more objectivist and positivistic perspective, the researcher's biography and subjectivity need to be removed or minimised in a struggle to build reliability: different researchers should produce more or less the same answers or data when working with the same people if research is to be considered valid. There is, in such a perspective, a truth and nothing but a truth waiting to be revealed, regardless of who interviews or the nature of the interaction.

On description and using the moment

Description and perception – and thus interviews – are highly creative and dynamic acts. The quality of biographical interviews will depend on what we as researchers bring to the encounter, not least our awareness of immediate and wider contexts. This includes sensitivity towards what is happening when we first encounter the other.

Naomi Stadlen (2004) helps us to think about what can be involved. She describes two people, separately, witnessing and responding to the same situation. We can imagine them as researchers and that Stadlen is one of these. (Maybe you can think of yourself in this situation and how you might respond.) Each of the researcher/observers enters the same house, in turn (we can think of this as a setting for a biographical interview) and notices the bathroom with the door open. There is a tube of toothpaste on the floor:

> Its top has rolled goodness knows where. A toothbrush with some paste on it lies unused on the rim of the sink. Someone must have been disturbed who was about to brush their teeth. That person is in the next room. She's a woman, a mother with her baby. What is she doing? Well, how you answer that question depends on you yourself and what you see when you look at her. (Stadlen, 2004: 258)

Stadlen offers one interpretation, with a potentially gendered dimension. The observer/researcher could perceive an unfortunate woman with a very demanding baby who could not wait while she brushed her teeth but kept crying. Such a person might feel, Stadlen writes, that babies ought never to have been invented. Stadlen then shares her interpretation, as a woman shaped by an immersion in and understanding of processes of caring over a long period. She makes her standpoint clear: that caring – despite its importance – is often culturally undervalued and goes unnoticed, often by men. We are not, in this view, neutral and passive observers but interpret, from the outset, whether consciously or not. She interprets the situation in a qualitatively different way:

> I see a totally exhausted-looking mother, pale and dark shadows under her eyes, who miraculously has the energy to sing and rock her baby in a way that he is starting to recognise. I see him relax, and his tense body seems to melt into her arms. He isn't crying now. His whole being is attentive to the music and wonderful rhythm of the mother who is comforting him so well. It takes a long time until he finally reaches sleep. When he does, the whole room seems at peace. Something momentous seems to have changed. It has been a journey, a transition from distress into harmony. The mother looks up with a warm smile. The miracle was hers, but perhaps you and I helped her by being there and seeing what she did as 'something'. (Stadlen, 2004: 258)

You might find the language unscientific and overly sentimental, yet the point remains that our subjectivity, and wider cultural understanding, shape our response and interpretation. This could be a first interview with a young mother as part of a biographical study of single mothers, pregnancy and raising a child. There is, potentially, rich material to begin an interview and yet we may barely notice. Or we may worry about departing from a prepared script for fear of being a bad or biased researcher. But good interviewing requires attentiveness to moment and context, to the emotional tone and qualities of a situation and how this can help or hinder our work. We might also, in our actions, as feminist researchers insist – by recognising that something important is happening and giving it words – build potentially more empowering forms of enquiry.

The contribution of feminist research and the positioning of the researcher

Feminist researchers have paid particular attention to interviewing and its potential for empowerment. Such research has often been conceived of as by women and for women. Feminism recognises that the presence of the researcher is always there:

> Basic to feminism is that 'the personal is political'. We suggest that this insistence on the crucial importance of the personal must also include an insistence on the importance, and also the presence, of the personal *within research experiences* as much as within any other experiences. (Stanley and Wise, 1993: 157, original emphasis)

Stanley and Wise go on to stress that:

> all research involves, as its basis, an interaction, a relationship, between researcher and researched … Because the basis of all research is a relationship, this necessarily involves the presence of the researcher *as a person*. Personhood cannot be left behind, cannot be left out of the research process … We see the presence of the researcher's self as central in all research. (1993: 161)

Feminist interviewers can strive to build more equal and democratic relationships so that the interview becomes more like a conversation. Feminists often take issue with notions of detachment for the sake of it, and maintain that the researcher should answer questions if asked by the participant, even if these are about the researcher's life. Oakley (1992) outlined what she felt a feminist approach to interviewing should be, in an essay entitled 'Interviewing Women'. For Oakley, answering questions was important for building up rapport with her interviewees: she called this 'no intimacy without reciprocity' (1992: 49).

In writing about her research on *Becoming a Mother* (1979), Oakley stated that she kept in contact with some of the women after the research had finished and even attended the birth of some of their children and in some cases became a friend. We are not suggesting that qualities of detachment are irrelevant to interviewing, rather that it might be important to come alongside, to understand, to be reflexive, as well as to cultivate some analytic detachment, in the research relationship. There may be parallels with therapeutic processes in which the therapist needs to develop a capacity for absorption in another's story, alongside, paradoxically, having internal mental space for thinking about what is happening.

There are further questions to think about, which various feminist researchers, such as Sherna Berger Gluck, Daphne Patai and Susan Armitage, have raised (Armitage and Gluck, 2006; Gluck and Patai, 1991). These are about the authority of interviews and the need for self-, but also cultural and historical, awareness. Whose story are we hearing, whose memory or understanding of a situation is being evoked? They challenge the idea of the traditional interviewer as sole source of authority and emphasise the importance of a wider contextual understanding of why particular people may tell particular stories at particular times. Gluck, for instance, has re-interrogated her research with Palestinian women and how the assumptions of an emerging feminist consciousness should be tempered by understanding of wider political influences on story telling – the pressure, for instance, for political conformity at particular historical moments (Armitage and Gluck, 2006). Parents in studies of family support programmes can repeat dominant, ideologically inspired accounts of their situations: that problems are essentially theirs, as is the responsibility for sorting them out. Of course, this can be an important 'finding' in its own right but researchers can also think of how to engage people, reflexively, in considering what may shape the stories they tell.

Only women?

Many feminists argue that only women can interview women because they share and understand a woman's experiences. For Oakley, 'a feminist interviewing women is by definition both "inside" the culture and participating in that which she is observing' (1992: 57). Others, such as Harding, disagree and point out that 'significant contributions to other emancipation movements have been made by thinkers who were not themselves members of the group to be emancipated' (1987: 11). This is an issue for Gluck and Patai (1991), given the diversity and complexity of women's experience, and of how gender may interact with class, race, sexuality and other structuring processes. Who is the insider in such contexts?

Barbara was involved in a project about participation and non-participation in further education in Scotland in partnership with Jim Gallacher and the Centre for Research in Lifelong Learning at Glasgow Caledonian University. The Scottish Office Education and Industry Department (SOEID) funded the project. Biographical interviews were used and Barbara was anxious about whether working-class Scottish men would open up and tell her their life history, or whether a male interviewer would be more appropriate. However, in practice this was not a problem and the men talked at length, and covered at times, very personal issues.

Linden has written of how we can exploit our own experiences of marginality – of feeling like outsiders and being ignored – to understand other's lives, including the troubled career of a lesbian doctor, Aidene Croft, who was introduced in Chapter 4. She was alienated from what she experienced as a highly gendered medical culture. But she learned, over time, that being silenced and misunderstood enabled her to understand the silences and evasions of patients; and that this was as important as the more scientific aspects of medicine. Mirroring this, in the research, Linden drew on feelings of marginalisation in his own life at a time of change and difficulty, which included unhappiness in a particular university and pressure to take early retirement (West, 2001). All of us, at some time or another, feel left out, ignored, powerless or silenced, which provides resources to better empathise with and more fully understand what someone else has experienced. Our subjectivities can be a source of evidence and understanding as well as bias. But using them requires thought, self-awareness and transparency in doing and reporting research.

Psychoanalytic perspectives

There are other ways of thinking about biographical interviews and a number of researchers draw on psychoanalytic insights (Frosh et al., 2005; Hollway and Jefferson, 2000; Roper, 2003; West, 1996, 2001). Unconscious factors, on the whole, have been neglected in research, despite abundant evidence of the role they play in everyday encounters. Yet, over the last two decades, numerous researchers have questioned the neglect, as they use more in-depth interviews: processes of transference, counter-transference and defence are seen to operate in research as much as in therapeutic or counselling situations (King, 1995; Roper, 2003; Thomson, 1994; West, 1996, 2001).

Dennis Brown and Jonathan Pedder (1991), from a psychotherapeutic perspective, note how we transfer feelings and attitudes developed in earlier experiences, especially where there are no particular clues as to how we should react. The emotional tone of an interview, fuelled by the power dynamics in the relationship, can be shaped by traces of past relationships and familiar patterns of response. An interviewer, like a therapist, might, unconsciously, represent significant others from a person's history, while the interviewer may feel protective, repulsed, attracted or even angry towards the interviewee in the counter-transference.

Linden has written of how interviewees can give the answers they think, unconsciously, the researcher wants. This can be a form of defence against anxiety. 'Brenda' was an Access student and during her interviews (which took place over a period of four years as she, and others, progressed through higher education), she began to notice how her story of motivation was changing, not least as Linden shared aspects of his own history. She observed a tendency to appease powerful male figures, including Linden, which reached back to difficult experiences in early childhood with an emotionally abusive father. Past and present intertwined because of abusive behaviour by her husband (West, 1996).

In a first interview, Brenda said she wanted to be a teacher, giving the kind of answer that adult learners often do, because vocational reasons – 'I'm getting a better job' – tend to be more respectable and acceptable than anything personal. Over time, Brenda was able to reflect on her motives in greater depth and her understanding changed substantially (helped also by being in counselling at the time):

> It was just the fear of being alone and that fear is still there a little bit, this sense of isolation … and I try very hard not to do that with my children, consciously. I guess it's there, as the children have got older they have spoken freely and I have encouraged them to speak freely about their feelings. At the same time, I have also recognised they need space and privacy to build their own lives; because that once again was something I wasn't given. So there we are; so that's why I am doing a course. … My mother was very protective with me and over anxious. Always worrying about things, I could never ever find my own space, my own freedom because she was always over anxious … Because there has been a lot of co-dependency there with my mother and I needed to unhook myself from that. … It goes back I think to when I used to look after her when she was very sick, cooking and washing her down, when I was very young. There was a bond formed through that and perhaps it wasn't a healthy bond, letting a child be free, and there was that co-dependency from the point of view of 'I shouldn't do that if I was you' and 'I shouldn't do that' and 'be careful, you'll fall' and usually I did! I was caught climbing trees when I was twelve and was severely punished, and it wasn't a particularly high tree, I only went up to where the branches begin to break out from the trunk. There was quite a lot of enforced punishment there, and so in a way I became co-dependent on them because I felt I lacked confidence to venture in any risk taking. So again the course for me is risk taking, and I am enjoying it … Just to rebuild the house a little bit – instead of it being on sand, I am aiming to get that house a little bit on rock. So in turn that would make me feel my own person, I would really discover who I am and not who other people want me to be. (West, 1996: 51–2)

Brenda was in counselling at the time and had become confident in talking about her family history. She talked too about her husband and how participation in higher education, and the sense of a more cohesive self and narrative engendered, was helping her feel more of a subject in her own life rather than an object serving others' needs.

Various researchers (Hollway and Jefferson, 2000) have noted how anxiety and defensiveness find ubiquitous expression in interviews. There is a defended as well as social subject to consider, just as there is a need to move beyond crude notions of the rational, cognitively driven, information-processing subject that has dominated social research and how we think of interviews. Conventionally, aspects of story telling – when 'objective' evidence does not fit what people say – have been considered 'irrational' (Hollway and Jefferson, 2000). Biographical perspectives help us see such irrationality in a different, more rational light.

Differing approaches to interviews

Biographical researchers favour relatively open and in-depth interviews, using only the most general of guides to enable the subjects to construct and explore a sense of their own cultural and psychological worlds (Plummer, 2001). But if biographical researchers interview in relatively open-ended ways, there are different approaches. Some researchers initially ask a person to tell their life story, while others provide a checklist of questions, partly to put interviewees at their ease. Free association techniques, derived from psychotherapeutic insights, may be encouraged, in which openness of expression is valued even when there may be no logical or rational relationship between the topic at hand and what an interviewee is saying. People can be asked to say what comes to their minds, which can open up rich areas of enquiry and new possibilities for understanding lives (Hollway and Jefferson, 2000). But there are ethical dangers – of opening up a Pandora's box – that need to be addressed (see Chapter 10).

Debates about how to conduct biographical interviews have taken place in a new trans-European study of non-traditional learners and retention in higher education. This involves researchers from eight universities across Europe, including ourselves. The debate has partly focused on the role of the researcher and the structuring of interviews. One perspective is influenced by German biographical-interpretative methods (Alheit, 1982, 1995; Apitzsch and Inowlocki, 2000; Chamberlayne et al., 2004; Rosenthal, 2004; Schutze, 1992; Wengraf, 2000). Interviews, in this view, are to be divided into distinct phases with the aim of encouraging informants to speak extensively and freely with minimum intrusion by the interviewer. The interviewer – having explained the purpose of the study – begins with a single, open-ended question, such as: 'Please tell me about your learning life history'. The interview is conducted in what is called a methodologically controlled way, in that the storyteller must have trust as well as understand that the material will be treated confidentially and that s/he is also in control of things (Alheit, 1982). A second phase involves more structured questions, shaped by the researcher's theoretical interests. An outline interview begins to look, as follows:

1st phase. 'Tell me about your educational life history'.
2nd phase. Questions are asked about, among other things:

- Family
- Social background (class, gender, ethnicity)
- Mentors – people who supported them as a learner
- Structural barriers/support
- Access and university experience.

The subsequent narratives are subject to intense group analysis followed by more focused interviews. There has been a great deal of discussion about this particular approach and how asking such an opening question could be threatening, especially for vulnerable people unused to such situations. Another approach is to provide a checklist of topics to be covered, which can help the interviewee have a better sense of the ground to be covered.

Paul Thompson (2000) provides useful guidance about doing biographical interviews, in his case around the importance of working out some questions beforehand, to build confidence and to avoid apologetic confusion. Interviewees can detect embarrassment, confusion and anxiety, so we need to feel as confident as we can in what we do and to interview in a way that is appropriate for us. If some biographical researchers ask the person to tell their life history, others favour more interactive interviewing. As Paul Thompson (2000) observes, asking a question such as 'Tell me the story of your life' can produce disappointing, brief and even terse results. Stories can often flow more freely when questions are asked: the narrative interview can in fact suppress the interviewer just as much as a survey instrument. 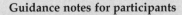Some very vulnerable people might take a long time to feel confident about the purpose of a study (is this surveillance?) and what might be involved for them. In the Sure Start research, we took a great deal of time to explain who we were, the nature of the research and who and what it was for; and we identified topics we wanted to know more about. This put people more at ease. In the example below, contact was made with families by telephone and letter. They already had some understanding of the study. At the first meeting, we provided four sheets of paper: one explained the project, one outlined our ethical code and one was a consent form to be signed. The other explained the sorts of topics to be covered:

Guidance notes for participants

We want to record your experiences of Sure Start and how your thoughts and feelings might change, and to consider why, over the lifetime of the project. We wish to understand this in the context of your life history and present circumstances.

We would like to conduct a number of interviews, over a period of time, to chart your relationship with the project.

Some initial topics

1. A bit about you, your child/children and family; a bit of life history.
2. Sure Start, what it is and how you came to be involved.
3. The details of your involvement and impact on and in your family, including as a parent.
4. The local community and perceptions of Sure Start.
5. Community involvement in running Sure Start.
6. Experiences of community workers, professionals and professional agencies.
7. What might get in the way of Sure Start being a success?
8. Other issues that you might like to raise.

Using such a checklist can be important for the researcher as well as her subjects. It can help build clarity and a feeling of being organised, which will be communicated to interviewees. Disorganisation can be unsettling for everyone concerned. Introducing the research and its procedures, with good and tested documentation, provides a firm foundation for biographical work.

Peter Alheit (1982) has produced a set of rules for conducting interviews, which are worth considering. A summary of these is given in the box below:

Rule 1: Prepare an interview carefully. Interviews in which people tell their story need not be viewed as television interviews ... You the listener must prepare yourself just as much as the one telling the story...

Rule 2: Interview only people who really interest you on account of their own person or problem ... It may be that one interviews people one cannot stand ... [but] your interest will provide the opportunity of conducting a successful interview. So feigned interest is dangerous.

Rule 3: State openly the purpose of your interview: it is the interviewees who are the experts – not you ... they have a right to know what is going to happen.

Rule 4: Say something about yourself as well ... you are the listener, but prior to the interview you talk about yourself ... who you are and what you do.

Rule 5: You need time.

Rule 6: Make sure that the rules of telling the story are really 'ratified' at the beginning of the interview: ... if s/he is uncertain ('where shall I begin?'), give an instruction: 'just begin with your childhood'.

Rule 7: Remain in the background as much as possible ... perhaps you'll be worried by a long pause; try to decide whether the interviewee needs this to think things over ... or there is no more air left.

Rule 8: Avoid questions such as 'why?' and 'what for?': so ask 'how did that happen?' or 'what happened then?'

Rule 9: Postpone concrete questions to a follow-up phase.

Rule 10: Do not be afraid of making mistakes: take rules seriously but do not be pedantic ... Learn your lessons and write down further rules (Alheit, 1982: 4–6).

Such suggested 'rules' merit careful consideration and discussion by biographical researchers.

The interview as transitional space

At a more conceptual level, we can think of interviews as spaces for learning in which there may be changes in the interviewee's understanding and more confident story telling. This may be especially true in longitudinal studies. Sometimes one-off interviews barely scratch the surface. In the research with doctors (West, 2001), initial interviews begged many more questions than they provided answers. Over time, the doctors explored their training and the medical habitus, in greater depth, setting this in the context of life histories (including their own illness narratives) as well as the practices and cultures in which they were embedded. They began to focus on the problematic relationship between self-knowledge, their own psychological histories and emotional interactions with particular patients (West, 2001).

Donald Winnicott, as described in Chapter 4, developed the idea of transitional space to explore processes of self-negotiation that take place between people, including in biographical interviews (Winnicott, 1971). Winnicott noted that transitional spaces appear across a life – in initial separations from prime caregivers but also in higher education or research – and that story telling represents a transitional area of experience in which the self is constantly negotiating its position in relation to others. The self may initially use predictable scripts, reflecting dominant ideologies, but may come to question these in the light of new experience, including in the interview process. Shifts in the quality of authorship, and agency, can take place when people feel encouraged to tell stories and feel really listened to and understood. New senses of legitimacy and self-understanding, via greater narrative coherence and acceptance in the eyes of significant others, may begin to develop (Sclater, 2004).

How to create stronger senses of agency in human interactions, especially when dealing with vulnerable people, has been a preoccupation of some of those working in counselling, psychotherapeutic settings or guidance settings (Egan, 1994). Emphasis is given to building rapport through empathy and serious listening; to the importance of using open questions ('tell me about …'); to the requirement to focus on here-and-now, concrete experience as a starting point; and to minimal encouragers (such as 'I see' or 'I understand') alongside silence (not feeling obliged to break silence). Importance is also attached to reflecting back what a person has said (mirroring a person's thoughts and feelings to encourage exploration); or the role of summarising (in order to progress). Such procedures can be applied to biographical interviewing. It is important, for instance, to take the emotional temperature of an interview, on a regular basis; and even to challenge what people say but in empathic and digestible ways, so that contradictions can be explored and alternative perspectives can emerge (Gould, 2009).

Starting

Starting an interview is clearly crucial, whether a first or subsequent one. In the research on trainee teachers with placements in challenging London schools, the aim was to chronicle the lived experience of classrooms and the cultures of schools, as part of interrogating the emotional aspects of learning and managing transitional processes (West, 2006, 2008a). Interviews would often begin by reference to an immediate experience or concrete situation. The following example comes from a second interview with Rupal, whom you met in Chapter 5. She talked, as we entered the room, of being in her own classroom, this time, and how important it was. We encouraged her to continue and switched on the recorder:

Rupal: It seems like I have come a very long way. To be honest I can't even ... the day that we met last time seems so long ago. So much has happened since and I can see that I have developed a lot in the time. I have become, I don't know, I can just see that maybe I have become a better teacher. I know what I am doing a little bit more. A bit more controlled with what I am doing. And I think that is making more of a difference. I think the kids have gotten used to me as well, which makes a big difference. The kids are starting to trust me. I am just happy it's over. I can't believe I got through term.

Linden: When we talked ... last time you took us on a journey really. You kind of, I felt I was in a classroom with you with various groups of people and we explored issues of discipline ... racism ... a sense of well should I be doing this at all? Some stress and strain I think in you ...

Rupal: I think when we met I had been teaching for two weeks I think it was ... There was a lot going on with me not having my own room as I was saying before and just being crowded with other people and so on ... I think I moved in here just after half term. Before that things started to settle down with my year 10 group. Things started to get a lot better. Some of the kids I was told I might need to get tough with and they are actually doing work in my lessons. And then two of the kids in my class, I think this was after we met, started to abuse me ... calling me names singing songs about me in one of my lessons ... Ok. Well there were just two children who were renowned to be terrors ... So when they came into the lesson they were already upset. And it just carried on through the lesson. In the end I had to call 'on-call' to come and take them away because I wouldn't have them in my lesson. I was shaking by the end of the lesson ... Yeah it was hard because the minute that had happened an 'on-call' came in and they took them away. I had to carry on teaching. I was only half way though the lesson. I was like 'oh my God'. And it was just really hard to compose myself again and think and try and separate myself from that situation. And I am sure that some of the other students noticed that I was a bit on edge. It was difficult ...

Rupal proceeded to tell more stories of particular incidents, in some detail, and talked of a lack of space in the school, or time in the formal aspects of training, to consider these. The research served as a kind of transitional space: she read her transcripts, which raised important issues of the meaning of what she was doing and her capacity to be a teacher and thought a great deal about her work and its meaning.

Finishing an interview

Finishing an interview can be as important as starting. We can ask participants if they would like to add anything or talk about something that has not been mentioned. When the participant feels they have finished, the recorder can be switched off but a conversation might continue. This may be a general 'chat' before thanking the person for their time and contribution. This space is important as it allows people to 'wind down' rather than asking them to leave straightaway. Sometimes participants may return to talking about aspects of their life history so it is essential to remember the material and to write it down immediately afterwards. You may even ask if you can switch on the recorder again.

Practising, using recorders and transcribing

Clearly practice, including doing pilot interviews, makes more perfect, as people like Paul Thompson (2000) suggest. We should try things out and get feedback from critical friends, research supervisors or fellow students on what we do and how others experience us. Conducting pilot interviews can help clarify themes and the importance of remaining open to new and unanticipated possibilities. Such interviews can be transcribed and material discussed in research workshops. We can interrogate our own role in the interviews as well as the nature of people's responses to us, via audio-visual replays. At a very practical level, we need to get used to our technology and feel competent in handling it.

Some biographical researchers prefer to take detailed notes rather than use digital or tape recorders (Horsdal, 2002). We favour recording interviews, partly to enable us to listen more attentively, but their presence needs to be talked about with our interviewees. In running workshops for doctoral students, the use of recorders can be a major topic for discussion. One would-be biographical researcher, after being interviewed, felt he was talking to two people: the interviewer and the recorder. He was aware that someone else – a transcriber – would listen to the material and this made him feel, initially, uneasy. On the other hand, most people will accept the use of recorders and soon forget their presence (although remaining anxious, perhaps, as to who will have access to the material). We need to talk openly about such matters with our subjects as part of building good and reflexive practice.

We normally transcribe our interviews, in full. People are given copies (and tapes or discs if they wish) to read, 'correct' or amend, before a following interview. However, the best laid plans can go awry because transcriptions are not completed on time. We easily underestimate the resource and time implications, given that it can take upwards of nine hours to transcribe an hour of recording. We transcribe recordings in accordance with oral history conventions, in contrast to the more elaborate procedures of linguistic analysis, partly reflecting the philosophical and interpretative stance of our work as well as our interests.

The text is transcribed in full and in its narrative form and no attempt is made to force the speech into a written or grammatical correctness. Pauses are indicated by three dots and where material is abbreviated or omitted in the process of editing or quotation, four dots are used. Interpolations are indicated by the use of brackets. Use is also made of some punctuation, in order to break the text, but this is done in ways consistent with the rhythms and patterns of speech. Interviewees are also given the right to correct transcripts as they see fit but we encourage them to preserve the rhythms of the spoken word. Yet people can ask for their material to be made more 'grammatical' – which happened in the study of doctors – for fear of seeming incoherent and uncertain, not least to colleagues and even the researcher. They can be exercised by how confused and contradictory they seem and want to iron this out and produce more 'acceptable' accounts. This may be especially problematic when working with relatively advantaged, confident or powerful people, like doctors, although it is by no means true of everyone. When such issues do arise, however, they need to be sensitively managed. (For a discussion on issues in transcription in biographical and oral history research, see the article by Francis Good, 2006; see also Humphries, 1984; Perks and Thomson, 2006; P. Thompson, 2000). It is important to emphasise that conventions can vary and some place greater emphasis on fully verbatim accounts. Here, everything is to be included, if possible – ums, ars, and pauses – and the mms and yeses of the interviewer. This can be important and fertile ground for analysis and potentially valuable inferences of meaning.

Literary-inspired and conversational analysis can go to great lengths. Every line is numbered and every pause recorded and timed. Every minute feature of conversation is noted (Elwyn and Gwyn, 1998). This can be important for detailed analysis of small segments of text – and for interrogating what may be happening between people, at least linguistically, in particular moments – but there is a danger of unreadability, and getting lost in the detail of language use (Hollway, 1989; Kleinman and Copp, 1993; West, 1996). Notwithstanding, aspects of an interview can get lost in transcription, including the music of speech as well as subliminal information, and it is important to listen to recordings as well as to read transcripts. Listening while travelling in a car, for instance, can evoke the sights and smells of an interview once more: in one case, the sound of sirens and agitated city noises in the recording of an interview with a doctor was evocative of the troubling context in which he worked. But in the end, as Good observes:

> we must learn to live with the fact that transcription of the spoken word is more of an art than an exact science … the best we can do is carefully consider the options, which may be suitable for any given set of objectives, and then follow this up with a systematic and consistent editing style. (2006: 365)

Being a good enough biographical interviewer

We may have left you feeling anxious about interviewing but it needs to be thought of as a learning and developmental process in its own right. This is partly because doing biographical research often prompts us to think about our own lives as well as to learn about the effects we may have on others and them on us. We have also to accept that some interviews do not work well and recorders go wrong. Some people will not want to talk or be guarded and we have to respect this. Particular doctors said little or nothing in the GP study, at least at times, fearful, as they may have been, of exposing 'weakness' in a litigious, blame-full culture.

Sometimes people simply do not turn up and we feel upset and rejected. These things happen to everyone. But the unpredictability of research can work to our benefit. When interviewing a young single mother in a parenting project in East London, there was no room available at the youth centre, despite one having been booked. We met, instead, in a caretaker's room – more of a cupboard really – into which the caretaker entered, a couple of times, despite being asked not to. It might have been a disaster but we both laughed and it strengthened the research relationship (West, 2007).

Key points

- The interview is central to much biographical research and we need to think of it as a relationship as well as in more technical terms.
- Biographical researchers can disagree on interviews and interviewing: as, for instance, between narrative and interactive approaches.
- We have to think about intersubjective processes and the defended as well as social subject, which includes our own difficulties in dealing with certain topics.
- Practice does make more perfect.

FURTHER READING

Good, F. (2006) 'Voice, Ear and Text', in R. Perks and A. Thomson (eds) *The Oral History Reader* (2nd edn). London: Routledge.

Oakley, A. (1988) 'Interviewing Women: A Contradiction in Terms', in H. Roberts (ed.) *Doing Feminist Research.* London: Routledge.

Stadlen, N. (2004) *What Mothers Do Especially When it Looks Like Nothing.* London: Piatkus.

Thompson, P. (2000) *The Voice of the Past* (3rd edn). Oxford: Oxford University Press.

DISCUSSION QUESTIONS

1. Have you ever done an interview? What are your memories of this?

2. Have you ever been interviewed about aspects of your life? How did this make you feel?

3. How might you respond if an interviewer asked you to tell your life story, as in the narrative approach?

4. If you were to be interviewed about your learning biography, are there any topics or issues that might cause anxiety?

ACTIVITIES

1. Try out an exploratory pilot interview with a colleague or friend. Choose a topic, such as being a parent or son/daughter, or take a broader approach and ask about his or her learning life history. Prepare an explanatory note and a list of topics (and also introduce your ethical codes; see Chapter 10). Find a room and practise with your recording equipment. Allow time to think about the process with your collaborator.

2. Becky Thompson undertook a study about women with eating disorders and talked about the stress which the interview process caused her – consider the following extract:

   > I sometimes found myself trying to escape from the pain of their stories as they spoke. Many of the women have been multiply victimized including enduring poverty, sexual abuse, exposure to high levels of violence, and emotional and physical torture. One way I tried to escape the pain of their stories was by interrupting them with comments such as: 'I know what you mean' or 'I went through a similar thing'... Recognizing psychological consequences of interviewing on the researcher elucidates dilemmas involved in using feminist interviewing techniques ... (I had to sort out) when making a comment during an interview is actual support and when it is dysfunctional rescuing ... sitting with the pain may be the only response that doesn't cheapen the power of its recounting. But sitting with the intimacy of such silence is intense and often left me completely drained after the interviews. I also noticed that my immediate desire to comfort them was my wanting to escape the pain myself and wanting someone to comfort me ... I sometimes had to remind myself that the woman's ability to retell a traumatic story meant she had already survived the worst of the pain. (Thompson, 1990: 24, 27)

   - What is your reaction to Becky Thompson's experience?
   - What do you think about the ways in which she dealt with it?
   - How do you think you would react to listening to painful stories?

8
Making Sense of Biography

Analysis

I take someone else's words (someone I respect and trust and who trusts me), slowly read her text, try to understand her intention behind her choice of words, try to place myself in her place so that I feel inside her mind and heart, search for her meaning before I impose new words or meaning of my own, imagine what might be so important to her to say that I must take care not to lose her meaning. Only then do I allow new words to flow from my fingers – the words are mine, yet hers as well. (Nancy Goldberger, 1997, quoted in Belenky et al., 1997: XV)

Overview

In this chapter:

- We look at organising narrative material for analysis.
- We share our humanistic and subjectivist approaches to analysing biographical material.
- We relate our analytical procedures to theoretical and epistemological perspectives.
- We consider whether understanding best derives from an appreciation of the whole, or gestalt of a life, or through disaggregating data.
- We introduce other ways of analysing texts, including more 'objectivist' orientations.

Introduction

Analysing biographies is time-consuming yet important and rewarding; it helps bring coherence to material and facilitates the development of theoretical understanding. Analysis helps us to make sense of a person's story but also to move beyond description, as important as this is, to refine understanding in more systematic and sustained ways.

The process of analysis can be confusing for those new to research, especially as there are different ways of doing it and varying perspectives on the nature of narrative material. This chapter provides an overview of our own approaches, shaped, to an extent, by sociological and psychological perspectives but also by a humanistic orientation. We consider, briefly, how others analyse material and reflect on the advantages and disadvantages of different ways of working. We should reiterate, however, that the stages of doing research – interviewing, analysing and writing up – cannot or should not be rigidly separated. We are, as discussed in the last chapter, actively involved in interpretation and analysis from the outset while description is a profoundly interpretative act. Moreover, especially when working longitudinally, interviews can develop a dynamic, iterative, analytical character in their own terms, testing and retesting hypotheses with the subjects of our research as active collaborators. What may, at first sight, seem a linear progress from description to analysis becomes, on close scrutiny, a deeply intertwined patch-working of description, interpretation and theorising.

John Creswell argues that analysing data is 'a formidable task for qualitative researchers' (1998: 139). Biographical interviews can produce mountains of material and we may feel that we are 'drowning'. Transcripts may be read and re-read several times, which takes time. If you are writing a PhD or Masters thesis, do not underestimate the time needed; but do not wait either to finish or transcribe interviews. Analysis can begin during interviews and you can think about your material, and your subjects, when driving home or sitting on the train after an interview. You will start to live the material and be engrossed by it. You can, early on, start to read transcripts and highlight paragraphs, sentences or words which relate to your research questions. This is particularly important if you are undertaking several interviews. Begin analysis as soon as you have a transcript, and even before, in listening to a tape: this helps to inform future interviews and can lead to a review of interview themes and/or questions. David Silverman has argued that: 'in most qualitative research, unless you are analysing data more or less from day 1 you will always have to play catch up' (2006: 150).

We emphasise that there is no one 'correct' way of analysing biographical data, although some researchers may claim, as academics tend to, that their analytical techniques and procedures provide the more definitive answer. You will need to read about, experiment and decide on an appropriate approach for you. The approach chosen will also depend upon your focus and your theoretical understanding of research itself. Doing research, as noted throughout the book, begs many questions about the nature of being human, or of how we make sense of another's life and of the role and reliability of story telling.

If you are a member of a research team, you may have little choice about analytical approaches because this has been decided by the person co-ordinating the project. When analysing stories, you also need to be thinking ahead about how you are going to present the stories, in written form, for your thesis, article, conference paper or book. Are you looking for one or possibly two or three 'good' story(ies) as luminous case studies or do you want to analyse and write thematically, drawing from several or even all the transcripts? A further question is whether you want the data, as much as possible, to speak for itself, because of its richness, or as a means to give voice to those who may have been silenced, as in some feminist work; there may be relatively minimal interpretation in such contexts. Or you may think that extensive interpretation is necessary because people may not realise the significance of what they say, or how they are 'storied'. Narratives, as observed, can be structured by powerful discourses of which individual narrators may barely be aware.

Humanistic and subjectivist approaches to analysis

We favour a more humanistic orientation to analysis, although from different disciplinary perspectives. The humanistic approach, shaped, in part by feminism, places the subjects of our work more at the centre of the process, including analysis. The relationship between researcher and researched is an intersubjective one with the putative voices of interviewees, or struggles for voice, being a prime focus and source of reference, located within understanding of the importance of relationship in research. Theories are built in that light, as cogently expressed by Goldberger (1997), above.

We believe that social science should take seriously its humanistic foundations, derived from the idea of human beings as active creators of their worlds as well as being created by them. We would emphasise the capacity of human beings to reflexively understand, including in the research setting – a potentially transitional space for collaborative learning – how they may be structured or positioned by discourse. This is an element in building what we have termed critical realism: listening attentively to diverse voices but also being sensitive to how people can be storied, including by researchers. We need to address the interplay of language and subjectivity, immediacy and memory, self and other, if we wish to build really reflexive research.

Research itself is understood as a potentially empowering act, via listening and valuing what people say, even when this may be muddled and contradictory (this can tell us, as noted, a great deal of how a particular life has been understood and narrated). But the tension between letting 'data speak for itself' and building more abstracted categories, and thus moving away from what people actually say, remains. For feminist researchers like Joan Acker, Kate Barry and Johanna Esseveld, it provides a fundamental dilemma: 'in the actual task of analysis, we initially found ourselves moving back and forth between letting the data "speak for itself" and using abstracted categories' (Acker et al., 1991: 143).

Abstract categories or typologies bring the risk of taking us far from the embedded complexity of lived experience; conversely, abstraction is necessary, as is comparison with other lives, to explore patterns and build theory which help illuminate more of the particular. Feminist analysis, from the outset, has been preoccupied with this tension and associated questions of representation: the need to let women's voices be heard yet relate such a process to theories of women's oppression of which the women concerned may be conceptually unaware.

Barbara's approach to analysis

We want to share our different, if philosophically overlapping, approaches to analysing biographical material. There are some essential steps in doing analysis, from Barbara's perspective, which find parallels in Linden's work. The stages are as follows:

- You need to listen to the tapes several times as well as read the transcribed version.
- Start to read through stories as soon as they have been transcribed highlighting or underlining key paragraphs, sentences or words.
- When reading through for the first time, start to think about and identify key concepts, words, themes.
- Think about the questions that your data is generating.
- Immerse yourself in your data.
- Read through your transcripts a second time and make notes (coding) on the transcripts. This could involve summarising a statement, for example, attitudes towards schooling and/or identifying a concept such as class or gender.
- If you are selecting a sample of transcripts for analysis, identify the ones you want to use, bearing in mind your research questions.
- Re-read again and again in order to code and relate the stories to theoretical and conceptual frameworks.
- Think about whether your data relates to existing theory, disagrees with existing data or generates new ideas/theory.
- You may want to make summary notes about each life story.
- If you are undertaking a longitudinal study, you will need to look at all of the interviews undertaken by a participant together in order to compare and identify changes in a person's life.
- Refer to your field notes and research diary.

Remember when reading transcripts that people generally do not tell their life story as a linear progression of events but move backwards and forwards between different times and experiences. The stories, therefore, may appear confused and muddled. If you are working with another researcher or as part of a research team, you will need to discuss your interpretations of transcripts together. In some research teams, everyone reads all the transcripts, but each team member has responsibility for analysing a sample of stories in depth. The more you read the transcripts, the more familiar you will become with them. You also need to decide:

- What is important?
- What is unimportant in relation to the research objectives and can, therefore, be left out? (However, do not discard data totally as it may be useful to you in the future.)
- What themes are emerging? Do not worry if ideas and inspiration do not come straightaway. They will the more you absorb and think about the data.
- You need to think about your data all the time, even when doing ordinary everyday things.

Choosing what to leave in and what to leave out is difficult. Acker et al. explain their response to this problem:

> Our feminist commitment had led us to collect data that were difficult to analyze and had provided us with so much information that it was difficult to choose what was 'essential'; at the same time we tried to give a picture that provided a 'totality'.

> Our solution to this series of problems was to present a number of 'life histories', expressed largely in the women's own words, to typify what we thought were particular to patterns of change. (1991: 143)

Immersing ourselves in participants' stories enables us to come to know them well. It can bring back memories of the interviews themselves and even the pain and emotion experienced as interviewers in what Linden terms the counter-transference. Becky Thompson has written of the stress researchers can experience in interviewing and how this can re-emerge in analysis:

> While I was transcribing each woman's words, I felt as if I were doing the interview again: I could see the woman's face and hear her exclamations and pain ... While analyzing the interviews, I experienced some of the same types of protective responses that survivors experience following trauma. For example, while immediately following the interviews, I could retell the woman's story almost verbatim, within two or three days. I had a hard time remembering basic aspects of the women's experience ... sometimes I found myself changing their stories in my memory and in doing so, was minimizing the abuse they had suffered ... while I was transcribing interviews, I would typically fall asleep soon after beginning to transcribe each interview. This had nothing to do with whether I needed sleep or not. Rather (it) was another way of coping with the extreme stress and pain of painstakingly chronicling (what) many of the women experienced. (Thompson, 1990: 30–2)

Thompson, in these remarks, captures experiences that many biographical researchers have shared. Biographical research can take us into difficult, even disturbing, territory.

Coding

Having listened to the tapes and read through the transcripts, Barbara begins the process of coding. Coding helps to make sense of the data. Amanda Coffey and Paul Atkinson recommend three helpful stages in qualitative coding: 'noticing relevant phenomena'; 'collecting examples of those phenomena'; and 'analysing those phenomena in order to find commonalities, differences, patterns and structures' (1996: 29).

Coding is a process by which data are broken down, conceptualised and put back together in new ways (Strauss and Corbin, 1990). You may have some ideas about possible codes before reading the transcripts based on your research questions and from undertaking the interviews. Coding involves identifying concepts and themes as you read the interviews, making notes of these in the margins as well as any overall patterns which emerge in comparing transcripts. As you read further interviews, new codings can develop and even contradict earlier ones. For grounded theorists, coding is an important procedure with a strict series of stages to be followed but this is not a position either of us adopt, for a range of reasons (see below).

Most of Barbara's research, as illustrated, focuses on the learning experiences of working-class adults in community, further and higher education. She is interested in how gender, class and ethnicity impact on the learning process and how adult students develop (or not) a learning identity, which helps them to be successful (or otherwise) in formal learning environments. Barbara writes: I draw on the work of Bourdieu and his concepts of habitus, underpinned by my feminist/Marxist perspectives. For Bourdieu (1997), the habitus is a collectively created sum of variables, organised mental and physical manifestations of dispositions – or ways of being in the world – which are embodied in individual people. How each individual practises them, however, can vary, depending on experience. If people are positioned by the habitus, they can also come to position themselves, in new ways, via internalising new narrative and emotional resources.

When reading individual transcripts, I am looking for shared experiences and patterns which connect across the transcripts so that the individual stories become collective ones. I am also looking at how structure and structural inequalities impact upon biographies. At the same time, I am identifying whether and how individuals have been able to use their agency to seek to change, in however small a way, their structural location in society and hence the interaction of structure and agency. In studying the lives of adult learners, I have noticed that in particular moments in a life, structural forces might predominate, while at other times, agency is stronger. To illustrate the collectivity in people's biographies, I want to draw on quotations from interviews with adult students in higher education. They are talking about their experiences of schooling and working-class parental attitudes. Themes were repeated across numerous transcripts:

> I thought I was just an ordinary working-class woman who would go and get a job. The thought of doing anything else at that time just didn't enter my head. And I wanted to be earning too. I wanted the money, but I never thought about college or anything like that.

> I started school in 1969. Girls went to school, just did it and then got married. You know, had a little job then got married so there's no encouragement whatsoever … it was just the norm. Women just got married and children and that was it.

> [I]t wasn't until later that I felt quite resentful about the experience I had at school … I just feel there was a lot of potential that I had that was totally wasted because assumptions were made about me. Too young at the time to know but I do feel it came back to my background and my family and where I lived and that influenced how they treated me and that's why college never got mentioned … I think the system could have done more for me. (female)

> I went to see the careers teacher and he sort of steered the kids from the council estate (social housing) away from university and towards the steel works. At the same time at home I used to go and talk to my parents and say 'look I've done this at school … I got really good marks for English' and they weren't really interested. Then I said about going to university and it was 'university what are you talking about? Your granddad was in the steel works, father was in the steel works and that's where you are going to go'. (male)

The following illustrates how to code a transcript. Mark (whom we introduced in Chapter 5) is the black working-class adult student taking a 2+2 Social Studies degree. Here, Mark is talking about the transition from college to university:

I kind of see it as the analogy of jumping into the swimming pool. Everybody is going to go under for some amount of time and that's in the case	Transition Awareness of transition
of the first weeks finding out where you are and where's the Ramphal Building and what's Ramphal for a start. The you know getting use to all the	Learning a new environment
language. That's the hardest thing when you first come on any course. What's a module? You know	Academic language
before I came on the course a module was something in space and now they are saying that I have to choose four modules. The 2+2 co-ordinator and that lot came over and talked about this and I hadn't a clue what I was going to do when I got to Warwick. What's all the majors and minors about and although people came and explained you still don't know. You don't really	Learning a new student language
know what it is about until you finish. Have I chosen rightly? So yes you go under and it's a matter of time if you stay under or when you come out. But I came	Uncertainty
over to Warwick a few times before and checked out the place and got to know it and I got used to the	Confidence
feeling of being the odd one out. You know a lot of the students are younger so there is the age thing for me that made me feel the odd one out. Also I am not an ideal student in the way I look I suppose. I am the working-class dodgy looking geezer and with respect	Age issues Marginalisation Class issues Identity
quite a lot of people at Warwick are middle class and they cross over the road from me usually … I had some dealings with Warwick so it wasn't as intimidating for me.	Familiarity

Such an approach to coding seeks to identify different dimensions of the narrative and how these relate to a wider theoretical understanding of class (and/or gender/race) in English society; and of what may be involved, by way of identity work, in negotiating class and/or gender issues within higher education. We have glimpses of how identity is under negotiation in the process of telling and interpreting his story. Getting to this stage – of having rich interview material, of being aware of how the subject is making sense of a situation, and connecting this with a body of sociological theory – marks an important developmental stage in the research journey.

Here is a summary of Barbara's analytical stages:

- The first stage is to reflect upon each interview immediately afterwards and jot down my thoughts and reflections.
- Each interview is transcribed straightaway.

- Once a transcript is returned typed, I send the transcript to the participant to see if they are happy with this or want to add/change anything.
- I read a transcript through for the first time highlighting parts of the story which I think are interesting and relevant to the research questions. I listen to the recording.
- I read the transcripts several times. On the second reading, I begin to add comments in the margin such as the impact of gender, reasons for returning to learn, a critical incident, etc. The more you read the transcripts, the more you get to know the person.
- I write a summary about each person and identify themes such as initial schooling experiences, impact of the family on studying and links between past and present lives. I include relevant quotes from the transcript in the summary. This helps me to remember the individual interviewee's story. I use the summaries to choose which stories to use for the writing stage.
- For reasons of anonymity, I change the names of participants.
- I identify common themes and issues across the stories. For example, several women stated that they were expected to leave school at the earliest possible age and go into female jobs such as secretarial, nursing or factory work before settling down to have a family.
- I think about what the stories are telling me and whether or not they relate to other literature in the field.
- I relate the data to theory, drawing on existing knowledge but also looking out for what may be new.
- Much of my research is European (European Union funded) and cross-national. Within the team, we have different approaches to analysing biographical data. We discuss and explain our different approaches at team meetings in order to understand each other's way of analysing stories. My colleagues at the Centre for Research in the Education of Adults (CREA), University of Barcelona, use a dialogical approach to analysis (see below) which actively involves participants in the process. Contrastingly, Peter Alheit at Goettingen University, Germany, uses a more detached and 'scientific' approach (see below).

Linden's approach to analysis

There are similarities between Linden and Barbara's approaches but differences too, partly reflecting disciplinary assumptions but also varying experiences in doing research. In Linden's approach, echoing Barbara's feminist orientation, subjects are encouraged to think of themselves as active participants in interpreting and making theoretical sense of narratives as part of a learning relationship.

Linden has also wrestled, like other biographical researchers (see Hollway and Jefferson, 2000), with the fundamental epistemological question as to how we can best make sense of narrative material and the experience of doing research. There are two possible stances, among others, although, in practice, these may overlap. The first insists on breaking down data into its constituent parts, believing, like grounded theorists, for example, that this is necessary to manage the complexity of the material, as well as to build theoretical insights in some systematic way. The second stems from a need to understand the overall form, or gestalt of lives, for appreciating the significance of the detail. This perspective draws, to an extent, on psychodynamics and phenomenology and finds expression in the work of Fritz Schutze (1992) and the German biographical-interpretative school. Gestalt derives from the premise that there is a sort of order, form or patterning, or hidden agenda in lives, which can be found in our data (Hollway and Jefferson, 2000). Linden tends to this second view, as explained below.

Linden also emphasises the importance of working with subjects, over time, to analyse as well as generate material. He writes: 'I used grounded theory in earlier work, as I sought to manage the material gathered, over a period of years' (West, 1996). Grounded theory seemed the solution, offering, in its very terminology, a way of rooting conceptual insight, pragmatically and tentatively, in people's rich data, rather than overly abstract categories. Data, according to grounded theorists like Anselm Strauss and Juliet Corbin (1990), have to be systematically compared for similarities and differences. Observations, sentences, paragraphs are coded, each element is given a name or coding and every coded item is then placed into a series of categories. My study, at home, was overwhelmed with piles of paper, by codings and classifications to be endlessly worked and reworked, constructed and reconstructed, in what seemed an endless play of possibilities. I felt lost, at times. Words and whole transcripts can mean different things to different people, but also to the researcher, and I felt it essential to talk further with participants about particular experiences and their meaning as well as the ambiguities and uncertainties that infused texts. The research relationship itself, in such a context, became a focus for analytical work.

Relationships could develop over many cycles of interviews and over years. Interviews could become dynamic and collaborative spaces for interpretation and analysis as well as for the development of the narrative itself. Moreover, prematurely coding and disaggregating individual narratives, and aggregating these with material from other interviews, carried a danger of losing some of the contextual meaning or wholeness of the material. Each fragment was embedded in, or made meaningful by, the entire life. The experience of the young mother, referred to in Chapter 5, when speaking out at a meeting with professionals, might simply have been coded 'agency', and placed in a category pile, alongside similar material from other mothers. It could then have been written up as part of a story of collective struggle for agency and voice. But this, while legitimate, risked losing some of the individual significance of the experience and its biographical poignancy. Here was a woman who, as a child, felt no one really listened, either at home or school. She was bullied and humiliated. She saw herself, until recently, as 'simply' a mum stuck at home. She was experiencing a potential break-up of an abusive relationship at the time of the research, while sensing the possibility of becoming more of a subject in her life. There was gestalt in the material: of abuse, silencing, self-deprecation, struggle, but also of resilience, forged, in part, by feeling understood in the transitional spaces of the family support programme and of the new relationships this provided. She also felt listened to and respected in the research.

Why a particular experience might be considered epiphanal could only be grasped by reference to the whole story (West, 2007; West and Carlson, 2006, 2007).

Using and developing a proforma

I developed a proforma as an analytic space through which to understand more of the whole, including the relationship in the here and now, which might provide clues to how a life had been lived. Use of the proforma was rooted in an intense immersion in transcripts and in listening to recordings as well as considering the auto/biographical resonance of particular stories. The proforma was a space to identify and refine themes from each interview and illustrate them with extensive quotation. And to chronicle how themes develop and even change, over time. Extensive notes on process issues were included, such as the possible workings of power but also potentially unconscious factors such as transference and counter-transference. The proforma was also a research diary for recording experiences as researchers, all of which combined, iteratively, to create an evolving document of a life. I incorporated extracts or notes from the wider literature when theories or even a poem could help make sense of material. The intention was to integrate data, interpretation, theory and process insights into a living document. Proformas can provide space to 'play' imaginatively and thoughtfully with every aspect of our engagement with others and their stories.

The material below consists of extracts from a proforma of a trainee teacher based in the Teach First project, introduced in Chapter 5. She, 'Anna', was another of the 17 trainees with a placement in a 'challenging' London school (West, 2006, 2008a). The research focused, especially, on the emotional dimensions of learning to be a teacher. Teach First was devised in response to problems in teacher recruitment and retention and achieved prominence by being a business-led initiative and recruiting graduates from 'elite' universities. Note has also been made of the rhetoric of 'learning to lead' in the programme. Discourses of heroism and of the importance of leadership from the 'gifted and talented' infuse the programme (Hutchings, 2007).

Anna was placed in a shiny new business academy, sponsored by a particular company and replacing what was deemed to be a failing school. Such academies, which involve private-sector resources and even management styles, have been considered a prime means to transform public education. The research, as observed, was focused on processes of learning, both informal and formal, in the context of the school and the wider Teach First programme. This included how Anna managed this important transition in her own life. Her proforma is long, covering three cycles of interviews and containing material of diverse kinds. The study developed over two years and generated rich material on learning – in a lifewide, lifelong and holistic sense – encompassing anxiety, vulnerability, frustration, anger, muddle and self-doubt, but also resilience, progress and achievement. There is evidence of the interplay of self and the cultural context of the programme, and of interactions between past and present in connecting experiences in her family of origin with those in the school.

Biographical Interview Proforma

The proforma provides a way of recording key issues to do with the content and process of interviews, in relation to a specific person, in some standardised format that can be shared within the research team. It includes diverse aspects of the experience, including difficult material as well as our own feelings in the interviews and subsequent reflections. Field notes and diary material as well as extracts and comments from our reading are also integrated.

The themes. These surround initial impressions; interactions with schools including colleagues and pupils; interactions with other trainees; processes of managing changing identities; the interplay of the personal and the professional, past and present, etc. It should encompass significant moments of learning, in the broadest lifewide sense, which can include very informal processes. This section might include themes to be explored further with the participant in subsequent interviews.

A second aspect has to do with the *process* of the interview and observations about the nature of the interaction, including issues of power, defensiveness, etc.

The third, more *ethnographic* dimension, centres on the circumstances of the interview, including interruptions, and general impressions of the setting and of what might have been happening in and around it.

The fourth examines, over time, the sense, if any, of *an emerging gestalt* in the material: are there patterns in learning, and/or in managing change and transition, as viewed from a biographical perspective?

Themes

The first interview started with a difficult issue, after an especially fraught visit by some teacher assessors. Anna was struggling with this and a sense of letting herself down:

Letting herself down

Well, it is interesting actually because …. I am in the thick of it at the moment … I had my … assessment … and my paper work was OK and everything, but my, the lesson that the assessors observed was abysmal, abysmal sort of a lesson, behaviourally, that the class it felt like a lesson in November, felt that I hadn't progressed at all and my reaction still, when something goes wrong in those sorts of situations, and I really hope that professionally this changes, is to get very upset and I cried with my assessor for about 45 minutes after the lesson.

… And at the time I thought god thank god that there is a woman because at that time I felt very much, I don't know why, I think I just … but I cried for a while after that.

Anna talked at length about feeling unsupported in the school, despite a rhetoric of this being a supportive and stimulating environment. A similar theme emerges in the second interview:

There is a tension there and the management are very concerned to be the cutting edge of education. There is, the sort of restructuring of the way it works, I am not sure that we talked about it last time, but the fact that there was no middle management. There is no sort of heads of department, and heads of year …. It is there are six management plus all the other teachers and that has sort of been, apparently it has been kind of taken from business structures. It is the sort of cutting edge of what people think education should be now, but there is a tension there with the people who are on the ground, the everyday teachers who are … finding it hard to deliver what they want … especially in a community that are fairly switched off from education per se …

Teaching, she added, does not come naturally to her. There is a strong theme of working through issues in relation to her parents – including a struggle to separate – born of a difficult family history; all this despite a persona of academic success and confidence.

Families

Anna began to talk at length, in a second interview, about her family and her father's depression and serious difficulties in her parents' marriage, in the context of her own learning life history and current preoccupations:

… with my dad, very depressed although he recovered quite quickly, I think … he became disaffected with teaching as some teachers do sort of 20 years into it, or whatever … It got better and over those two years things got better and now they have got a friendship … as a 12 year old I distinctly remember going out for dinner or lunch or something with my dad, and saying to him, I am old enough now, get divorced. I am old enough, sort it out …

Anna felt she needed to help out with these family difficulties. Yet the family's influence was positive too and her spiritual values were strong, in a growing sense of vocation. She is passionate about some of the children and committed to a wider social and spiritual purpose for schools and education. But teaching is not thought of as a long-term career. Anna talks of her passion lying elsewhere but gets caught up in a variety of school initiatives, including, as the second interview makes clear, those to enable the academy to generate profit. She also talks about the difficulty of letting go of her family and breaking free. The themes of anxiety, and needing to get everything right, and struggles to separate and individuate, against a backcloth of fragility are strong. She worries too about getting things right in the interview. There is a defended self in the anxiety over what I might think about her struggles over the assessment.

Process

This is an extract from her second interview, which broadens out into a series of reflections on her family and finding her own feet:

I think probably I am in the process of beginning to break away from [my family]. There is a huge ... influence that I feel, my family and my feelings towards my family have had on my decisions. I feel I am beginning to break away from it, or at least learn to work with it and I think, you know you kind of think well why does that, why has she talked about family so much, you know this interview is generally, the sort of content of it, is professional, it is about your professional life and things like that, but then, family is in everything.

A gestalt?

Anna recognises a possible gestalt in a need to escape parental imperatives, alongside their vulnerability and a requirement to look after them. This includes the 'parent managers' of the school. There are issues about the research representing a kind of reflexive learning space that the project itself seems to lack. Issues to do with family intertwine with the play of wider forces in education. There is the culture of Teach First, which is partly seen as distant, business-orientated and 'slightly flashy'. This includes meeting with her business mentor, who is a City high flyer yet spends a lot of their first meeting talking about her own problems in a relationship. Anna listens to this, in characteristic ways. If aspects of the academy – where all is not what it seems and there is a gulf between teachers and management – bother her, she also wants to work with management, recognising their faults, and to contribute to the well-being of the school, in the interests of the children. Despite the appearance of academic success, her narrative is grounded in vulnerability and anxiety, as well as resilience and strong spiritual and family values, which help her keep on keeping on in a difficult environment.

This is just a brief, edited extract. It should be added that the two researchers working on the project completed a proforma separately and then compared notes to build a comparative and questioning dimension. We are all partial in what we perceive while we may avoid, perhaps for unconscious reasons, material with which we are uncomfortable. Anna represented an academic success story and in certain respects was managing her Teach First experiences rather well. I, Linden, was especially engrossed in her material, which included the sense of conflict between her values and aspects of the school and the Teach First programme. I was struggling to make sense of what Teach First represented and the shifting boundaries between public and private sectors in education. The research was also controversial. We, the researchers, were located in the university responsible for the teacher training, which inevitably evoked anxiety among senior managers. Reference was made, time and again, in discussions with us, to a specially commissioned evaluation of the project, which appeared, despite reservations, to be generally supportive. The evaluation identified a number of innovative features in the programme, such as recruitment and selection procedures as well as the creation of an *esprit de corps* (Hutchings et al., 2006). This, in fact, made us more determined to understand the world, empathically and openly, through Anna's eyes and those of the other research subjects, wherever this might take us. And to think reflexively about our values and assumptions and the need to be open to what the project might achieve.

There is also mention, in the proforma, of feeling paternal towards Anna and having concern for her family problems. There is reference to my own family history and the need to look after parents, through educational achievement. There were, in these senses, strong auto/biographical dimensions. There are notes on the experience of doing research: of the difficult boundaries between research and therapy. An interdisciplinary perspective informed the analysis, including the ideology of Teach First itself, alongside the psychosocial factors at work in Anna's life. Attention was also given to her struggles for agency and to the resources Anna draws on for this, which included other Teach First trainees alongside her family and their strong values. The richness of the material, and the analysis, was also the product of a strengthening research relationship with Anna.

Other ways of analysing biographical narratives

This final section offers a brief overview of other approaches, which have influenced our work or are important to consider. Dialogical approaches, for instance, actively seek to engage participants as explicit collaborators in processes of analysis, attempting to break down the power relationship between researchers and researched. Beverly Skeggs, for instance, as a feminist, has used a dialogical approach, which she calls 'interpretation through dialogue' (1997: 30). She explains that in analysing the stories of working-class women studying in further education, 'I discussed my ideas and interpretations with them and they would challenge, contradict, confirm etc' (1997: 30). However, using a dialogical approach can cause dilemmas, as Skeggs illustrates. She positioned the women in her study as working class but the women themselves rejected this interpretation. She kept to her theoretical perspective and rejected the women's viewpoint but did reflect, at length, on this kind of problem.

There is a commitment to dialogical forms of analysis among educators working with marginalised groups for collective change: for example, in the work, already referred to, of the Centre for Research on the Education of Adults at the University of Barcelona. This is undertaken from what is called a 'critical methodological base', set within 'a communicative paradigm'. Analysis is rooted in intersubjective dialogue and the creation of an egalitarian relationship between the researcher and the researched. Dialogic societies need dialogical research inquiries, so the argument proceeds, that enable subjects to analyse the changes that are taking place (Flecha and Gómez, 2006). Researchers pay close attention, working with their collaborators, to the analysis of situations, phenomena and interactions that are seen to create barriers to people's inclusion in particular social practices or exclusion from social benefits.

Grounded theory

Grounded theory, as observed, has played an important role in biographical research. It was developed by Barney Glaser and Anselm Strauss (1967) in their book *The Discovery of Grounded Theory*. However, many researchers claiming to use grounded theory do not follow the procedures strictly, which involves a systematic approach to analysing data, using three stages of careful coding (open, axial, selective). The intention is to generate theory systematically from the data, so that researchers do not begin their analysis with a preconceived theoretical framework. For Glaser, a key principle is that the researcher should use a 'codified procedure for analysing data ... which allows readers to understand how the analyst obtained his/her theory from the data' (1992: 227).

Michele Moore explains why she used grounded theory in analysing the life story of a disabled person:

> Grounded theory was chosen as the best analytic tool for making sense of David's story because it offers a well-established approach to ensuring that ideas and recommendations which the researcher develops and makes emerge from the data, are grounded in what key participants have contributed through their words and experiences. Grounded theory gives an analytic qualitative approach explicitly concerned with seeking out theoretical explanations for what is going on in any given research situation, and is sufficiently adaptable to be fitted to projects in which both the research methodology and the process of analysis are developing in unpredictable ways. (2004: 119)

There have been various refinements to grounded theory, which incorporate, for example, psychoanalytic awareness of the motivation not to know on the part of both subjects and researchers. In these perspectives, the interviewee can produce, to an extent, self-defensive biographical accounts, which may avoid difficult forms of knowledge or learning about self. Tom Wengraf (2000) applies this to researchers too: we may be motivated not to know certain things that might be upsetting or disturbing, which, in turn, affects what is heard and reported as well as analysed. Wengraf recommends a mix of the biographical-interpretative method (based on a distinction between the told life and the lived life, in which the latter is forged from what is termed hard objective evidence) and the 'constant comparative method' (derived from grounded theory) which involves teams of researchers generating multiple hypotheses until the knowledge and imagination of the researchers are exhausted. Hypotheses are then applied to further material for acceptance or rejection. However, if these varied applications of grounded theory offer a thorough approach to analysis, they also bring the danger of neglecting the potential of the research relationship itself for analytical work; and of research subjects to act as co-analysts. The role of researchers themselves can also be neglected or obscured. This includes how their own counter-transference and biographies can be sources of insight, which can get lost in the requirement to appear 'objective'.

'Objectivist' approaches

Some researchers are much less concerned with issues of subjectivity and how the researcher's subjectivity may shape the analysis. They prefer to highlight, instead, how the researcher brings methodological rigour and specialist theoretical understanding, which can, it might be argued, be undervalued in the rhetoric of collaboration. Among some Danish researchers, the emphasis is on group-based interpretation of texts (transcripts) of interviews and collective discussions in a research team, focusing specifically on the relation between language and (life) experience. A distinction is made between the description of lives, on the one hand, and life history, on the other. The former is the told life, as previously noted, while the latter is the interpreted life by researchers. Use may be made of critical theory or psychoanalytic ideas in suggesting that stories and subjectivity are more complex than implied by notions of conscious and transparent self-presentation. In-depth hermeneutic interpretation procedures, especially working in interdisciplinary groups, are employed, drawing on the literature of socialisation, identity and learning theory as well as psychoanalysis. There is an especial focus on what is termed narrative structures in texts (West et al., 2007).

Peter Alheit has been influential in the development of these approaches (1995). He provides a comprehensive approach to analysing data, which includes using 'memoing' or diary keeping, and the careful gathering of ideas and data as they emerge, from whatever source. There is intensive discussion of emerging categories within a research team, drawing on diaries, transcripts, notes and other material. The interconnections between separate observations and transcripts become clear, over time, in an iterative process, which may evoke eureka moments for researchers. In working on transcripts, Alheit makes use of ideas of 'structural description' or 'narrative structure', developed by Schutze and colleagues. This exploits how the narrator herself structures the narrative and her 'performative' approach. Texts are subdivided into narrative units, which encompass how the narrator weighs and evaluates her material. Attention is paid to how narrators describe changes in their biographical processes, and in themselves, and of how life course trajectories may become actual life-course patterns. Alheit draws an important distinction in analysis between the felt experiences of a life, including the degree to which subjects conceive of their lives as under their control, and structuring processes in society, embodied in narrative descriptions, which evoke the contrary feeling that lives are not their own.

Computer-based analysis

Finally, there may be a temptation to believe that computers can solve analytic problems, frustrations and differences. In recent years, the number of computer software packages available for analysis has increased. Key ones used are NUDIST, N-Vivo and Atlas in an approach often labelled computer-assisted analysis of qualitative data (CAQDAS). There are now several textbooks, which explain how to use such computer packages. Computer software can map complex interview material through marking text with a range of researcher-driven thematic issues (Frisch, 2006). It can help with coding, content analysis and sampling of data and is useful for researchers using a grounded theory approach. It can enable narrative material to be organised, sorted and rearranged in different ways. It becomes possible to cross-reference the emotional intensity of story telling and even body language can be referenced, if using videos (Frisch, 2006). Computer software also has the advantage of speed. For example, once the coding has been established, the software can identify particular words and comments in the transcripts and count the number of times phrases are used. Researchers may find the software especially useful if they have a large number of transcripts to analyse and compare and are working in a team.

But there is a downside. Computer-based analysis can fragment data and there is a danger of clerical forms of coding predominating and for more refined analysis to be neglected, in the hope that a computer can generate solutions (Hollway and Jefferson, 2000). Analysing narrative data, we suggest, is a deeply intuitive, subtle, inter-subjective as well as a challenging process: intellectually, epistemologically and in terms of the researcher's self-knowledge. This may defy computerisation. We feel, from our experience of attempting to use computer-based analysis, that it can also overly objectify as well as simplify the analytic process and risks devaluing and dehumanising the subjects at the heart of the research, including the researcher.

Conclusion

This chapter has offered a flavour of different approaches to analysing biographical data. Which analytical method you adopt will depend upon your disciplinary background and your theoretical and epistemological perspectives. Hopefully, this chapter will help you to decide which method you prefer or what you think makes most sense in terms of how best we can come to know about another's life as well as our own. Analysis, as stated, is essential in helping us to use narrative material to build more refined and grounded forms of psychosocial understanding. If we are motivated by the humanistic imperative to respect narrators and what they are trying to say, we have an equal obligation to think about the nature of the material and how this ought not simply to be accepted at face value. We have to find a balance between potentially competing imperatives.

Key points

- There are different approaches to analysis, rooted in different disciplines and understandings of being human in social and cultural contexts.
- Researchers may be positioned in more humanistic and/or subjectivist analytic orientations or more objectivist ones. The former tend to emphasise a wider purpose for research – contributing to the humanist project, for instance – as well as the importance of dialogue and collaboration.
- There is a major philosophical difference permeating analysis: do we make better sense of data by finding ways of understanding the overall pattern of a life, or by building our understanding from the fragments? Often, analysis may involve some synthesis of these different ways.

(Continued)

(Continued)

- Sociologists can have a slightly different focus in their analytical work in comparison with those of a more psychological bent: the former may be concerned to build categories and typologies while the latter are more focused on the complex particularities of a life.
- Other researchers will emphasise the importance of theoretical understanding and methodological rigour in analysis, which may be neglected in the rhetoric of dialogue or collaboration.
- It is important to try out different approaches, including computer-assisted analysis. But there are major dangers of reductionism and of denying some of the richness and complexity that human beings bring to analysing biographical narratives.

FURTHER READING

Alheit, P. (1995) *Taking the Knocks*. London: Cassell Education.

Lewins, A. and Silver, C. (2007) *Using Software in Qualitative Research*. London: Sage.

Goodley, D., Lawthom, R., Clough, P. and Moore, M. (2004) *Researching Life Stories: Method, Theory and Analyses in a Biographical Age*. London: Routledge Falmer. See Chapters 8 and 9 in which the authors outline their analytical approaches to their research from four different theoretical perspectives.

West, L. (1996) *Beyond Fragments*. London: Taylor and Frances. See Chapter 2.

West, L. (2001) *Doctors on the Edge*. London: Free Association Books. See Chapter 3.

DISCUSSION QUESTIONS

1. Where do your prime interests as a biographical researcher lie? Do you have a more psychological or sociological bent? How might this affect how you read and analyse narrative material?

2. How important do you think it is to involve research subjects in analysing material? What are the benefits of this and what might be the disadvantages?

ACTIVITIES

1. Coding activity: look at the following extract from Claire's life history. She is a doctor (a General Practitioner) in a deprived area of London. The story is taken from Linden West's (2001) book, *Doctors on the Edge*. She is talking about her life as a doctor and her family. Read the quote and code what she is saying. (If you are working in pairs, compare your coding and discuss.)

(Continued)

(Continued)

I feel very guilty, because I sort of failed, but that is because of the standards I set myself.

… I find it very hard to be a good GP (doctor) and to be a good mother and to be a good wife, because I set very high standards all the time. And therefore it makes it much easier to fail and I know that is a fault. I mean for instance I hate upsetting anybody. I wouldn't want to upset someone, patient, colleague, husband, child – whatever. I don't like, I always try and consider other people first. I mean I do value myself and I do look after myself but I don't like causing any upset at all. So yes it is very easy for me to end up feeling guilty because I feel I should be there and it does make it difficult. I was saying I didn't see my husband as he didn't get in until eleven and I was in bed by that time … So I do find it difficult when it is all the clinical issues of making sure that you are totally up to date and can deal with all those issues, and all the emotional issues. Not letting your patients down or your family. I mean my daughter said to me this morning, 'But mummy it is parents' assembly. Why aren't you coming?' 'I have to go to work darling' … It is very hard, it is very hard. That is why I go home at the end of the day and I am exhausted. Yes, I could have easier mornings if I stuck to the old model of the doctor. 'Hello what is wrong with you? OK fine, here you are, off you go', I mean I can do that. We can all do that in three minutes. One of the things I have changed when I came here was that I said I have got to have ten minutes for every consultation, whatever it is, however small. Even the extra is fine. I will just do longer surgeries, which is actually what I do. I do longer surgeries.

2. Try analysing a transcript of your own life (you may have been interviewed, or should be, by a friend or colleague). Immerse yourself in the text and, using the kind of proforma described above, begin to structure your material into themes and process issues (what may be missing or what is difficult to say, as well as how the interviewer might have affected your story), and consider any potential gestalt or patterning in your material. Think about how the overall patterns can help in making more sense of different parts of your narrative.

9
Representing the Stories

Writing Up

Arguably, we are all writers. Letters or emails to friends, memos for our work colleagues, or even grocery lists are all forms of writing. The act of writing, then, is something that all literate people engage in almost daily. However, when it comes to writing research reports, we tend to become afraid and uncomfortable. We put off assignments for weeks and reluctantly turn our attention to the task of writing hours before the work is due. (Amir Marvasti, 2004: 119)

Overview

In this chapter:

- We consider the nature of biographical research writing and how it often straddles boundaries between creative and analytic forms of writing.
- Some examples are given of what we consider to be 'good' biographical research writing.
- A number of issues are explored from getting started in writing to different ways of representing others, and self, in texts.

Introduction

Writing is a deeply creative process but not always an easy one. It raises questions of how to represent lives in their complex and interconnected personal, social, psychological, as well as historic, dimensions. Biographical researchers, like others, struggle with these issues: when we read an academic paper or book, we may see a polished outcome of a journey, which at times will have been slow and painful. In writing this book, we have spent hours thinking about and discussing its content and style, before, during and after producing various drafts. Modifications were made many times before sending it to our publisher for comment. Then, further work was necessary. We start by illustrating how biographical writing can be challenging and how such writing often transgresses a number of boundaries: between creative/literary and imaginative writing, and more detached, analytical or academic work. Or between an ability to chronicle raw experience and to write in theoretically developed ways.

Dissolving boundaries?

In parts of the academy, including in educational and research settings for would-be professionals, the use of personal material and the personal pronoun may still be deemed inappropriate. Peter Dorman, an experienced teacher educator, now uses auto/biographical methods in his work with undergraduates. Many of his trainee teachers come from fairly conventional British backgrounds but have visited India and taught in Indian schools, as part of their degree programme. Peter writes below about encouraging them to write, reflexively and biographically, about these experiences:

> To begin with the first troubling question, that of voice. The trainees who travelled to India were drawn from a year group. I have been disturbed for some years by the requirement that when our Year 3 undergraduates carry out research that this must not be written in the first person. That they should be absent from the writing even when examining what are clearly issues which relate directly to their own life histories. Thus parents of autistic children, or students who have been bullied, must absent themselves and their own experience from the emotionally dehydrated writing process ... The distinction is crucial and lies at the heart of the auto/ biographical approach adopted. (Dorman, 2008)

Peter describes conflicts with colleagues – some from scientific backgrounds – about writing and representation. Like other academic educationalists (see Woods, 1993), he has come to believe passionately in the need for students – and himself – to bring their personal history and experience, not least when they feel shaken to the core, directly into writing. Conventional academic work, he notes, can dehydrate the creative process and disenchant writer-students.

Susan Krieger in her plea for a more humanistic, transparent style in social research writing, challenges how academic writing has traditionally been positioned:

> Some of us have become increasingly dissatisfied with the tone of remote authority commonly used in the writing of social science and with the way the personality of an author gets lost in social science texts ... Social science is premised on minimizing the self, viewing it as a contaminant, transcending it, denying it, protecting its vulnerability ... we paint pictures in which we hope not to exist; or if we exist ... are subordinate or nearly invisible. (1991: 47, 116)

Feminist researchers have questioned the subordination and invisibility of self and subjectivity and actively paint this into research portraiture. However, this raises obvious questions. The forms of biographical writing to which we aspire problematise the boundaries between creative writing and writing for academic purpose; between more literary styles of representation and the need for detachment. We may seek both to illuminate the conscious experiencing of lives in ways analogous to novelists like Virginia Woolf, Jane Austen or Edith Wharton, yet to do far more than this in theorising our material. However, Woolf, Austen and Wharton were biographers and ethnographers of their times too. Wharton explicitly drew on contemporary social theory, and the distinctions between literature and academic writing can get blurred (Lee, 2008).

Creative writing

Celia Hunt (Hunt and Sampson, 2006; Hunt and West, 2006) specialises in the use of creative writing as a developmental, even a therapeutic tool, and convenes Masters and Doctoral programmes to this end. People participate in these programmes to strengthen their creative writing through a deeper engagement with self and self-experience; or use creative writing to explore life transitions such as the move from work to retirement; or learn how to use creative writing as a developmental or therapeutic tool with groups and individuals in health care, therapy and education. Part of the work students undertake is experiential, involving an exploration of themselves through imagery and metaphor, and re-writing of personal narratives through fiction; or through more explicit auto/biography.

Such writing, at first sight, may appear different from a research paper, a PhD or a book on biographical research. We wonder about the differences. Celia Hunt and Fiona Sampson (2006) pose the question of how to access, but also objectify, raw experience to build reflexivity in writing in the context of their work with students. They consider the importance of attending to the imaginative body in order to allow creativity full reign. They note how being overly critical, prematurely, may stifle this. Yet they also insist that it is important to cultivate a capacity for distance, to bring things into some order and think about them; to shape, edit and be critical. There is in this process a sort of doubling rather than an extinction of self and subjectivity: we immerse ourselves in what others are doing and thinking while standing outside this and observing what we are doing. Creative and biographical writing are not, in these terms, complete opposites: the contemporary anthropologist will imaginatively immerse herself in another culture, on its terms, suspending assumptions absorbed from her own culture, yet will also draw reflexively from parallels in her own culture and experience in building detachment and understanding.

We argue for a more holistic perspective on academic writing, at least in biographical research: for the cultivation of detachment alongside immersion in the other's world. Yet there are some differences between writing good literature and biographical research, if of emphasis and not kind. Joan Acker, Kate Barry and Johanna Esseveld, as feminist sociologists, discuss this issue:

> We are probably faced with another unresolvable dilemma: working from a perspective in which we are trained to want to give a reasoned and connected account, we face live material that is constantly in the process of transformation, that is not organized in the way of academic theories. Virginia Woolf, among other novelists, may give a better account of the conscious experiencing of life in all its episodic and unorganized ways than we sociologists can achieve. However, as sociologists we can find representations of such experience that allow us to build a sociology for women, a sociology that connects with real experience at that level to its structural determination in the wider society. What distinguishes us from those who are not social scientists lies in our method of systematically attempting to reconstruct social reality and to put these systematic reconstructions into a social theory which we share with other social scientists. (Acker et al., 1991: 149)

To repeat, however, these may be differences of degree rather than of kind. To build detached and theoretical understanding requires the capacity to experience and represent 'real' lives and situations, including our own. We are in a border country between creative writing and academic purpose in which there are tensions but also rich possibilities.

Faction

Biographical researchers may explicitly traverse academic conventions. Under the influence of postmodernism, researchers like Peter Clough have experimented with different ways of telling stories, to illuminate more of the complexities of human experience. This includes producing fictional accounts. Here, boundaries dissolve or become deliberately blurred. Clough (2004) writes of Frank, a fictional character and the effects of teaching on his life. Yet Frank's story is based on Clough's own experiences of teaching. In developing a fictional character, Clough aims to: 'raise questions about the role of the author in the creation of stories (social scientific or literary) and about the nature of the data which are so created' (2004: 66). Clough chose to fictionalise because this was 'a story designed to provoke something of the self in the reader' (2004: 183, 184). Fictional stories can stir a collective consciousness of problematic issues and illuminate what is often obscure or deeply personal. The writer can allow situations to develop in relatively uninhibited ways, like good literature. Clough believes that some of the 'truths' of teaching have been neglected in research and fiction gets us nearer to them. We may have been taught to think of fact and fiction as opposites – truth and untruth – but good fiction creates different kinds of narrative truth, speaking to the muddle, mess, conflict, anger, resentment, revelation and resilience that we all experience. We come to understand others and our own situations, as Rustin (2000) observed, in new and deeper ways through such writing. Nonetheless, most biographical researchers strive to ground their writing in the narrative material, and no more.

Examples of good biographical writing

It is worth entering some examples of good writing in this border country. Edward Thompson (1980) embodies the ability to combine theoretical insight with provocative narrative, grounded in imaginative empathy and engagement with the lives of ordinary people. There are three other texts quoted below that embody good biographical writing. The first extract comes from Al Thomson's (1994) book *Anzac Memories: Living with the Legend*.

> I had a military childhood. For the first twelve years of my life, from 1960 until 1972, my father was a senior infantry officer in the Australian army. With my two brothers, I grew up in army barracks in different parts of Australia and around the world. We were surrounded by soldiers and soldiering. My earliest memories are of
>
> *(Continued)*

(Continued)

starched khaki and green-clad men parading across asphalt squares, trooping and wheeling to echoed commands. When I was five, my father took his battalion to Borneo to fight the secret war of confrontation against the Indonesians. While the men were away, the army brats marched up and down in makeshift uniforms, childhood imitations of our soldier fathers ... My family war myths show how only some experiences become highlighted in remembering, while others are repressed and silenced ... The Anzac tradition that I grew up with articulated a selective view of family history and generalized it as an influential version of the nation's wartime past. But one of the lessons of growing up in a relatively powerful family and class is recognition that its members do not simply, or conspiratorially, impose their views upon society. Their views are pervasive because of public power, but they are sincerely believed and propagated. (Thomson, 1994: 3–5)

Thomson evocatively describes how martial music and marching men still make his spine tingle and that patriotic ritual and rhetoric can fill the need for a sense of purpose and proud collective identity. But other things get silenced and Thomson engages with stories that do not fit the dominant account or ideology. His interviews with Anzac veterans stem too from dis-ease about his own family in which other stories, including those of the women, were marginalised. This is writing that draws the reader into personal experience and dilemmas – ones with which we easily identify – but uses this to historicise problems around the meshing of power and story telling, and of how some stories are repressed. The researcher's job is to challenge this, even when difficult and painful issues are raised. There is a mix here of the creative – in the evocation of childhood – with the capacity for solid historical work.

The second example is taken from Carolyn Steedman (1986), who combines the skills of the biographer and storyteller with, in her case, a rich feminist, psychoanalytic, sociological and historical imagination. The extract comes from the introductory chapter of *Landscape for a Good Woman*.

My mother's longing shaped my own childhood. From a Lancashire mill town and a working-class twenties childhood she came away wanting: fine clothes, glamour, money; to be what she wasn't. However that longing was produced in her distant childhood, what she actually wanted were real things, real entities, things she materially lacked, things that a culture and a social system withheld from her ... and the story of the two lives that follows points ... to a consideration of what people – particularly working-class children of the recent past – come to understand of themselves when all they possess is their labour, and what becomes of class consciousness when it is a structure of feeling that can be learned in childhood, with one of its components a proper envy, the desire of people for the things of the earth.

Class and gender are the bits and pieces from which psychological selfhood is made. (Steedman, 1986: 6–7)

Phillipe Bourgois provides the third example, in a chapter with the intriguing title of 'In Search of Horatio Alger: Culture and Ideology in the Crack Economy'.

> The heavyset, white undercover cop pushed me across the ice cream counter, spreading my legs and poking me around the groin. As he came dangerously close to the bulge in my right pocket, I hissed in his ear 'it's a tape recorder'. He snapped backwards releasing his left hand's grip on my neck, and whispered a barely audible 'sorry'. Apparently he thought he had clumsily intercepted an undercover from another unit instead of an anthropologist, because before I could get a look at his face, he had left the bodega grocery store-cum-numbers-joint. Meanwhile the marijuana sellers stationed in front of the bodega that Gato and I had just entered to buy beer saw that the undercover had been rough with me and suddenly felt safe and relieved. They were finally confident that I was a white addict rather than an undercover.
>
> I told Gato to grab the change on my $10 bill from the cashier as I hurried to leave this embarrassing scene. At the doorway, however, I was blocked by Bennie, a thin teenager barging through the door to mug us. Bennie pushed me to the side and lunged at the loose dollar bills in Gato's hand, the change from the beers. 'That's my money now Gato – give it to me,' he shouted. I started with a loud 'Hey! Yo, what are you talking about, that's my money! Get away from it'. But one look at the teenager's contorted face and narrowed eyes stopped me halfway through the sentence. Gato's underbreath mutter of 'be careful – my man is dusted' was redundant. I was ready to give up the eight – and more if necessary – to avoid any out-of-control violence from a mugger high on angel dust. (Bourgois, 2002: 171)

Bourgois, like Thompson and Steedman, breaks away from the traditional mould of academic writing, in his case by beginning with a rich descriptive scene in a literary style. The first three and a half pages seem more akin to fiction but bring the fieldwork to life. Such writing makes us want to read more. Thomson and Steedman's styles are also direct, accessible, personal, and analytic too.

What makes such writing fit for purpose? Our list would include an openness to the autobiographical roots of research; the capacity to write in clear, simple prose and to evoke childhood or adult desire; the ability to use commonplace examples, and ordinary experience, such as children's play, to stir up strong feelings and associations in the reader. The writing connects public issues with private experience. The child plays, the mother desires, while the academic writer works in disciplined and imaginative ways to paint a bigger historical and/or psychosocial picture.

Writing and the self

Writing parallels the research process itself in serving as a transitional space, or container, for experiments in story telling and analysis. This is a space for experiment with narratives of the other, and of self, and for working on our identities as we project aspects of who we are into creative activity, mould them in new ways and introject them in changed form. Biography is the art of the retrospective but research and writing are equally part of the fabric of ongoing experience. We tell stories which are not merely about ourselves but also an integral part of them. We come to live autobiographically; or in short, we create narrative identities. Paul John Eakin (2008) explores the intimate, dynamic connection between ourselves and our stories, between narrative and identity in everyday life. He draws on a wide range of biographical writings including the *New York Times* series 'Portraits of Grief' memorialising the victims of 9/11. He uses insights into self and identity formation from developmental psychology, cultural anthropology and neurobiology. In his account, the self-fashioning in which we routinely, even automatically, engage is largely conditioned by social norms and biological necessities. We are taught by others how to say who we are, while at the same time our sense of self is shaped decisively by our lives in and as bodies. For Eakin, biography can become an act of self-determination, no matter what the circumstances, and he stresses its adaptive and dynamic value as an art that helps anchor our shifting selves, and those of others, in time.

Choices and other matters

There are more choices to make and practical questions to consider in how to represent lives. One approach is to let people speak for themselves, to greater or lesser extents, although an element of selection and editing always takes place. Another approach is to use direct quotation sparingly in comparison to our interpretations and theory building. Laurel Richardson notes that 'we are using our authority and privileges' (1990: 12), regardless: 'No matter how we stage the text, we – as authors – are doing the staging. As we speak about the people we study, we also speak for them. As we inscribe their lives, we bestow meaning and promulgate values' (1990: 12).

How then to stage material in ways that do justice to our narrators and their complexity, however much we remain in charge? We can seek to build a more democratic relationship in writing, building on what may have been established at the interview stage. The transcripts, diaries and reflections of our narrators are fully interspersed with interpretation while the writing can be explicitly democratic as the researcher and researched write together.

Rebecca Lawthom (2004) adopted such an approach with her participant Colleen Stamford in telling the story of transformations in a life, from marriage to becoming a lesbian. Linden has occupied a middle ground, where rich narrative material is quoted extensively, alongside interpretation. The following example is from an encounter with a doctor experiencing a difficult day. The transcript is quoted at length because of its capacity to evoke confused feelings, and guilt, that can lie at the heart of professional practice. Dr Ambi worked in a difficult area of inner London, and like many ethnic minority doctors felt it necessary, always, to give of his best, in a culture where doctors like him, he thought, were not always appreciated.

> I want to tell you about what happened over the weekend ... I am so engrossed in my work and my mind is working overtime all the time, even when I am at home and am thinking how can I develop this, write down on a piece of paper and bring

it here and in the early morning. I just write and map it out, do all that, and my eldest daughter said to me – 'Daddy you are going to lose me soon, because you don't sit and talk to me' and she had a go at me and my wife as well and so this emptiness is something which I may not have picked up … But at the same time we think we are giving the best for them. We try to do everything. But when she came out with this, she said – 'if you think I am thinking this way', I have two other daughters. So all this stemmed from my last girl. She doing her GCSEs now and she came and cried the other day because she had missed a question. She was aiming for A and she is not going to get it … She wants to get into medicine. So I am struggling what I should do. Should I do all this and then be a proud professional or whether I am leaving an empty space for my children … we had this bust up … Physical and financial aspects they recognise that we do all what we can, but emotionally not doing at all … I think if you get too much engrossed in your professional thing it can leave the emptiness in us … (West, 2001: 68)

The doctor was suffering from stress and had recently been in hospital. But he said he was a fortunate man who never allowed himself to forget from whence he came (West, 2001: 68). The quotation is long but important in enabling the reader to know more about this doctor, in his own words, and to understand the delicate interplay of the personal and professional. The lengthy quote (which has been edited for this chapter) brings raw, ragged experience to life while prompting questions about its meaning. Barbara tends to opt for similar ground, attempting to balance raw material and the voices of participants with sociological understanding.

How many cases?

At a relatively mundane level, perhaps, we have to ask ourselves whether we will use one case study or engage with issues more thematically, drawing on several lives in a particular chapter or research paper. Barbara uses both approaches in her research on class and gender. In her chapter 'Recovering Class and the Collective in the Stories of Adult Learners' (Merrill, 2007), she chose to use themes and illustrate them with quotes from several of her participants. The themes chosen were:

- Schooling, Family and Class
- 'Get Me Out of Here: There Has Got to be More to Life Than This'
- Re-entering Education: Problematical Experiences
- Cultural Experiences of Learning
- Improving Employment Prospects.

In a journal article written with Beth Crossan, John Field and Jim Gallacher (2003) – 'Understanding Participation in Learning for Non-Traditional Adult Learners: Learning Careers and the Construction of Learning Identities (Crossan et al., 2003) – Barbara, and her colleagues, decided to focus on two case studies, one female, one male, in representing experiences of participation and non-participation in further education in Scotland. Choosing just two case studies can offer more in-depth understanding of particular lives, with less editing of the narrative. But there are still issues, with several transcripts, of who and what to choose as well as on what basis. In the Scottish study, Barbara and her colleagues selected a male (Dave) and a female (Jane) to illuminate the gendered dimensions of learning lives, because of its importance across all the material. 'Jane' was a participant in education and 'Dave' was not. In the eventual article, the choice of Jane and Dave was justified, as follows:

> Clearly, this evidence base will not support too many hard and fast conclusions. We are using these two narratives, not to provide a formal typology, but heuristically, in order to explore the usefulness of our modified concept of learning career in understanding engagement with learning. (Crossan et al., 2003: 59)

Using several life stories in, say, an article, can mean that individual narratives are used in partial ways. However, such an approach is useful for building and refining typologies. For Barbara, the approach was helpful in her book chapter, referred to above (Merrill, 2007), as she sought to employ 'rich' individual life histories to illuminate collective experiences of class and gender. But people, as noted earlier, may get upset when their material is elided with that of others, for purposes they may not appreciate.

Linden has used one or two 'good stories' or 'telling' case studies to reveal key themes across a number of biographies in especially acute and/or complex ways. In the work on adults and their motivation (West, 1996), he chose two people to illustrate and illuminate various themes across the whole sample. Brenda, whom we met in Chapter 7, and Paul, came from the Medway Towns in Kent. He was a working-class man in his late 30s and she a slightly older woman. They shared a number of biographical features in common. Both were socially marginalised people who struggled to manage disturbing changes in their lives. In Paul's case, wider scripts of class, in Brenda's, of gender, intruded into and shaped the narratives. Both had more 'secret' stories too, of being abused in childhood and of having little encouragement to know and experience themselves as they really were. Time, instead, was spent appeasing parents or defending against their abuse, the consequences of which had resonated across their lives and relationships. Although particular aspects of the material were distinct, their stories echoed themes across the entire sample; other cases were then used to explore specific issues in other lives.

Textual poachers

In biographical writing, we continually refer to the texts and theories of others, even if this is unstated. There is a process of intertextuality at the heart of biographical writing. Other authors shape what we do as we draw upon their theory(ies) and narrative styles. We may draw on others to support our analysis and conclusions; or we refer to them to critique their or even our own work. We are in this sense part of a community of writers. Plummer (2001) refers to social researchers as being 'textual poachers', to capture this process. Throughout this present book, we refer to many different authors and have inserted quotes from texts that we feel are particularly useful and relevant. Referring to other authors is part of being scholarly, academic and honest about our interdependence as writers, academics and people.

In using the work of other social researchers, however, we have to be careful about issues of plagiarism. For students, it is important to be aware of this and what it means. All departments and universities have policies on plagiarism. There are now electronic aids to help tutors identify cases of plagiarism. It is crucial that you strive to use your own words and not the words of others, and if you do, to be explicit and accurate in citing reference(s).

Starting to write

Writing should not be left to the end of research but should begin early in a project. If you are writing a thesis, produce draft chapters, such as the introduction, early on; it can be changed, perhaps radically, in the light of experience. Write about why you chose the topic for research and begin the literature review, before or during fieldwork. Many students are anxious about starting to write, which can be related to concerns about the level, standards and conventions of postgraduate work.

Beginning to write, biographically or autobiographically, can be exciting, if perplexing. The following examples come from two PhD students. Both have struggled to find authentic authorial voices in an academic context when combining the personal with an intellectual register. Wilma Fraser (2007), in drafting a paper, turned to an esteemed relative – the Gaelic poet, Sorley Maclean – in search of a form of writing that was personal, political, academic and analytical at the same time:

> One of Maclean's greatest achievements, and gift to Gaeldom, was his ability to universalise from the local; his community, his culture, was his well-spring; but it fed and informed his responses to the horrors and madnesses of the twentieth century. Whilst family responsibilities prevented him from fighting Franco, he served in World War Two and was severely wounded at El Alamein ... His hatred of fascism and colonialism and his early espousal of communism were also nurtured by an upbringing in the Free Presbyterian Church. (Fraser, 2007: 5)

Wilma draws in other people of importance in thinking about her research topic (adult education and the cultural imagination). These include academics like George Davie (1961), author of *The Democratic Intellect* and feminists such as Jean Barr (2006) who have challenged aspects of Scottish educational thought, including the primacy of reason and the neglect of marginalised voices. Wilma writes:

> Those are ... links; the fifth, the 'hand' that 'pens' these lines ... but the sixth, the 'unifying sensibility', is the one to be interrogated in the forthcoming pages. Of course there is a distinction between the lines and the author of the lines; there is the consciousness which writes and the lifeworld which frames, shapes and informs that consciousness. There are the slips and assurances, the contingencies and contradictions; the five decades of experience which form both my 'spiritual geology' as well as my 'emotional geography', all 'at once part of (my) personal apparatus of feeling'. (Fraser, 2007: 8)

If the hand penning the lines is hers, as is the unifying sensibility, she is nonetheless part of an imaginative community, building on the inspiration and insights of many others.

It took Wilma much time and many drafts, as well as soul searching, to reach this stage and to find, for her, the beginnings of a confident authorial PhD voice. Elizabeth Chapman Hoult (2007), another PhD student, experienced a similar struggle in combining the personal and the academic, in her case on the topic of resilience in adult learning. She struggled to apply 'blocks' of sociological theory, in particular the work of Bourdieu, to the lives of others as well as her own:

> I am uncomfortable, therefore, with an unaccompanied application of Bourdieu's theory of capital to my own story and the stories of the other learners in the study. So the primary purpose of this section of the autobiography is to try to find out what happened in my formative years that enabled me to perform an active subjectivity and to develop a resilient identity as a learner in the subsequent years of formal education (part one of the autobiography) and as an adult learner (to follow).

> … In order to gain access to those years I decided to interview my mum. My mum's presence in the text has opened up my thinking and writing considerably and helped me to find a way through the apparent closure that is a feature of Bourdieu's work. The allowance of space for the mother in the text has a long history in women's writing … 'Woolf experimented all her life, in both her autobiography and fiction, with this problem of how to allow the mother's presence into a writing that has traditionally not permitted her a place.' By giving my mum a place in the text my writing has been liberated in terms of the academic discourse as well as in terms of my thinking about language and learning and it has taken me into new territories relating to the interchange between resilience and resistance.

If writing is hard, it can provide imaginative space for building resilience and resistance, and for forging more of a self in the process, in a kind of communion with others.

Who is my audience?

There are more prosaic questions to ask: 'who is my audience'? Two other questions can follow: 'how will they read and interpret it'? And 'why are they reading it – for what purpose'? Knowing who our readers are is important, as we may vary our style of writing for particular audiences. Writing a research report for a funding body is different to writing for fellow academics; while writing aimed at policy makers or practitioners can require different styles. Writing always and inevitably has to be sensitive to its audience:

> Reading is an active process, and no text can have a completely fixed meaning. When we write – and hence inscribe certain preferred interpretations in our books, dissertations and papers – we do so with an implied audience of readers. (Coffey and Atkinson, 1996: 118)

It is important to think about writing for specific non-academic audiences such as practitioners and policy makers: our work, we feel, should be accessible to those outside the ivory tower; and in a sense our writing should always be governed by a concern to communicate as widely as possible. Written work for non-academic audiences needs to be jargon-free and not overly weighed down by sociological or psychological terminology. Yet the avoidance of jargon and the capacity to express complexity in simple ways is desirable in all writing. However, documents aimed at policy makers have to be brief and we may need to learn to use life stories in more focused ways: to help policy makers or others identify how the practices of institutions, such as universities, can be improved.

An example

Barbara co-ordinated two EU Socrates Grundtvig projects focusing on adult students and entitled 'Learning in Higher Education' and 'Promoting Reflective Independent Learning in Higher Education'. Both studies used life history approaches and both produced practical outputs. These included handbooks with one aimed at adult students and one at lecturers and support and guidance workers in higher education. Quotes from the students' life stories are used to illustrate strategies to improve teaching and learning approaches in higher education.

How to structure a thesis or research report is also an issue. Undergraduate or postgraduate thesis writing can be governed by formal conventions in terms of types of chapters. The traditional approach is to structure chapters in the following manner:

- Abstract/Summary
- Preface/Introduction
- Context and Literature Review
- Existing theory in the field
- Outline of methodology used
- Presentation of data and analysis – this may be more than one chapter
- Findings and relationship to existing theory
- Conclusion
- References
- Appendix.

Academic conference organisers can also require a particular structure for a paper. But structures can be talked about and may vary. The review of literature may be interspersed across chapters and autobiographical material introduced and developed at different stages in a book, for instance, as part of a dialogue with specific narrators (around themes of masculinity, for example, in Linden's book on doctors (West, 2001)). University guidelines also need to be considered but also challenged. A few years ago, Barbara examined a PhD, which she felt was written in a rigid, overly objectivist style, with no personal pronouns and the voices of participants got lost. Barbara was critical of this only to learn that the university required the format.

Making time, finding space

Writing can be a lonely experience (even when part of a research team), sitting in a room on our own with a computer. Everything has to be drafted, read and re-read, re-drafted and refined, many times over. When Barbara is writing a first draft, she is thinking quickly and is more anxious to get her thoughts down rather than worrying unduly about her English style and grammar. Linden does the same and often simply goes with a flow, which sometimes works well, if sometimes not.

Almost all writing is limited by word restrictions. Editing is necessary not only in relation to grammar and style but also length. All the chapters in this book were too long and the material required extensive editing. Some chapters had to be edited drastically; one being reduced from 11,000 to 7000 words. Editing is a hard process because it means abandoning part of our creation. We can get angry and resentful that our precious work is to be pruned and that voices or ideas may be lost; but this is almost always for the better. Once a chapter, article or book is finished, it is helpful to persuade a 'critical friend' to read and comment. There is always material that can be jettisoned or refined in producing a more readable text.

We do need to find a space for writing: an environment that makes us feel comfortable, a room of our own if we can. In one of the United Kingdom's leading newspapers (*The Guardian*), there has been a weekly item in the Arts Review section featuring a photograph of a writer's room with an explanation of why and how the space is decorated and furnished. Although we have offices at our universities, most writing is done at home because it is quieter. Barbara's desk sits in front of a window and overlooks the garden. There are photographs of family scattered around the room alongside paintings of sunny Provencal landscapes, which she is deeply fond of, and diverse artefacts. Linden has prints of places where he has lived. There are candles, photographs and chaos, all having biographical significance. They help create a transitional space for creative work – one redolent with good and/or significant objects – to encourage and evoke meaning making and self-expression. Objects to engage with when the going is tough are important because they may answer, so to speak, the question of why we strive to be biographical researchers at all and remind us that our writing matters.

Writing: a problem rarely discussed

Some of the processes explored in this chapter have traditionally been neglected in the academy. Writing has, at times, in Plummer's words, been 'the dark secret of social science' (2001: 168). The actual experiences of writing a journal article, a book chapter or a book get lost or overly sanitised. Barbara has talked about writing with colleagues who are friends and was reassured to discover that others shared difficult, messy experiences, including times of giant despair. Everyone admitted that it could be hard to write and that they might sit for hours and produce barely a paragraph. On days like this, it is best to leave writing alone. Linden has felt stymied and talked at length with a friend who is a professional writer – of plays for radio and television – about 'blocks', and what they represent and how to overcome them. We all get them at times. (See Marvasti (2004) who identifies some tips to overcome writer's block.) Luckily, it is not always so and there can be good days when our writing flows. Books or chapters on writing for academic purposes have begun to appear more widely: see Kristin Esterberg (2002), Amir Marvasti (2004) and David Silverman (2006). There is also Howard Becker's (1986) *Writing for Social Scientists*, Laurel Richardson's (1990) *Writing Strategies: Reaching Diverse Audiences*, Adrian Holliday's (2007) *Doing and Writing Qualitative Research* and Harry F. Wolcott's (1997) *Writing Up Qualitative Research*, among others.

Summary

Writing is a visible, tangible and public outcome of research, constructed by the researcher in interaction with others and a range of discursive possibilities. Writing combines a creative and systematic way of representing lives, including our own. For some biographical researchers, writing is particularly important because it provides a platform for making known the lives of the marginalised; or of neglected aspects of lives, like the politics and psychology of desire. In telling the stories of others, and ourselves, we need, as researchers, to think about what matters to us and why. The process of biographical writing is also a process of self-creation in which we can come to think and feel in new ways: it is about being retrospective and prospective in a mix of science and art.

   If you are just starting a research career and/or writing an undergraduate or postgraduate thesis and are feeling anxious, it is important to repeat the fact that even experienced researchers find writing hard at times. What is often essential is to start writing rather than putting it off. You need to find a style with which you are happy, but it takes time. It is important to remember that in biographical research, there is great scope for experiment, play and innovation, and to speak to audience(s) in new ways. Remember that a piece of research can be written up in different ways, for different audiences, and in different formats. Persevere: writing a first piece of work, and, eventually, perhaps, seeing it published, can be a memorable biographical moment.

Key points

- Biographical writing transcends or even transgresses conventional distinctions between literary and academic genres, the creative and systematic, the intuitive and logical, fact and fiction.
- Writing is not always easy. All of us have good and bad days.
- There are choices to make about how to represent the lives of others.

(Continued)

(Continued)

- Writing always requires drafting and re-drafting.
- It is important to experiment and find a writing style which suits you, drawing on others who inspire you.

FURTHER READING

Esterberg, K.G. (2002) *Qualitative Methods in Social Research.* Boston: McGraw-Hill. This has a useful chapter on writing.

Gilbert, N. (2001) *Researching Social Life.* London: Sage. This has a useful chapter on writing.

Holliday, A. (2007) *Doing and Writing Qualitative Research* (2nd edn). London: Sage.

Richardson, L. (1990) *Writing Strategies: Reaching Diverse Audiences.* Newbury Park: Sage.

Wolcott, H.F. (1990) *Writing-up Qualitative Research.* Newbury Park: Sage.

DISCUSSION QUESTIONS

1. Think of an academic book or a journal article that you have enjoyed reading and consider why.
2. What might be the role of fiction in biographical writing and research?

ACTIVITIES

1. Choose a journal article from within your discipline, one that focuses on biographical research. What did you like or dislike about the writing style? Was the language clear and accessible? Is it written in a traditional academic style or does it experiment with a more informal style? Did the introduction 'grab' and interest you? (This activity can also be undertaken in small groups or in a pair.)
2. Choose a transcript of one of your participants, decide how you will write her/his story and produce a first draft; and then discuss this with a critical friend.

10
Is Biographical Research Valid and Ethical?

Too much research activity is based upon minimal involvement with a given group of people (referred to as participants), often over a short period of time allotted by funding ... before the researcher moves on to another hot topic in order to enhance their research résumé ... The current climate of research production is in danger of missing out on the gifts of longer term ... relationships with people who can enhance a researcher's knowledge of the world. When Plummer (1983) argues that we need to know our informants from the inside, he is hinting at the need to work relationally, emotionally and empathically with the people whose stories we are hoping to tell. (Dan Goodley, 2004b: 165–6)

Overview

In this chapter:

- We examine how validity means different things to different social researchers. Claims to validity may be rooted in notions of reliable procedures as well as statistical principles. Biographical researchers often claim validity on the grounds of the verisimilitude, or the lifelikeness and plausibility of narrative material.
- We see how many biographical researchers are concerned with chronicling the distinctiveness of biographies but also how they may be representative of wider aspects of the human condition.
- We explore the importance of ethical issues in conducting biographical/life history research.
- We note that good ethical practice requires researchers to be proactive and to consider the values informing their work.
- There may be an overlap between biographical research and therapeutic processes but it is important to distinguish between them.

Validity

This chapter returns to two key issues that have been present throughout the book: validity and ethics. We have noted how the validity of biographical research can be challenged from a variety of perspectives, including by historians and post-structuralists. So in what senses can the research discussed in the book be regarded as valid? The topic is constantly debated and to be faced every time we undertake biographical research. There are profound differences around the meaning of validity in social research; between those, for instance, who model their work on the procedures and criteria of the natural sciences, and those who insist that the study of psychosocial phenomena requires a different kind and quality of relating and understanding, and thus criterion of validity.

There are also differences within the 'family' of biographical researchers as to what makes research valid: some insist, from a 'realist' perspective, that validity lies in the degree to which their work is a convincing account of the past; others consider this potentially naive and are concerned as much with the interplay of past and present, researcher and researched, representation and reality, immediacy and memory. These, they insist, are legitimate topics for study in their own right. We take more of what we have termed a critical realist position. Validity, from this perspective, partly derives from generating some account of the past, of what it was like from the inside, but this can only be done in conditional ways. The past is always a provisional construct, mediated through the present, including the workings of language and relationship. Some post-structuralists occupy this ground while others question the preoccupations of biographical research altogether. Life stories, in this latter view, become little more than language games shaped by competing discourses, power/knowledge formations and regimes of truth, about which the subjects at their heart may be unaware (Foucault, 1978, 1979a, 1979b).

History and validity

The post-structuralist claim that we are missing some larger point has echoes among certain humanistic critics too. We have noted how a prominent historian of adult education (Fieldhouse, 1996) has questioned 'the present enthusiasm for life histories' among contemporary researchers. For Roger Fieldhouse, the historian's task is to locate evidence to inform the development of wider understanding of conflict and change processes, rather than generating endless detail. History, for Fieldhouse, is a site of struggle between power and powerlessness, progressive and reactionary social forces, and over human values, as well as between competing versions of the good society and how this is to be realised. If histories from below and the narratives of ordinary people matter, as in the work of Edward Thompson, their validity lies in building convincing connections between individual histories and wider social theory as well as humanistic purposes. Thompson's research, for instance, contributed to building a less deferential working-class culture, as well as to illuminating how people make more of their own histories, collectively, if never in conditions of their own choosing (Fieldhouse, 1997).

We have suggested that biographical researchers need theory to help make sense of the detail. We are also motivated by wider, humanistic purposes: of how research can help build a more just social order. Detail, in our view, is crucial: rich or thick description – and really getting to know something of the other, from the inside – is essential for understanding and evoking new insights into people's experiences. Linden referred in Chapter 1 to the cultural and psychological importance of an apparently trivial gift from his father, when he, Linden, went to university. Bacon, sausage and fruit were of intensely personal significance yet also pregnant with historical and social meaning. The gift can tell us a great deal about one parent's experiences of living in a century dominated by world war, as well as of gendered relations. It is also representative of a bigger picture. This might include structuring forces in human relationships, encompassing the difficulties of intimacy among men and how this finds expression in everyday encounters.

Conventional views

However, many conventional research textbooks discuss validity in different terms. Validity, at root, in much mainstream social research, is seen to lie in statistical significance, standardised procedures, reliability, replication and generalisability. Significance refers to the probability that a result derived from the study of a sample could not have been found by chance. Standardisation has to do with using the same, well-tested instruments, in consistent ways (compare this with the open-endedness and unpredictability of many biographical interviews). Reliability is a preoccupation of hard methodologists, who insist on using the same instrument (like an interview) in identical ways; researchers must behave in exactly the same manner in every encounter. If another researcher undertook the same piece of work, on the same terms, in the same setting, they should arrive at essentially the same results; if, that is, the research is to be valid (Blaxter et al., 2006; Plummer, 2001). Generalisability is also a statistical concept: the greater the numbers in the sample, and the more representative they are of a parent group, the more valid the research will be. The language and assumptions of biographical researchers can be quite different. The fact that Barbara's research interviews, derived from her sociological perspectives, can produce different kinds of data to Linden's, even if working with the same or similar people, does not render it invalid. Research, for both of us, is relational and dynamic, and the researcher, and what s/he brings, has to be taken into account. We can generate rich but also varying accounts of what it has meant to live a life, to be a parent, a professional or learner in higher education: variety is not the antithesis of validity.

It is worth noting, at this point, that the Latin root of valid – validus – means strong, powerful and effective. Strength could be defined by reference to narrative richness, to the quality of our knowing and its power to speak to others in new ways. Effectiveness might emanate from our capacity, as researchers, to create good transitional spaces in which people feel respected and encouraged to find and experiment with voice. Furthermore, as Plummer notes, it will 'simply not do to … standardise everything in advance, for this would be a distorted and hence invalid story' (2001: 155). What matters is the quality of research relationship, and the extent to which this facilitates deeper forms of insight and wider meaning. Research, as Wendy Hollway and Tony Jefferson note, can be highly generalisable, but deeply flawed: 'one person's unique defensive structures cannot simply be read off from their social, demographic characteristics' (2000: 127). We need, always, to keep in mind the rich individual biography or good story. If a particular person – a man, for example – is deeply fearful of crime and defies the norm, researchers should not simply and reductively dismiss this as 'irrationality'. It is bad science.

Family matters

However, biographical researchers may seek to establish validity in the eyes of research communities via some notion of representativity for their work. A biographical sample may be constructed on the basis of categories used in large quantitative studies, for instance. As observed, Hollway and Jefferson (2000) made use of data from the British Crime Survey to construct their sample, with a view to establishing that biographical research could contribute to an understanding of the fear of crime across different categories of people. Tom Schuller and colleagues (2007), as also previously observed, used data from the 1958 and 1970 British Birth Cohort Studies, to choose a purposive sample for biographical study, in their case of the wider benefits of learning. But, as Hollway and Jefferson demonstrate, people who can be classified in similar ways according to demographic characteristics, may turn out to be quite different from one another, when using biographical methods. The claim to validity of biographical research lies, fundamentally, in challenging epistemological reductionism and superficiality.

Biographical research, in fact, provokes profound questions about the validity of other approaches and the generalisations drawn from them. The following case study is drawn from Linden's research (with Andrea Carlson) among the families in a Sure Start project. This demonstrates how spending time – over cycles of interviews – with a family, and getting to know something of their experiences from the inside, can build subtleties of understanding easily lost or missed completely in other methods. This is especially so when researchers pre-select what is to be measured or explored: or when researchers assume they know which questions to ask, and fail, as a consequence, to learn.

There is currently a major debate about the 'impact' of Sure Start on children and families. The national evaluation of Sure Start, as observed, draws on a large data set. Researchers have, it seems, failed to detect any measurable developmental, behavioural or language changes between children living in Sure Start areas and those living outside in similar communities. Linden and Andrea wrote:

> 'But we spent many hours with individual families (as well as staff), and the auto/biographical design enabled us to explore the meanings of experience, in depth and over time, in ways that other kinds of research rarely do. The study was able to chronicle subtle changes in the relationship between, for example, a young mother, professionals and a child, as she began to understand more of the origins of a speech defect'.

Mandy was a single parent, with two children, aged 2 and 5, who had suffered the death of another child. Her oldest child was 2 ½ when Mandy and her husband separated and her son felt it 'badly':

> 'He became very hard to handle, very abusive, the only way I could get around it was actually having him in my bed at night and that seemed to calm him down

(Continued)

(Continued)

a lot. He actually only went back in his own bedroom when she [a daughter] went in her bedroom as well. So they are now both in a bedroom together and they won't go to bed unless the other one is there. But he did react badly to start with. He couldn't understand why daddy had left this house. He withdrew into himself partly'.

Mandy recognised that her son's speech problem began at this point. He was always being taunted, she said, and called a wimp because he would cry at the slightest thing. He struggled to speak ... Mandy was advised to seek help for herself, to deal with her loss, and began to see 'a Sure Start counsellor' on a weekly basis.

'At the time she was helping me through my pregnancy ... because I was on my own and she helped me come to terms with losing my other daughter, and she just made things easier. Sure Start as a whole made things a lot easier for me and if they hadn't of been around I don't know where I would be right now, whether I would actually be here or whether the children would actually be here I don't know'.

The counsellor would sit and listen and Mandy would cry and 'it wouldn't matter if it was in front of her because everything was just so open with her'. The counsellor was 'a rock', enabling her to be open about her feelings rather than hide them away. Mandy also participated in various Sure Start courses. She studied children's behaviour and hoped she might find work via Sure Start, which would be an important step in her life. Mandy had taken GCSEs (an examination taken at secondary school) and worked in a range of jobs. But most of her adult life had been taken up with kids, she said ... Sure Start became a real resource. Mandy, with the help of a speech therapist and a health visitor – who were working as part of a team and were able to give her time and attention, in non-paternalistic ways – learned to understand the origins of the speech defect, and how this was not her fault or irredeemable. (West and Carlson, 2007: 40–51)

The relationship between the particular – Mandy's story – and the more general objectives and achievements of a project like Sure Start, can be understood in new ways: in terms of changing qualities of inter-professional practice, the marshalling of interdisciplinary expertise and subtle shifts in subjective understanding. Links can be built with the biographical experiences of other parents, using theoretical and opportunistic sampling. Sampling, as noted, in biographical research, is driven by a need to engage with particulars but also to relate these to wider social understanding and representativeness.

For certain biographical researchers, a single case study can be both unique and representative and can provide the basis for important theoretical development, despite accusations of atypicality or even of the eccentricity of single cases. Unique and original things can be learned. Freud used individual case histories to interrogate complex aspects of the human psyche: his story of the Wolf Man provided the detail to build theories of sexuality in childhood and the development of character structure (Gay, 1988). Many historians (and most writers) make use of the single case to reveal aspects of uniqueness and representativeness. The particular, in this view, is never entirely unique in any case. Mike Rustin (2000), we have noted, argues that the validity of individual cases rests in their capacity to generate understanding of how people make their worlds in interaction with others, in diverse ways. One good case study can, in its luminosity, reveal the self-reflection, decision and action, and/or the ambivalence, pain, loss, messiness and satisfaction in a life that has resonance and meaning for us all. This is an everyday assumption in psychoanalytic thinking as well as in imaginative writing. Medea, Macbeth, Faust and Vladimir are all individual creations yet provide points of common reference 'because their creators have identified in them some previously unrecognised but nevertheless recognisable social being' (Rustin, 2000: 49).

Humanism, validity and its meanings

A final word, for now, on post-structuralist critiques of biographical research and of the idea that life stories, and the selves composing them, are little more than effects of language. Ken Plummer (2001) has addressed these criticisms, arguing, as we do, that language and symbolic activity are central to human life, in social constructivist terms – except that humans are also reflexive, dialogical, inter-subjective, learning creatures. They can interrogate how language and discourse works in and through them. However, biographical researchers must also pay attention to language and power; and to how texts are created in relationship, including in research (as they must attend also to what is difficult to say, or what may escape language altogether, as in memory in feeling or unconscious processes). The language, gender and even the clothing, accent and speech patterns of the researcher can affect the interviewee. Post-structuralist and postmodern sensibilities have taught how power/knowledge can 'story' the other and ourselves, as well as the extent to which the old humanist idea of an autonomous self and story is problematic. But a humanistic ambition can still survive and prosper, in focusing on how lives, individually and collectively, are and have been enriched, and made more varied and fruitful, by the actions of people themselves (Plummer, 2001).

The importance of ethics

We now turn to the ethics of biographical research, having noted throughout the book that biographical research – or research of any kind – raises diverse ethical questions. We focus on specific examples of ethical problems from our own and others' work, which include the boundary between research and therapeutic processes. We address very practical matters: maintaining confidentiality; the importance of obtaining consent from participants; and questions about ownership in research. We offer a set of principles as a basis for good, ethical and effective biographical work.

> **Definition**
>
> Ethics are a set of guidelines, principles and codes which in the case of research are used to guide the behaviour of the researcher when conducting research.

For Tim May, the use of ethics in research is important because:

> The development and application of research ethics is required not only to maintain public confidence and to try to protect individuals and groups from the illegitimate use of research findings, but also to ensure its status as a legitimate and worthwhile undertaking. (2001: 67)

Being ethical is partly, as feminists advocate, to do with thinking proactively about the values we bring to our work: concerning what is just and right in a research relationship rather than simply avoiding harm. This can include being respectful and thinking of what we can do in our behaviour and responses to empower the other. Fundamentally, being ethical stems from treating people as full human beings: knowing, creative subjects in their own right, rather than as repositories of 'data' to be extracted and understood by us alone. Doing research is not value-neutral and biographical research deals with sensitive issues and often injustice. It is important to think about this and adopt a considered ethical stance in relation to the subject and subjects of our work. Biographical research can be a fundamentally humanistic as well as a respectful endeavour, and it is important not to lose sight of this in the desire to get results.

There is, however, a danger of being overly intrusive in people's lives. At the extreme, it may become like an act of surveillance or voyeurism. We need to remember that we are asking individuals to give their time, to open up and tell their life story to a relative stranger, which can include intimate and even disturbing material. They are not usually paid for the purpose and do not benefit from the career enhancement this can bring to us as researchers. We generally leave those we have researched behind, as we present their stories to public audiences, to some extent, on our terms. These are difficult matters, especially at a time when the public confessional can dominate the mass media and emotional disclosure appears ubiquitous. The soul has become, some insist, a legitimate target for surveillance, rather like the body in earlier times (Edwards, 1997). We need to ask what we are doing, why and on whose behalf.

We should also think about our – the researcher's – well-being as well as about our motives. Some topics require biographical researchers to enter potentially difficult environments. Female researchers may feel vulnerable or anxious about interviewing men alone in their homes. This was a big issue in researching families (West and Carlson, 2007). A man or woman researcher entering a house alone can expose themselves to risk, which can include threats from partners. In these instances, researchers may choose to work as a team, although this is not always possible. We have also observed how researching disturbance and pain in others can disturb the researcher: this needs to be incorporated into our ethical frames.

Thinking further about ethics

We are suggesting that it is important to have a set of ethical questions constantly in our minds:

- How can we make the relationship between our participants and researchers as equal as possible and avoid exploitation?
- How can we ensure that our participants are fully involved in the research process, including analysing material?
- How do we deal with painful, sensitive and emotional issues? What might we choose not to ask, and why?
- How do we ensure confidentiality, privacy and anonymity, particularly in situations where it might be easy to work out who the participant is?

The following actions should be avoided, as they can be profoundly unethical, but in practice, some, like not revealing identities, can be problematic:

- breaking confidentiality
- revealing identities
- using and exploiting participants
- breaking trust
- promising more than the research/researcher can do, for example, in relation to changing policy, or their material conditions
- misrepresenting participants in our text
- not sharing transcripts or research findings with participants.

No matter how experienced as researchers we might be, ethical issues perpetually surface. We remember specific issues from our research, which have affected us. Here are some examples:

I (Barbara) was involved in a project about participation and non-participation in further education in Scotland funded by the Scottish Office Education and Industry Department (SOEID) (see Chapter 7). The aim of this project was to widen participation in FE by improving policy and practice in Scotland. Using good research practice, we informed all participants about the aims and objectives of the project. Many of the men we interviewed were long-term unemployed (10–20 years). One of the men I interviewed – Jim – was in this category. I interviewed him at a community centre, which helps unemployed people with job applications and also offers courses such as IT. Jim wanted to get a job but realised that as he had no qualifications and had been unemployed for over 10 years, he was unlikely to do so. At the end of the interview, he stressed that he hoped that his story and this research project would make SOEID improve policy and practice for people like him. I told him

(Continued)

(Continued)

that we would be presenting our findings and recommendations to SOEID and we (the research team) hoped that they would listen to these so that some things could be improved. He was so optimistic that the Scottish Office would listen and make improvements but I could not promise him that. It made me feel powerless as a researcher and worried whether such projects can be in danger of raising false hopes.

I, Linden, in the study of doctors, their work and learning, was aware, in a first interview with Dr Claire Barker, that gender, in any explicit sense, was absent from the material, yet it came to occupy a central place in her evolving story. She was too busy getting through the day and week to give work, home, and the norms, which underlay the distribution of emotional labour, much thought, she said. Her two children were there, at the first interview, playing while we talked. Claire made a conscious effort, on her day off, to give the children the time and attention she could. She wondered why she was talking to me, except she was interested in the topic. She worked three and a half days a week, at present, but this was often full-time when on-call. She tried to keep home and work separate but was not always successful. Her husband was a highly successful professional man and they were, at one level, a fortunate family.

The story changed, three months later. She had thought about the issues raised in the previous interview. She was happy, she said, afterwards, but her main thought had been about 'a very rosy view of being a female GP and having a family and it isn't as easy as I made out on that occasion'. The transcript had captured most of what she felt at the time, but the issue she really wanted to address was the conflict between being a female doctor and a mother at the same time. Later on, in a further interview, she thought of withdrawing from the research, because of the troubling issues raised and I reminded her of her right to do so at any stage, and that she could do so at that precise moment and all her material would be destroyed. Being reminded, she said, was empowering and she decided to carry on, yet remained concerned at the difficulties of being all things to all people, which the research so clearly exposed. After the research was long finished, I heard she was suffering from mental health problems and worried about this and if the research had contributed, in some way. I wrote to the sociologist John Berger, whose classic study of a family doctor (Berger and Mohr, 1967) was influential in my own work, partly out of concern about the possible effects of research. Dr John Sassall, who was the focus of Berger's study, committed suicide. Berger wrote to me that 'I now begin with his violent death, and, from it look back with increased tenderness on what he set out to do and what he offered to others, for as long as he could endure' (West, 2001: 212).

Of course, we can be narcissistic in assuming what we have done is central to subsequent difficulty. There is a danger too of infantilising people. Yet biographical research enters difficult, disturbing territory and we need to take care. This should perhaps include having regular supervision (Dominicé, 2000). Our best intent can raise unexpected ethical issues. Care was taken to explain to all the doctors that their narrative material would be quoted extensively in the book, although details would be altered to protect confidentiality and preserve anonymity. There might be risks of recognition too and they should be aware of this when telling their stories and checking transcripts.

(Continued)

(Continued)

Medicine can be a small world and particular doctors questioned, at the end of the process, the use of extensive quotation in the eventual book. One doctor thought it should have been kept to a minimum. We may not know or fail to appreciate the effect of seeing words, and worlds, in the public domain. Of course, the opposite can be the case: particular people can celebrate their story being told, as in the case of a gay doctor. His narrative of problematic, counter-transference experiences with particular patients – including with a young man who reminded him of aspects of himself – was felt to be important material in contributing to the debate about neglected areas of doctor/patient relationships. He was glad to see the material in the public domain.

Ethical guidelines

In recent years, ethical issues and the need to make explicit codes of ethics have become more important. Each discipline, via a professional body, has a set of ethical guidelines for academics to follow. Linden adheres to those of the British Psychological Society (www.bps.org.uk) as well as the British Educational Research Association (BERA) and those of his own university. Barbara draws on those of the British Sociological Association (www.britsoc.co.uk). These are available on websites. Each UK university has had to produce ethical guidelines. At Warwick, for example, there is a 'University Statement on the Ethical Conduct of Research and Guidelines on Ethical Practice' and a University Research Ethics Committee to oversee this, and similar practices operate at Canterbury Christ Church. As a postdoctoral student, it is important to be aware of ethical guidelines issued by disciplinary bodies as well as those of a host institution.

We now turn to some other important ethical issues.

Informed consent

It is essential that all participants enter the research process voluntarily and willingly through 'informed consent' and that they are aware of their rights as a participant. In Chapter 6, an example was given of part of a consent form used by Linden. The form ends with an agreement on the use of the research material and the signature of the participant is required. Here is an example from Linden's work with doctors:

General Practitioners, Health and Learning in the Inner-city

Conditions of Use Form

1. I agree to the material on tape and transcript being used for research purposes as part of the above project, subject to the conditions specified in the Notes of

(Continued)

(Continued)

Guidance attached to this form. I understand access to it is restricted to Linden West, unless specific, additional agreement is obtained.
2. I request/do not request (delete as appropriate) that my anonymity is preserved in the use of material via the use of pseudonyms, etc.
3. Any other comments.

Signed:
Name (please print):
Address and telephone number:
Date:

The form ensures that a formal agreement is reached by both sides but importantly protects the research subject and allows him/her to leave the research project or to qualify the use of material. However, Michelle Fine et al. (2003) remind us that a consent form raises dilemmas and contradictions too, because it begs questions such as 'What is consent? And for whom?' (2003: 177); and it highlights and reinforces power differences between researched and researcher:

> The informed consent form forced us to confront and contend with the explicitly differential relationships between respondents and ourselves; it became a crude tool – a conscience – to remind us of our accountability and position. Stripping us of our illusions of friendship and reciprocity. (2003: 178)

On the other hand, space can be provided to raise such questions with research subjects, and in some detail, as happened with Dr Claire Barker.

Payment to participants is sometimes considered unethical but there can be situations when researchers feel it is necessary, when, for example, interviewing people who are poor. In a study of unemployed people participating in training schemes run by community organisations in Coventry, Barbara, and her co-researcher Mick Carpenter, decided to pay participants their bus fares and gave them a shop token. We felt this to be justified because the participants had little or no money for bus fares and otherwise would not have come for interview.

Confidentiality, privacy and intimacy

Building and conserving trust is crucial in biographical research. Participants are narrating life stories which can contain, as described, very intimate material. Altering a person's name is essential to ensure confidentiality and privacy. Using a pseudonym can be agreed with collaborators, including the actual name to be used. Giving the location of the research a pseudonym too can facilitate confidentiality and privacy. The value of biographical research is that it provides in-depth material and thick description but participants, and situations, have also to be disguised; where this is difficult, it needs to be made clear and discussed. It was an issue in the study of doctors and can be difficult in work in a small community or institution. Barbara was recently involved in pilot research, funded by her university, to examine student experiences of a foundation degree (a degree which combines vocational and academic study) in further education colleges. One participant contacted a research assistant after reading her transcript. She was anxious because she had been critical of the college. She had been diagnosed with dyslexia and other problems and felt that the college had not done enough to support her. We were examining different foundation degree programmes and named them in our report, because we wanted to see if there were differences in student experience between programmes. But she was the only Asian woman on the programme, so we used a non-Asian name. We assured her that the report was not going to the colleges and omitted some of the more critical comments made. We also promised her that she would not be visible if the material was used in other publications. But the negotiations were difficult.

Increasingly, in the UK, there is an expectancy on the part of funding bodies that project data will be placed in a data set, located on a website. The Economic Social Research Council (ESRC) is linked to a data set called Qualidata, specifically designed to bring together data from different studies, around a number of themes; other social researchers can then use the material. Although the database is only accessible to social researchers, it nonetheless raises serious ethical questions. Biographical transcripts frequently contain intimate details and painful stories may be placed into diverse quasi-public arenas, which may make an interviewee feel overly exposed. This was true with some of the parents in Linden's work with families; yet a colleague, in questioning the interpretation of texts, argued that all raw data should be made available to researchers, in the interests of transparency and public debate. This is a difficult area, because stories may have initially been shared on the basis of only one or two people seeing the raw data, and after giving assurances that its wider use would have to be agreed. The moves by funding bodies to encourage freer access to raw data can be worrying and certain kinds of research could be rendered more or less impossible.

Power relationships

Ann Oakley (1992) takes us into further, relational territory. She explains, explicitly, why as a feminist she did not adhere to the 'textbook code of ethics with regard to interviewing women ... I did not regard it as reasonable to adopt a purely exploitative attitude to interviewees as sources of data' (1992: 48). (Her original 1979 study had looked at motherhood.) Instead of keeping a distance and being objective, in a traditional sense, she began to see the women as friends and answered any questions that they asked her. Breaking down conventional researched and researcher boundaries and seeking to build more equal partnerships, is one kind of ethical practice.

Linden and Barbara share a similar feminist ethical position, in relation to interviewing, in that we aim not to exploit interviewees. We may also share our experiences, at particular moments. However, Irving Seidman has written that sharing aspects of ourselves can still be exploitative – a kind of seductive imperialism – however supposedly egalitarian:

Interviewing as exploitation is a serious concern and provides a contradiction and tension in my work that I have not fully resolved ... at a deeper level, there is a more basic question of research for whom, by whom and to what end. (Seidman, 1991: 24–5)

In contrast, Barbara has worked on European projects with German colleagues who adopt a more traditional, 'objective' ethical stance when conducting biographical interviews. They do not enter into a conversation with participants at all, in the name of keeping research 'scientific' and themselves detached.

Covert action

Occasionally, social science research stirs up deeply controversial ethical questions, particularly in relation to covert participant observation. Do the ends justify the means? The famous Laud Humphreys' (1970) PhD sociological study illustrates this in an acute form. He undertook research into homosexual acts in America at a time when society was virulently homophobic and homosexuality was a criminal act in many states.

Humphreys used covert participant observation to join a group of homosexuals in Chicago who performed homosexual acts in public toilets known as 'tearooms'. He was given the role of 'watch-queen' – the person who acted as a look-out at the 'tearooms'. This role enabled him to observe the behaviour of the men. Unknown to the participants, he recorded the car number plates of the men who visited the 'tearooms'. The focus of his research then changed. Humphreys altered his appearance and worked as a market researcher for a health survey of men. Using his contacts in the police force, he was able to obtain the names and addresses of the men, many of whom were married and had children, through the car number plates. He then interviewed them in their homes as part of the health survey research. The names and addresses of the men were kept in a safety deposit box and later destroyed. His PhD research caused outrage in the research community because it violated privacy and there was the potential that the men could have been arrested by the police. Some sociologists thought that he should not have been awarded his PhD degree. For Humphreys, however, the end justified the means in order to understand the behaviour of a group that little was known about. Other sociologists supported Humphreys as they felt that his research helped to make people aware of homosexuality and undermine stereotypes and prejudice.

Researchers have become covert members of right-wing groups (Nigel Fielding, 1981) or delinquent gangs, involved in breaking the law (Phillipe Bourgois, 2002). Like Humphreys, such researchers argue the end justified the means. Fielding (1981), who joined the National Front in the UK, hoped his research would expose racist politics and help persuade people not to join such organisations. Bourgois (2002) joined a group of Puerto Ricans involved in drug dealing in New York. His aim was to make people aware of the oppression and poverty they faced. Bourgois explains: 'The foregoing summary of my fieldwork is merely a personalized glimpse of the day-to-day struggle for survival, *and for meaning,* by the people who comprise the extraordinary statistics on inner-city crack and crime (2002: 174, original emphasis).

Although biographical methods may not immerse the researcher in such dramatic and dangerous situations, they nevertheless raise profound ethical questions: of confidentiality, privacy and of the nature of the relationship we have with our subjects. Like Fielding and Bourgois, each of us has to consider, carefully and constantly, the purpose of research and the morality of what we do.

Biographical research and therapy

There is a potentially difficult boundary issue between biographical research and therapy. Thinking back to Chapter 7, and to other case study material used in the book, note has been made of how, in researching lives, we can enter unpredictable and potentially disturbing territory. Becky Thompson (1990), for instance, described how many of the women she interviewed had been multiply victimized, enduring poverty, sexual abuse, exposure to high levels of violence, and emotional and physical torture. There can be psychological consequences in interviewing – for researcher and the researchee – which need to be thought about. Linden's work has straddled a border country between research and therapy and boundaries can on occasions get blurred (Hunt and West, 2006).

A number of researchers (Frosh et al., 2005; Hollway and Jefferson, 2000) have looked to the clinical style of psychoanalytic psychotherapy as a model in their research practice when exploring, for instance, the defended dimensions of story telling and research relationships. Use has been made of 'free association' techniques – an idea borrowed from psychoanalysis – in which people are encouraged to report whatever comes into their mind, however trivial or apparently irrational. This is done to provide some access to what may be unconscious processes, such as defences against anxiety.

However, ethical questions are raised. Free association can lead to especially distressing, even traumatic events resurfacing in contexts where there is no long-term structure of support. But a 'no harm at any cost to the participant' principle can preclude interpretative work that assigns motives other than those articulated by participants. Moreover, well-being can depend on making the causes of distress more conscious, in a sufficiently good and containing environment that the research might generate. Recognising anxiety or defensiveness need not be harmful if the researcher is guided by values of honesty, sympathy and respect and there is a good containing environment (Hollway and Jefferson, 2000). On the other hand, if people are not trained as psychotherapists, they may not recognise or fully understand what they do, or risk. Interviews can take an unexpected turn: simply to ask someone about their experience, at times of difficulty and stress, can lead to material simply pouring forth and the research relationship may prove to be insufficient as a container. Researchers need to arrange for diverse agencies to be available (this was done in the case of the Sure Start study) as sources of possible referral and potential support, at times of need.

However, research subjects can also welcome the opportunity to understand themselves, and their biographies, in new ways. Take Paul, in Linden's study of adult learner motivation (West, 1996). The following extract provides a different perspective on boundary questions:

> The pain in describing particular incidents had been intense. We discussed the ethics of life history research and whether it was appropriate to explore family history in this way. I shared some psychoanalytic ideas about patterns in relationships, and thoughts about projecting good and positive fragments of self on to others in ways which might denude the psyche of its strength and cohesion. This, coupled with humiliation as a child, and social marginality, could explain some of the emptiness he so often experienced. I thought transference had affected our relationship and described how other people, in conditions of uncertainty, may represent traces of past relationships which are reproduced in the present. He was interested in these ideas and wanted to know more. We talked around them, particularly the ethics of the process and Paul insisted that the research had been of great value and that he had always felt able to say no to any questions. He thought better of himself now. He had found the interviews therapeutic and said I should stop worrying. The project, like higher education, had provided a supportive framework in which to claim and piece together more of his life. If it had not been a positive experience, he insisted, he would simply have said so and left. (West, 1996: 70–1)

Notwithstanding, research is not therapy, however therapeutic it can be, and important distinctions need to be made. In psychoanalytic clinical settings, the analyst works, via a therapeutic alliance, to enable the person to recognise his/her defences, including in the here and now of the relationship with the therapist. Existing forms of relating could have evoked constant feelings of meaninglessness or emptiness. Defences might include the repression of what is unacceptable to consciousness; or denial of unhappy experience, like a disastrous affair or an examination failure. Disliked parts of the self and/or difficult feelings may be projected on to others: they may be denigrated as greedy or selfish when these characteristics belong closer to home. There can be rationalisation, like the fox in Aesop's fable who, on realising he could not reach the grapes, consoled himself with the belief that they were sour anyway (Brown and Pedder, 1991). In analytic contexts, addressing defences is achieved in a long-term relationship, with a trained person. The researcher is not necessarily trained in these terms and should not in any case seek to don such a mantle, however seductive, even when qualified as a psychotherapist. If there is a danger of infantilising people, there is an opposite problem of exposing them in inappropriate ways. The difficulty, sometimes, of deciding how best to manage such situations is why supervision is essential.

Summary

Articulating a set of ethical principles is of fundamental importance for guiding our approaches to research and for shaping our relationships with participants. We must interrogate the values that inform our practice, including how we construct the other:

not least whether, in effect, we see people as data, or as knowing, creative, living subjects, like ourselves, demanding fundamental respect. There is also the possibility, in the increasing 'professionalisation' of ethics, and its narrow focus on avoiding harm, that the subjects of research continue to be used in instrumental and even dehumanising ways. 'Mainstream' ethics, for instance, might emphasise the importance of value neutrality in research but this is deeply problematic. We may feel far from neutral when working with a Heidi or Joe (see Chapter 5) and strive instead towards collaboration, co-operation, equality and empowerment. But we also have to consider the danger of constructing the other in the light of our own needs or political agendas. There is a lot of ethical work to do but we agree with Clifford Christians (2003) when he suggests that the feminist emphasis on the personal and the social, as well as the location of research in everyday life, has led, irresistibly, to redefining ethics in more proactive, humanistic and empowering ways.

Key points

- The criteria as to what makes valid research varies in social research between those of a more scientistic and a more subjectivist orientation.
- Validity in biographical research does not lie in notions of reliability, replicability or the standardisation of research but in its capacity to generate new insights into human experience in particular, yet also representative, ways.
- Validity in biographical studies may mirror what makes for good literature, by reference to narrative richness and verisimilitude.
- Ethical issues need to be systematically addressed when conducting biographical research.
- Good ethical practice requires a proactive stance and a consideration of what creates empowering and mutually beneficial research.
- It is essential to obtain the informed consent of participants.
- As researchers, we must ensure, as much as possible, the confidentiality and privacy of our participants.
- It can be difficult to determine a clear boundary between research and therapy, but there are important differences of purpose and practice.

FURTHER READING

Christians, C.G. (2003) 'Ethics and Politics in Qualitative Research', in N.K. Denzin and Y.S. Lincoln (eds) *The Landscape of Qualitative Research.* Thousand Oaks, CA: Sage.

Fine, M., Weis, L., Weseen, S. and Wong, W. (2003) 'For Whom? Qualitative Research, Representations and Social Responsibilities', in N.K. Denzin and Y.S. Lincoln (eds) *The Landscape of Qualitative Research.* Thousand Oaks, CA: Sage.

May, T. (2001) 'Values and Ethics in the Research Process', in T. May, *Social Research: Issues, Methods and Process.* Buckingham: Open University Press.

DISCUSSION QUESTIONS

1. Read the extract about the Humphreys' study in this chapter (p. 174):

    (a) What are your reactions to the way he conducted his research?

    (b) Do you agree with him that the end justifies the means?

2. What would your code of ethics contain for a biographical study, and why?

ACTIVITIES

1. Do you think a single case study can offer valid research? Would you tend to look for larger samples, and, if so, why? Write a quick response and then consider the assumptions you are making about validity.
2. Subject disciplines have their own code of ethics which researchers are expected to follow. Look at the statements of ethical practice on the websites of the British Sociological Association and the British Psychological Association (www.britsoc.co.uk and www.bps.org.uk). Which statements do you feel are particularly relevant and important for biographical researchers? Are there any other points that you feel should be included?

11

On Being a Biographical Researcher

[C]ontinually work out and revise your views of the problems of history, the problems of biography, and the problems of social structure in which biography and history intersect. Keep your eyes open to the varieties of individuality, and to the modes of epochal change. (C. Wright Mills, 1973: 247)

Overview

In this chapter:

- We summarise and reflect on the central issues of the book, with its mix of theoretical, practical and self-reflexive concerns.
- We remind you of differences of purpose and approach within the biographical research community.
- We reflect on the journey of becoming a researcher and consider what it means to be a good researcher.

In this final chapter, we summarise some central issues in the book, concerning the theory and practice of biographical research. These include the different interests of biographical researchers, although, for many, the very cultural, economic and political change processes that have evoked the biographical age are a prime focus. We have documented the radical impulse that characterises much biographical research: the desire to recover neglected stories from marginalised groups and to give voice to their experiences and concerns. These aspirations, however, as illustrated, turned out to be more complicated than at first thought, and biographical researchers have developed more sophisticated understandings of truth, of the problematic nature of stories and memory, which includes how dominant stories in a wider culture, or myths, can shape individual narratives. We have considered the place of subjectivity and inter-subjectivity in research and how more 'scientific' orientations contrast with relational perspectives. There is the issue of the nature of theory in biographical research and the question of how to move between the particular and the general, and on what terms. There have been questions about the validity claims and ethics of biographical methods, and a concern that such research should be read more widely, perhaps combined with other approaches, not least by policy makers. We have noted too, time and again, how biographical researchers challenge and transgress boundaries: between academic disciplines, past and present, self and other, immediacy and memory, literary and academic genres.

We have also suggested that doing biographical research raises basic questions of what it is to be a researcher and can bring profound shifts of identity in its train. Biographical research often inhabits a border country between academic practice and soul searching of various kinds. Living the life of the biographical researcher can encourage openness and reflexivity towards what research actually is – including its emotional messiness – which often gets sanitised out of more conventional research accounts (Blackman, 2006). It can also make us think deeply about who we are and what we might be – which raises the question as to what makes a good researcher and, as constantly emphasised, the importance of using our own experience, alongside that of others, and of working with critical friends, supervisors and research communities to ensure that what we do – in generating narratives and interpreting and theorising them – is open to constant and critical scrutiny.

A research family: relatives, near and distant

We introduced notions of auto/biography in the first chapter, and deliberately so. There are differences of opinion among biographical researchers around the importance of what the researcher brings to the task and whether it is desirable to make the auto/biographical dimensions more explicit. In the German and Danish traditions, an attempt has been made to build more of an objective hermeneutics, partly to establish the efficacy of the biographical method in the academy, especially in sociology. In the UK, under the influence of feminism, oral history and post-structuralism (noted, especially, in Chapters 2, 3 and 4), there has been greater scepticism towards the positioning of research and researchers as overly 'objective'. Greater emphasis is given to intersubjectivity and to questioning whether the researcher can be easily separated from the 'object' of his/her enquiry. Reflexivity and the capacity for detachment, however, then become essential in building emotional as well as conceptual understanding (West et al., 2007).

Yet there remain shared assumptions in the biographical research family, although relationships, as in all families, can be distant and fraught. These include – reaching back to the Chicago School – respect for subjects as agents in making lives and of the constructed, malleable nature of the social order. And, as frequently observed, there is a widespread commitment to building interdisciplinary perspectives: biographies often mock single disciplinary presumptions or exclusive claims to know about lives, whether sociological or psychological. We require historical, psychological and sociological imaginations, maybe literary and poetic too, and in interconnected ways. Biography breeds eclecticism.

Feminism and intersubjectivity

The relational or intersubjectivist perspective at the heart of the book has been profoundly influenced by feminism. Liz Stanley (1992), whose work we have already mentioned at various points, draws persuasive attention to the dynamic inter-relationship between the constructions of our lives through autobiography and the construction of the life of others through biography. We write stories, she insisted, about ourselves by reference to, and by constructing, others' lives and selves, and we construct others via our own histories and experience. Yet the presence of the researcher, more often than not, remains uninterrogated. Intersubjectivity and auto/biography are still largely neglected in a great deal of social research, including in using biographical methods. This book represents, in part, a challenge to that neglect. Feminist researchers have also, over many years, challenged the idea that research is, or can be, carried out in an autonomous realm insulated from the wider society, its structures and dominant stories.

We have also emphasised that research is not simply a matter of generating words or evidence of life outside itself but is rather a form of living relationship, which shapes the story telling and its interpretation. Debate has constantly surfaced around these issues in conferences of the ESREA Research Network. This includes discussion between some German biographical researchers and ourselves about the nature of interviewing, as discussed in Chapter 7; not least between the narrative and interactive interview. Some researchers, in particular research cultures, position themselves as more objective and detached because this counts as good science.

We have not suggested that objectivity, or at least cultivating detachment, is unimportant, merely that it is frankly impossible to transcend completely our humanity; and can in certain senses be deeply undesirable. Our lives, and subjectivities, can be potentially rich resources for research as well as sources of bias and myopia. Yet there are dangers, as Molly Andrews (2007) illustrated in Chapter 3, of hearing what we want to hear and of projecting our needs on to others, however unconsciously. We have to think long and hard about what we do and to develop the habits of sustained reflexivity as well as humility. But there are potentially rich interpretive rewards in making use of our own biographies and subjectivities when engaging with others.

The term 'reflexivity' has been used throughout the text. It is a much quoted yet often under-theorised term. In social research, it can denote the necessary interrogation of self in relationship as a key element of the research process. But reflexivity can be treated as too straightforward and self-evident a psychological stance; and as overly rationalistic. Our feelings, in Linden's work on families, for example, can be important in making sense of the other while reflexivity easily becomes defensive, a way of 'policing' ourselves, to fit in with the norms of prevailing academic orthodoxies. They may help us feel secure and contained within a particular identity, but they can lead to stasis. Reflexivity requires sensitivity towards the self and others, to feelings as well as thoughts, and to what may be difficult for us, as researchers, to engage with and understand, because of our own life histories and psyches (Hunt and West, 2009, in press). We can, as various researchers note, be driven by avoidance as much as a desire to know. We, as researchers, have anxieties and needs in our own lives, not least when engaging with particular experiences, and we may resist, however unconsciously, knowing certain things. Learning, to repeat, is not inevitable in research or across whole lives.

As discussed in the last chapter, there are clear parallels in thinking about detachment and reflexivity in research and the practices of psychoanalytic psychotherapy, and there is a similar paradox at both their hearts. On the one hand, it is important – in therapeutic encounters – to fully immerse ourselves in the other's story, to listen attentively as well as respectfully. On the other, it is essential to achieve, or learn, the capacity for detachment and to think, carefully, about what is happening, which includes sensitivity towards what is difficult to narrate and our own feelings. A capacity to listen combines with a capacity to think; awareness of the other inter- acts with considering how we – as a therapist or researcher – might be feeling. The notion of the counter-transference is helpful, in that we can come to feel in research, as in therapy, something of what the other is experiencing, such as anxiety, doubt, muddle or distress. Tom Wengraf (2000) has perceptively noted how there can be two anxious people in a biographical interview and that counter-transference can be as important as transference in the relationships constituting research.

Transitional space and two orders of social research

Emphasis has been given, at various moments in the text, to the idea of biographi- cal research as a transitional space for learning for all the parties concerned. This includes, as illustrated especially in Chapter 5, the importance of creating a good enough environment for our subjects to consider and develop, as well as to change their stories, and to enhance, in the process, narrativity and agency. People are sto- ried as well as story tellers, their memories shaped by present needs, public myths and pervasive ideologies. The evidence is there in the work on families or in the sto- ries of Anzac veterans. Part of the researcher's task can be seen as one of creating good enough space for other possible stories to surface, for greater openness and reflexivity in relation to experience to develop. Of course, there can be ethical issues here that have also to be considered and research is not about challenging people's defences. But our responses and behaviour, in terms of curiosity and reflexivity, can shape the other and their enthusiasm to narrate and explore. If we are truly inter- ested in lives, our narrators will know this and can become more thoughtful and the quality of the research gets enhanced. There can be shifts from suspicion and anxiety towards greater trust; from people being storied to becoming more confi- dent agents and story tellers.

Mention was made, in the opening chapters, of the values of the researcher. Plummer (2001) notes that there can be two strands in social research that think and operate in quite different ways. Researchers may be motivated by compassion – for the Heidis of this world (see Chapter 5), for instance – or may feel that we should be as neutral as can be. There can be a tension between the influence of the human- ities, or of humanism, and traditional ideas of doing science. Such influences gen- erate differing assumptions: naming experience in the more 'scientific' perspective must be a neutral process. Biographical research and story telling in the more humanistic view are, at least in part, political acts to explore what or who may have been silenced or marginal in a given culture or sub-culture.

The particular and the general

The relationship between the particular and general has been a recurring theme. There is a concern among many biographical researchers to justify the method in terms of its capacity to produce generalisable forms of knowledge. Note has been made of how some researchers derive their samples from large representative data sets. The relative weighting to be given to the particular and to the general can reflect the researcher's disciplinary background. Using a crude dichotomy, this might mean that researchers from a psychological perspective favour the particular while sociologists the general. But it is not as clear-cut. As noted, the Chicago School sociologists focused on particulars. Yet their studies root the individual in a social context, using the life of an individual to generalise about others. The story of Stanley, for example, in Shaw's *The Jack Roller*, is carefully justified by reference to wider representational qualities.

In relation to Barbara's discipline – sociology – the issue of the particular and the general is fundamental because it raises questions of what is the dominant force in human behaviour: the individual or society/agency or structure (see Dawe's (1970) notion of the two sociologies). Some sociologists have striven for a middle ground, arguing for the importance of both, albeit in different ways, such as Pierre Bourdieu (habitus and capital), Anthony Giddens (structuration theory) and Margaret Archer (dualism).

Dan Goodley et al., in their study *Researching Life Stories* (2004), referenced on many occasions, focus on the lives of specific people yet the particular story can teach a great deal of what is general too. Goodley has narrated the life of Gerry, an adult with learning difficulties. Gerry expresses his thoughts and outlines his experiences of learning at a centre for people with learning difficulties, and how learning difficulties have affected his life as a whole. Although the story concerns just one person, Goodley uses the biography to discuss wide-ranging policy and practice issues for people with learning difficulties. He achieves this via the richness of the narrative, his closeness to his subject and by revealing, like good literature, what it means to be labelled as a pathological victim of impairment. Goodley reminds us, in the opening quote of Chapter 10 (2004b), of the importance of relationships in enhancing the quality of understanding the other, and also of the need to work emotionally and empathically with people (however difficult on occasions) whose stories we are helping create. Getting to know people demands real investment, emotional as well as intellectual. We see ourselves, and others we know, in writing of this kind. All of us, if to varying degrees, have been negatively labelled by powerful others and institutions. In Linden's work with the lesbian doctor, it was possible to exploit his own experiences of being an outsider, and of feeling marginal, at a particular point of transition in his life, to understand more fully the emotional, gendered and epistemological struggles of becoming a more effective and empathic physician.

In a similar vein, we have observed how many researchers, including feminist auto/biographers, use the particular to speak, in other ways, to the wider experiences of women. Carolyn Steedman's *Landscape for a Good Woman* (1986) locates interpretations of her own and her mother's life in the unique circumstances of an industrial town, and class location, but within a wider understanding of history and the interplay of the macro and micro. The central role in her mother's life, of maintaining households, is presented against a backcloth of a father killed at the Somme, as well as of economic depression. The general and the particular are woven into the texture of the most intimate of family and gendered experience.

Some historians and sociologists have always recognised how the particular can evoke and enrich our understanding of the general. There are many instances of powerful biographies speaking not simply for the person telling the story but for whole groups and cultures. These include the biographies of slaves, native Americans, holocaust survivors or gay people. This is what Ken Plummer refers to as 'collective autobiography', when 'A personal tale is now a story of a whole people' (2001: 91). Barbara, in her work, constantly seeks to remind us of the collective in individual narratives. In Linden's research on learning and change processes, the construction and dynamics of unique inner worlds are to be understood by reference to people being embedded in relationships, which are shaped in turn by structuring and discursive processes in the wider culture. Moreover, in Chapter 10 and elsewhere, we have also illustrated how conventional forms of generalisation, based, for instance, on categorising people according to demographic characteristics like class, gender and locality, uninformed by biographical understanding, may be profoundly problematic. Generalisation, in the final resort, can derive from a superficial understanding of people, their subjectivity and the meanings of what they do and think.

Theory and empiricism

Likewise, the place and nature of theory in biographical research has been a recurrent theme. It was central to debates in the Chicago School. Chicago School researchers emphasised the importance of gaining knowledge of social particulars, rather than relying on formal, overly abstract theory. Building on the philosophical traditions of pragmatism and formalism, they insisted that social forms – or patterns of interaction whose repetition accounted for the coherence and reproduction of social worlds – could only be fully understood by reference to the detail of everyday lives and the social actors at their core, rather than, for instance, by reference to an abstract quality called 'structure', understood by a detached, disembodied reason. There was a rejection of theories, in short, built in empirical vacuums. The theories of the biographical researcher are more middle range and experientially derived; tested, pragmatically, in terms of what works. Theory is crucial in interpreting narrative material and relating this to wider social and historical questions, but such theory is to be disciplined by or grounded in the stories of real people, in real-life contexts. Although 'fiction' or 'faction' may have a place too, we need to be explicit about what we are doing, that is exploring and illuminating illusive aspects of experience via the creative imagination, like the good novelist engaged in processes of truth seeking.

There are echoes of the theoretical humility needed in research in the writing of Edward P. Thompson, whose work has influenced the biographical tradition.

Thompson (1978), in his essay, *The Poverty of Theory*, explored the task of the historian and how we might best understand historical processes. Class, he observed, as quoted at the opening of Chapter 1, happens between people. Deference requires squires and labourers, experiencing and producing its character in everyday encounters. It is interesting that Thompson was in dispute with those versions of Marxism – such as the structuralist ideas of the French philosopher Althusser – which questioned whether people made history at all, and whether historical, or for that matter biographical, enquiry had any real validity. Theory, like mathematics, required no external validation, asserted Althusser: it was subject to its own verification, via rules of logic. The texts of Rousseau, for example, in his use of words and consistency of logic, are analysed by reference to rigorous philosophical or critical procedures. In this view, experience is considered a low level of mediation of the social world: it may generate no more than practical common sense. If the farmer knows, through experience, the seasons, or the sailor, the seas, both can remain mystified by class or cosmology. There are ironic echoes here of post-structuralist criticisms of biographical research: that people may be unaware of the discourses, as against the structural determinisms, that pervade them. What is at issue here is where understanding might lie and the importance of the subject in history.

Thompson argued that new experience, and the thoughts associated with it, can evoke new kinds of consciousness or forms of knowledge. People engage in thinking, he went on, mischievously, outside the academy: in tilling the fields, in building houses, and in making lives. As new experience marches into lives, in the form of poverty or a family support project, people can think, reflexively, about what may be happening. They may be encouraged to question poverty or the assumptions underlying social policy. The potentially rich and dynamic relationship between social being and consciousness, and how people can learn their world in new ways, gets lost in overly abstract theorising. New understanding, and radical insights, can thrust their way into the established order and lead to changes in how the world is experienced and understood.

Historical or biographical research, in these terms, is different from engaging with the proverbial philosopher's stone, which, when asked if it is real or how its existence might best be known, says nothing (Thompson, 1978). People talk back and can teach others by their experiences. In a similar vein, some postmodernist feminism has been criticised for being too detached from the experiences of many women (Merrill and Puigvert, 2001). Theory, for many biographical researchers, becomes less abstract and more situated, refined in the light of people's experiences of social life or the stories told about them. There is less presumption that the researcher has more and better knowledge. There is greater sensitivity towards the limits and illusions of logical and rational ways of knowing; greater concern, in a feminist and postmodern spirit, with differing ways of knowing. But theory does matter, as already emphasised, in illuminating what otherwise can seem chaotic, incomprehensible or meaningless. A father's gift of bacon, sausages and fruit takes on symbolic meaning when located within wider historical and gendered understanding. Yet such understanding is greatly enriched and extended by the detail.

Theory and subjectivity

The use and importance of Marxist and feminist theories in Barbara's research and writing stems from her life experiences as a working-class woman. The researcher and her biography are always there in working with others. In a way, biography and theory are dynamically linked as particular theories have helped to shape her values, actions and ways of seeing the world.

I cannot, Barbara writes, divorce theory and biography. As a young person, Marxist theory made sense to me and acted as a tool for understanding not only my individual and family life but the broader macro level of capitalist society and its inequalities. At about the same time, I became interested in Marxist feminist theory as it fused key experiences of my life: class and gender. Feminism and Marxism gave a purpose to my life and actions resulting in my participation in demonstrations, belonging to a Marxist and a feminist party, anti-racist organisations and involvement in establishing a left-wing teachers' organisation in Coventry.

I subscribed to Marxist humanism rather than those who espoused the more deterministic Marx, for, as Adam Schaff explains: 'From the outset of his theoretical inquiries, living human individuals were Marx's point of departure' (1970: 50). Marx's concept of praxis, linking theory and practice, particularly appealed:

> What is theory, what is practice? Wherein lies their difference? Theoretical is that which is hidden in my head only, practical is that which is spooking in many heads. What unites many heads, creates a mass, extends itself and thus finds its place in the world. If it is possible to create a new organ for the new principle, then this is a *praxis* which should never be missed. (Marx, 1843, published letter in a newspaper, original emphasis)

Marx too was also critical of abstract, theoretical philosophy:

> As every true philosophy is the spiritual quintessence of its age, the time must come about when philosophy will get in touch with the real world of its time and establish a reciprocal relationship with it not only internally, through its content, but also externally, through its phenomenal manifestation as well. (1842: 97–8)

Marxist theory, together with the writings of Bourdieu and C. Wright Mills, have helped me, Barbara continues, to link the macro and the micro, structure and agency and to reflect on their role not only in the lives of my family and myself but also the lives of the participants in my research. Importantly for me, research should strive to be about linking theory, experience and practice.

It is worth mentioning, from Linden's perspective, that theory has a relatively humble, if still important, place in psychoanalytic understanding. Theory is always to be interrogated in the light of clinical experience: its role is one of servant rather than master. However, the history of psychoanalytic psychotherapy has been riddled with 'theoretical' disputes, around the place and nature of sexuality, relationship and the desire to know in human life, for example. Yet, for many reasons, some of the intensity of theoretical debate has become less polarised in recent years, as greater emphasis is placed on qualities of relationship in therapeutic settings, and of grounding theory, eclectically, in its light, which includes developing research into clinical practice (see, for instance, Sayers, 2003).

Disciplinarity and interdisciplinarity

We have illustrated how biographical research propels us towards interdisciplinarity. Lives are lived at particular historical moments, shaped by specific social forces and discourses, to which people may respond in different and diverse ways. It is interesting that the history of biographical methods involved social psychologists and sociologists working closely together, as in the Chicago School. It was later, as sociology strove to be more scientistic and quantitative, that they tended to go their separate ways. The earlier collaboration, as observed, was grounded in some humility towards research subjects and a suspicion of overly abstract theorising.

We have made frequent reference to C. Wright Mills in the book. His contribution has been helpful in thinking about the interdisciplinarity of biographical research: his sociological imagination was a way of focusing on the prime task of researchers. Analysts were encouraged to understand the larger historical scene by reference to its meaning for the inner life. A biographical focus, in Wright Mill's writing, encourages the researcher to range from the most impersonal and remote transformations to the most intimate features of the human self and to consider the relations between the two (Wright Mills, 1970). C. Wright Mills challenges us to consider biography as a meeting point between the historical and the intimate, between structuring processes and struggles for human agency. Interdisciplinarity is combined with a humanistic purpose of seeking to build a more just social order.

The biographical research we have described, especially in Chapters 3 and 5, embodies the continuing power and resonance of this imperative (Frosh et al., 2005; Hollway and Jefferson, 2000; Salling Olesen, 2007a, 2007b; Weber, 2007). We illustrated how Weber (2007), for instance, focuses on gender and the learning processes of adult men training for work in the caring professions; how she draws on classic psychoanalytic insights into male struggles with intimacy while bringing culture, language and the material into the frame too. Gender is inherent in social structures, which stem from historic divisions of labour. It is reproduced or challenged within the scope of the accessible choices people can make. Salling Olesen (2007a), in his work on the professional identities and learning of GPs (see Chapters 4 and 5), uses psychoanalytic notions of defence – in understanding doctors' orientation to learning – alongside sociological awareness of modernisation processes and the pervasive power of scientistic forms of knowledge in the medical lifeworld. Psychological dynamics are seen, in his imagination, to be a product of social relations, a kind of embodied culture. His idea of critical theory synthesises elements from Marxism (social and historical factors) with psychoanalysis (in an embodied and symbolic sense, characterised by contradictions and tensions). The psychic processes – in which social relations are played out, internally – may be far from transparent and conscious (Salling Olesen, 2007b).

In Linden's work on families, the strength of the interdisciplinary and humanistic imperative is similarly chronicled. The struggles of Heidi, and people like her (in Chapter 5, for instance), to learn and become agents in their own lives, are to be understood as historical and social but also psychological. Biographies are located within the histories of whole communities as well as pervaded by the potentially demeaning scripts of class, gender and/or ethnicity, which are often projected onto the marginalised other and become internalised. But people can learn their way to challenge and change aspects of both their inner and outer worlds.

Being a researcher: learning the practice and living the life

We have sought in this book to combine the theory of biographical research with a concern for practical issues in becoming a more confident practitioner. Chapters 6 to 9 focused on such practicalities: from starting a project and choosing samples, to recording experience – using interviews – and moving on to analysis and the writing up of research. But these practical issues raise questions that are epistemological too and also about values and purpose. Sampling challenges us to think about the relative value of qualities and quantities and this may lead us to an understanding of validity close to that of good literature; or to the importance of generalising by drawing on the categories or evidence of large data sets as well as, perhaps, using substantial samples ourselves. However, we suggest, like Mike Rustin, that a single case study, in its luminosity, can be representative of the decisions, self-reflections and actions of the many (Rustin, 2000).

A further core argument of the book is that being a researcher entails a dual role: that of learner as well as researcher. They are not separate but intertwined. Research continues, even for the experienced, to be fundamentally about learning. Conferences and seminars – giving and listening to papers – are essential for understanding more of the richness, diversity and difficulties of biographical research. For the new researcher, they provide a forum for gaining new knowledge: of how to interview, analyse and write up biographical data, as well as how to present a paper. As a more experienced researcher, we continue to learn and change: to be surprised by a new idea or reinvigorated by older ones, for instance, in writing this book. Discussions with fellow academics, both in paper presentation sessions and outside of these, can be valuable and fruitful, including for writing books. Conferences remain good arenas for social networking, for making contacts and engaging with new communities of practice. At some point in your research career as a new researcher and/or PhD student, you will need to take the step of presenting a paper for the first time. This may be work-in-progress, rather than a more finished product. If possible, ask a critical friend(s) to read the paper before submitting it. Many conferences encourage presentations from PhD students and may offer bursaries to help with the financing and an award for the best student paper. Conferences provide the opportunity for new researchers to publish for the first time, via conference proceedings. That is how we started and continued on our journey, in dialogue with others.

Wider concerns and social policy

Reference has been made to how biographical methods reach parts of people's experience that other research may get nowhere near, and of how important aspects of the social world – such as crime and educational processes – may be understood in new, more nuanced ways, beyond the reductive variables of class, gender, ethnicity or place. There is, however, a challenge to communicate more of this to policy makers. For these reasons, some researchers argue for mixed method approaches as a complement to more widely accepted interdisciplinary collaboration. Biographical research has its own intrinsic merits but these may be enhanced, they suggest, when this is integrated with other forms of research (Schuller et al., 2007). Such integration, they continue, presents significant challenges to the research community. Tom Schuller and colleagues, as illustrated in Chapter 6 and elsewhere, describe how a large cohort study can provide data to enrich the use of individual biographies, while the latter can illuminate more of the complexities that larger studies merely allude to. There can be economies of scope here, they argue: combining qualitative and quantitative data produces more than the sum of the parts. Policy makers are also more comfortable with findings that can be generalised (Schuller et al., 2007). These suggestions are worthy of wider discussion because of the need to connect the work of the biographical researcher with the world of the policy maker.

Back to the future

We began this book by reference to our own biographies – as whole people as well as researchers – and the sense of changing identities when learning from and in research. Barbara thinks of herself as a sociologist, interested in the interaction between the macro/micro and agency/structure. Linden is more focused, at times, on the micro level and with what happens in the intimate spaces between people; with what biography, or auto/biography, can teach us about the workings of the inner world, located within an understanding of social relationships and unconscious processes but also what it can tell us about power and discourse. Yet we have come to understand more about each other and how and why we might think differently, as researchers, as well as in similar ways.

Writing the book has, in short, been a learning journey for us both. Other academic colleagues who know us were surprised to learn that we were writing a book on biographical methods together, because of the different disciplinary and intellectual traditions we come from. (Although we have presented several conference papers together, over a number of years.) Perhaps they imagined the process of writing would be riddled with heated debate, argument and unresolved difference. On the contrary, it has enabled us to reflect on what we do and who we are as researchers, and also the disciplinary and theoretical assumptions we make – even the words we use, like data or narrative. In our discussions of what to include and how to present biographical research, there have been differences yet a great deal of common ground.

Hopefully, these differences and commonalities will help you consider, as a new researcher – or as someone interested in adding the biographical method to your repertoire – where you stand and how you position yourself. Perhaps you will realise that it is possible to embrace different ways of seeing. The interdisciplinarity at the heart of the book has enabled us to be less dogmatic and humbler about what we do. Working together has enabled us to understand more fully the life of the other and their story and why we may think of research and auto/biographies in differing as well as similar ways. The similarities include the importance of generating rich description, of valuing what people say and their struggles for voice, but also of being aware of the socio-structural and psychological constraints to this. We need an eclectic imagination, and the capacity for mutual learning, in being a biographical researcher and in writing about its theory and practice.

Key points

- Biographical research offers a rich and rewarding approach to understanding, in a humanistic way, the lives of others but it also raises difficult questions about truth, memory, relationship, past and present, self and other.
- Differences exist within the family of biographical researchers, not least in how researchers position themselves.
- Being a biographical researcher can be a profound learning journey, one in which we have to decide where and how to position ourselves as well as recognising the importance of being sensitive to what we don't know and need to learn.

DISCUSSION QUESTIONS

- Reflect back on the book: what issues have most interested you and why?
- What is your position in relation to the objectivist/subjectivist debate and how the particular might be considered representative?
- In what ways does biographical research transgress boundaries and where might this lead you in thinking about being a researcher?

Glossary

Auto/biographical Being aware of the extent to which we use other's stories to make sense of our own biographies, as well as how we use our own to make sense of others' lives and experiences.

Biographical perspectives Using other people's lives as a basis for social research, such as understanding processes of learning, fear of crime, etc.

Defended self This is the idea, forged in psychoanalytic practice and theorising, that the self consists of unconscious as well as conscious aspects, rather than being a single unit. Such a self may be driven by defensiveness and anxiety surrounding threats to its well-being, in interaction with others, often in unconscious ways.

Formalism This is the perspective, which was influential in the Chicago School, that the purpose of sociology is to discover and depict social forms; these are patterns of interaction, the repetition of which explains the coherence and boundedness of particular social worlds.

Gestalt A notion that the whole is greater than the sum of the parts. Significance derives from understanding the place of particular experiences within some broader context, for example, a whole life.

Life history Life histories may be based on written accounts or transcriptions of interviews or other oral evidence. Life histories may be built up using biographical evidence, alongside other 'objective' sources, as well as by using the researcher's theoretical understanding.

Lifewide and lifelong learning The idea that learning, in and across all dimensions of experience, past and present, formal and informal, interconnects. Learning, in these terms, can be conceived of as a psychological orientation to experience, as a tendency to be relatively open to new experience, or, at another extreme, to fear and resist it. This can be rooted in early experience and the quality of our interactions with others.

Narratives These are important in a biographical perspective. We experience our lives through some conception of past, present and future. Such frames help bring coherence to the fragments of experience. Biographical researchers often pay great attention to the structuring and qualities of people's narratives.

Oral history This involves interviewing people about their experiences of events as part of developing an historical account.

Postmodernism   This celebrates the liberation of differences, or dialects, in which diverse ethnic, sexual, religious, cultural or aesthetic voices find more space. There is respect for a plurality of perspectives, rather than a single truth from a privileged perspective, while emphasis is given to local, contextual studies rather than grand narratives and methods that can homogenise or sanitise complex particulars.

Post-structuralist   The emphasis here is on what is seen to be the pervasive power of language and 'power-knowledge' formations to shape how we think and make sense of the world, including ourselves.

Pragmatism   This derives from the view that academics should concern themselves, in making sense of the social world, with understanding concrete situations. Rather, that is, than with overly abstract logic, or experience-distant theorising. Human beings, however, need abstractions, or theory, albeit of a more tentative kind, to create some coherent understanding of what can seem a chaotic world.

Psychosocial   An interdisciplinary perspective in social research, which is sensitive both to how society and culture can structure the way we think and feel about the world, but also how our psychologies have a life of their own. There is an interest in how psychoanalytic insights can contribute to an understanding of inner and outer dynamics in people's biographies.

Realism and critical realism   Realism is grounded in the idea that depths can be grasped, and lives more fully understood, via a mixture of careful observation, or gathering of data, alongside the use of theory. Realism can be seen to characterise, for instance, classical forms of psychoanalysis, with its mix of careful chronicling of a life, combined with theoretical insight into the role of the unconscious. Such integration can make a biography or life story more 'real'. Critical realism pays attention to the processes of generating the 'real', which includes what the researcher brings to the process, as well as the nature of the interaction and the role of language.

Symbolic interactionism   People give meaning to their experience, selves and bodies, as well as to their wider social worlds, via language and interactions with others, including the social order; analysis of such meanings is a core task for the social researcher.

References

Acker, J., Barry, K. and Esseveld, J. (1991) 'Objectivity and Truth: Problems in Doing Feminist Research', in M. Fonow and J.A. Cook (eds) *Beyond Methodology: Feminist Scholarship as Lived Research*. Bloomington and Indianapolis: Indiana University Press.

Ackroyd, P. (2000) *London: The Biography*. London: Chatto and Windus.

Alheit, P. (1982) *The Narrative Interview: An Introduction*. Bremen: University of Bremen Press.

Alheit, P. (1993) 'Transitorische Bildungsprozesse: Das "biographische Paradigma" in der Weiterbildung', in W. Mader (ed.) *Weiterbildung und Gesellschaft. Grundlagen wissenschaftlicher und beruflicher Praxis in der Bundesrepublik Deutschland* (2nd edn). Bremen: University of Bremen Press.

Alheit, P. (1995) *Taking the Knocks, Youth Unemployment and Biography – a Qualitative Analysis*. London: Cassell.

Alheit, P. and Dausien, B. (2007) 'Lifelong Learning and Biography: A Competitive Dynamic between the Macro and the Micro Level of Education', in L. West, B. Merrill, P. Alheit, A. Bron and A.S. Andersen (eds) *Using Biographical and Life History Approaches in the Study of Adult and Lifelong Learning*. Frankfurt-am-Main: Peter Lang.

Allport, G. (1937) *Personality*. New York: Holt.

Allport, G. (1964) *Letters from Jenny*. New York: Harcourt, Brace and World.

Andersen, A.S. and Trojaborg, R. (2007) 'Life History and Learning in Working Life', in L. West, B. Merrill, P. Alheit, A. Bron and A.S. Andersen (eds) *Using Biographical and Life History Approaches in the Study of Adult and Lifelong Learning, Across Europe*. Frankfurt-am-Main: Peter Lang.

Andrews, M. (2000) 'Texts in a Changing Context: Reconstructing Lives in East Germany', in P. Chamberlayne, J. Bornat and T. Wengraf (2000) (eds) *The Turn to Biographical Methods in Social Science*. London: Routledge.

Andrews, M. (2007) *Shaping History: Narratives of Political Change*. Cambridge: Cambridge University Press.

Apitzsch, U. and Inowlocki, L. (2000) 'Biographical Analysis: A "German" School?', in P. Chamberlayne, J. Bornat and T. Wengraf (2000) (eds) *The Turn to Biographical Methods in Social Science*. London: Routledge.

Armitage, S.H. and Gluck, S.B. (2006) 'Reflections on Women's Oral History', in R. Perks and A. Thomson (eds) *The Oral History Reader* (2nd edn). London: Routledge.

Armstrong, P. (1982) *The Use of the Life History Method in Social and Educational Research*, Newland Papers No. 7, Department of Continuing Education, The University of Hull.

Armstrong, P. (1998) 'Stories Adult Learners Tell ... Recent Research on How and Why Adults Learn', in J.C. Kimmel (ed.) *Proceedings of the 39th Annual Adult Education Research Conference (AERC)*. San Antonio, TX: University of the Incarnate Word. pp. 7–12.

Baena, R. (ed.) (2007) *Transculturing Auto/Biography: Forms of Life Writing*. London: Routledge.

Banks-Wallace, J. (1998) 'Emancipatory Potential of Storytelling in a Group', *Journal of Nursing Scholarship*, 30(1): 17–21.

Barley, S.R. (1989) 'Careers, Identities and Institutions: The Legacy of the Chicago School of Sociology', in M.B. Arthur, T.D. Hall and B.S. Lawrence (eds) *Handbook of Career Theory*. Cambridge: Cambridge University Press.

Barr, J. (2006) 'Reframing the Idea of an Educated Public', *Discourse*, 27(2): 225–39.

Becker, H.S. (1963) *Outsiders: Studies in the Sociology of Deviance*. New York: Free Press.

Becker, H.S. (1966) 'Introduction', in C. Shaw, *The Jack Roller: A Delinquent Boy's Own Story*. Chicago: The University of Chicago Press.

Becker, H.S. (1967) 'Whose Side Are We On?', *Social Problems*, Winter: 239–47.

Becker, H.S. (1986) *Writing for Social Scientists*. Chicago: University of Chicago Press.

Becker, H.S. (1998) *Tricks of the Trade: How to Think About Your Research While You're Doing It*. Chicago: University of Chicago Press.

Becker, H.S., Geer, B., Hughes, E.C. and Strauss, A. (1961/1977) *Boys in White: Student Culture in Medical School*. Chicago: Chicago University Press.

Belenky, M.F., Clinchy, B.M., Goldberger, N.R. and Tarule, J.M. (1997) *Women's Ways of Knowing: The Development of Self, Voice and Mind* (2nd edn). New York: Basic Books.

Berger, J. and Mohr, J. (1967) *A Fortunate Man: The Story of a Country Doctor*. London: Writers and Readers Co-op.

Berger, P. (1966) *Invitation to Sociology*. Harmondsworth: Penguin.

Bertaux, D. (ed.) (1981a) *Biography and Society*. Beverly Hills: Sage.

Bertaux, D. (1981b) 'From the Life-History Approach to the Transformation of Sociological Practice', in D. Bertaux (ed.) *Biography and Society*. Beverly Hills: Sage.

Bertaux, D. and Delcroix, C. (2000) 'Case Histories of Families and Social Processes: Enriching Sociology', in P. Chamberlayne, J. Bornat and T. Wengraf (eds) *The Turn to Biographical Methods in Social Science*. London: Routledge.

Biesta, G. (2006) *Beyond Learning: Democratic Education for a Human Future*. Boulder: Paradigm Publishers.

Biesta, G., Field, J., Goodson, I., Hodkinson, P. and MacLeod, F. (2008) *Learning Lives: Learning, Identity and Agency Across the Lifecourse*. London: TRLP/Institute of Education.

Blackman, S. (2006) 'Hidden Ethnography: Crossing Emotional Borders in Qualitative Accounts of Young People's Lives', *Sociology*, 41(4): 699–716.

Blaxter, L., Hughes, C. and Tight, M. (2006) *How to Research*. Buckingham: Open University Press.

Blumer, H. (1984) *The Chicago School of Sociology: Institutionalisation, Diversity and the Rise of Sociological Research*. Chicago: University of Chicago Press.

Blumer, H. (1986) *Symbolic Interactionism: Perspective and Method*. Berkeley: University of California Press.

Borenstein, A. (1978) *Redeeming the Sin: Social Science and Literature*. New York: Columbia University Press.

Bornat, J., Dimmock, B., Jones, D. and Peace, S. (2000) 'Researching the Implications of Family Change', in P. Chamberlayne, J. Bornat and T. Wengraf (eds) *The Turn to Biographical Methods in Social Science*. London: Routledge.

Bourdieu, P. (1997) *Outline of a Theory of Practice*, trans R. Nice. Cambridge: Cambridge University Press.

Bourgois, P. (2002) 'In Search of Horatio Alger: Culture and Ideology in the Crack Economy', in D. Weinburg (ed.) *Qualitative Research Methods*. Oxford: Blackwell Publishers.

Brewer, J.D. (2002) *Ethnography*. Buckingham: Open University Press.

Bron, A. (1999) 'The Price of Immigration. Life Stories of Two Poles in Sweden', *International Journal of Contemporary Sociology*, 36(2): 191–203.

Bron, A. (2002) 'Symbolic Interactionism as a Theoretical Position in Adult Education Research', in A. Bron and M. Schemmann (eds) *Social Science Theories in Adult Education Research*, Bochum Studies in International Adult Education, 3. Hamburg: LIT.

Bron, A. (2007) 'Learning, Language and Transition', in L. West, B. Merrill, P. Alheit and A. Siig Andersen (eds) *Using Biographical and Life History Approaches in the Study of Adult and Lifelong Learning Across Europe.* Frankfurt-am-Main: Peter Lang.

Brown, D. and Pedder, J. (1991) *Introduction to Psychotherapy: An Outline of Psychodynamic Principles and Practice.* London: Routledge.

Burgess, E.W. (1966) 'Discussion', in C. Shaw, *The Jack Roller: A Delinquent Boy's Own Story.* Chicago: The University of Chicago Press.

Burgess, R.G. (1984) *In the Field: An Introduction to Field Research.* London: Allen & Unwin.

Burke, P. (2002) *Accessing Education: Effectively Widening Participation.* Stoke-on-Trent: Trentham Books.

Burton, J. and Launer, J. (2003) *Supervision and Support in Primary Care.* Oxford: Radcliffe.

Butler, J. (1997) *The Psychic Life of Power: Theories in Subjection.* Stanford, CA: Stanford University Press.

Byng-Hall, J. (1990) 'The Power of Family Myths', in R. Samuel and P. Thompson (eds) *The Myths We Live By.* London: Routledge.

Calhoun, C. (1995) *Critical Social Theory.* Cambridge, MA: Blackwell Publishers.

Chamberlayne, P. and Spanò, A. (2000) 'Modernisation as Lived Experience: Contrasting Case Studies from the SOSTRIS Project', in P. Chamberlayne, J. Bornat and T. Wengraf (eds) *The Turn to Biographical Methods in Social Science.* London: Routledge.

Chamberlayne, P., Bornat, J. and Apitzsch, U. (2004) *Biographical Methods and Professional Practice.* Bristol: The Policy Press.

Chamberlayne, P., Bornat, J. and Wengraf, T. (eds) (2000) *The Turn to Biographical Methods in Social Science.* London: Routledge.

Chapman Hoult, E. (2007) 'Resilience in Adult Learning', work in progress, Canterbury Christ Church University, UK.

Christians, C.G. (2003) 'Ethics and Politics in Qualitative Research', in N.K. Denzin and Y.S. Lincoln (eds) *The Landscape of Qualitative Research.* Thousand Oaks, CA: Sage.

Clough, P. (2004) 'Frank's Life Story', in D. Goodley, R. Lawthom, P. Clough and M. Moore, *Researching Life Stories: Method, Theory, Analyses in a Biographical Age.* London: Routledge Falmer.

Coffey, A. and Atkinson, P. (1996) *Making Sense of Qualitative Data.* London: Sage.

Coffield, F. (1999) 'Breaking the Consensus: Lifelong Learning as Social Control', *British Journal of Educational Research*, 25(4): 479–99.

Cohen, G.A. (1988) *History, Labour and Freedom: A Defence.* Oxford: Oxford University Press.

Connell, R. (1995) *Masculinities.* London: Policy Press.

Corrigan, P. (1979) *Schooling the Smash Street Kids.* London: Macmillan.

Courtney, S. (1992) *Why Adults Learn: Towards a Theory of Participation in Adult Education.* London: Routledge.

Creswell, J.W. (1998) *Qualitative Inquiry and Research Design: Choosing Among Five Traditions.* Thousand Oaks, CA: Sage.

Crompton, R. (2008) *Class and Stratification.* London: Polity.

Crossan, B., Field, J., Gallacher, J. and Merrill, B. (2003) 'Understanding Participation in Learning for Non-Traditional Adult Learners: Learning Careers and the Construction of Learning Identities', *The British Journal of Educational Sociology*, 24(1): 55–67.

Crotty, M. (1998) *The Foundations of Social Research: Meaning and Perspective in the Research Process.* London: Sage.

Damasio, A. (2000) *The Feeling of What Happens: Body, Emotion and the Making of Consciousness.* London: Vintage.

Dausien, B. (2007) 'Learning from History? Experiences and Reflections from a German-Polish Time Witness Project', unpublished conference paper, Concepts of Learning – Conference of the ESREA Network on Life History and Biography, Roskilde University, Denmark, 1–4 March.

David, M. (2008) 'Foreword', in P. Frame and J. Burnett (eds) *Using Auto/biography in Learning and Teaching*, SEDA Paper, 120. London: SEDA Publications.

Davie, G. (1961) *The Democratic Intellect: Scotland and her Universities in the Nineteenth Century*. Edinburgh: Edinburgh University Press.

Davies, B. and Gannon, S. (2006) *Doing Collective Biography*. Maidenhead: Open University Press.

Dawe, A. (1970) 'The Two Sociologies', *The British Journal of Sociology*, 21(2): 207–18.

Daymond, M., Driver, D., Meintjes, S., Molema, L., Musengezi, C., Orford, M. and Rasebotsa, N. (eds) (2003) *Women Writing Africa. Vol. 1: The Southern Region*. New York: Feminist Press at CUNY.

Denzin, N. (1989a) *The Research Act*. Englewood Cliffs, NJ: Prentice Hall.

Denzin, N.K. (1989b) *Interpretative Biography*. Newbury Park, CA: Sage.

Denzin, N.K. (1992) *Symbolic Interactionism and Cultural Studies: The Politics of Interpretation*. Oxford: Blackwell.

Denzin, N.K. (1997) *Interpretive Ethnography: Ethnographic Practices for the 21st Century*. London: Sage.

Devine, F., Savage, M., Scott, J. and Crompton, R. (2005) *Rethinking Class: Cultures, Identities and Lifestyle*. New York: Palgrave Macmillan.

Dominicé, P. (2000) *Learning From Our Lives*. San Francisco: Jossey-Bass.

Dorman, P. (2008) 'Confusion of Horizons: Developing an Auto/biographical Imagination', Canterbury Christ Church University (part of a PhD submission).

Eakin, P.J. (2008) *Living Autobiographically: How We Create Identity in Narrative*. Ithaca: Cornell University Press.

Ecclestone, K. (2004) 'Therapeutic Stories in Adult Education: The Demoralisation of Critical Pedagogy', in C. Hunt (ed.) *Whose Story Now? (Re)generating Research in Adult Learning and Teaching. Proceedings of the 34th SCUTREA Conference*. Exeter: SCUTREA. pp. 55–62.

Edel, L. (1985) *Writing Lives: Principia Biographica*. London: W.W. Norton.

Edwards, R. (1993) *Mature Women Students: Separating or Connecting Family and Education*. London: Macmillan.

Edwards, R. (1997) *Changing Places? Flexibility, Lifelong Learning and a Learning Society*. London: Routledge.

Egan, G. (1994) *The Skilled Helper*. Pacific Grove, CA: Brooks/Cole Publishing Co.

Elqvist-Salzman, I. (1993) *Lärarina, kvinna, människan*. Stockholm: Carlssons.

Elwyn, G. and Gwyn, R. (1998) 'Stories we Hear and Stories we Tell ... Analysing Talk in Clinical Practice', in T. Greenhalgh and B. Hurwitz (eds) *Narrative Based Medicine: Dialogue and Discourse in Clinical Practice*. London: BMJ.

Eraut, M. (2004) 'Informal Learning in the Workplace', *Studies in Continuing Education*, 26(2): 247–73.

Erben, M. (1998) 'Biography and Research Method', in M. Erben (ed.) *Biography and Education: A Reader*. London: Falmer Press.

Erickson, E. (1959) 'Identity and the Life Cycle', *Psychological Issues*, 1: 509–600.

Erickson, E. (1963a) *Identity: Youth and Crisis*. London: Faber and Faber.

Erickson, E. (1963b) *Childhood and Society* (2nd edn). New York: Newton.

Esterberg, K.G. (2002) *Qualitative Methods in Social Research*. Boston: McGraw Hill.

Evans, R. (2004) *Learning Discourse: Learning Biographies, Embedded Speech and Discourse Identity in Students' Talk*. Frankfurt-am-Main: Peter Lang.

Falk Rafael, A. (1997) 'Advocating Oral History: A Research Methodology for Social Activism in Nursing', *Advances in Nursing Science,* 20(2): 32–44.

Fieldhouse, R. (1996) 'Mythmaking and Mortmain: A Response', *Studies in the Education of Adults,* 28(1): 117–20.

Fieldhouse, R. (1997) 'Adult Education History: Why Rake Up the Past?', Sixteenth Albert Mansbridge Memorial Lecture, Leeds, School of Continuing Education.

Fielding, N. (1981) *The National Front.* London: Routledge and Kegan Paul.

Fine, M. (1992) 'Passion, Politics and Power', in M. Fine (ed.) *Disruptive Voices: The Possibilities of Feminist Research.* Michigan: Michigan University Press.

Fine, M. and Gordon, S. (1992) 'Feminist Transformations of/despite Psychology,' in M. Fine (ed.) *Disruptive Voices: The Possibilities of Feminist Research.* Michigan: Michigan University Press.

Fine, M., Weis, L., Weseen, S. and Wong, W. (2003) 'For Whom? Qualitative Research, Representations and Social Responsibilities', in N.K. Denzin and Y.S. Lincoln (eds) *The Landscape of Qualitative Research.* Thousand Oaks, CA: Sage.

Finnegan, R. (2006) 'Family Myths, Memories and Interviewing', in R. Perks and A. Thomson (eds) *The Oral History Reader* (2nd edn). London: Routledge.

Fischer-Rosenthal, W. (1995) 'Schweighen-Reichfertigen: Biographische Arbeit im Umgang mit deutschen Vergangenheitan', in W. Fischer-Rosenthal and P. Alheit, in cooperation with E. Hoerning (eds) *Biographien in Deutschland.* Opladen: Westdeutscher Verlag.

Flecha, R. (2000) *Sharing Words: Theory and Practice of Dialogic Learning.* Lanham, MD: Rowman and Littlefield Publishers.

Flecha, R. and Gómez, J. (2006) 'Participatory Paradigms: Researching "with" rather than "on"', in M. Osborne, J. Gallacher and B. Crossan, *Researching Widening Access to Lifelong Learning: Issues and Approaches in International Research.* London: Routledge.

Flyvberg, B. (2004) 'Five Misunderstandings about Case Study Research', in C. Seale, G. Gobo, J. Gubrium and D. Silverman (eds) *Qualitative Research Practice.* London: Sage.

Foucault, M. (1978) *I, Pierre Rivière, Having Slaughtered My Mother, My Sister and My Brother…* Harmondsworth: Penguin.

Foucault, M. (1979a) 'What is an Author?', *Screen,* 20: 13–35.

Foucault, M. (1979b) *The History of Sexuality, Vol. 1.* London: Allen Lane.

Fraser, W. (2007) 'Adult Education and the Cultural Imagination', work in progress, Canterbury Christ Church University, UK.

Freire , P. (1972a) *Cultural Action for Freedom.* Harmondsworth: Penguin.

Freire, P. (1972b) *Pedagogy of the Oppressed.* Harmondsworth: Penguin.

Freire, P. (1976) *Education: The Practice of Freedom.* London: Writers and Readers Publishing Cooperative.

Freud, S. (1910/1963) *Leonardo de Vinci and a Memory of his Childhood.* Harmondsworth: Penguin.

Freud, S. (1977) *Case Histories: 'Dora' and Little Hans.* The Penguin Freud Library, Vol. 4. Harmondsworth: Pelican.

Frisch, M. (1990) *A Shared Authority: Essays on the Craft and Meanings of Oral and Public History.* Albany, NY: State University of New York Press.

Frisch, M. (2006) 'Oral History and the Digital Revolution: Toward a Post-documentary Sensibility', in R. Perks and A. Thomson (eds) *The Oral History Reader* (2nd edn). London: Routledge.

Frosh, S. (1989) *Psychoanalysis and Psychology: Minding the Gap.* London: Macmillan.

Frosh, S. (1991) *Identity Crisis; Modernity, Psychoanalysis and the Self.* London: Macmillan.

Frosh, S., Phoenix, A. and Pattman, R. (2005) 'Struggling Towards Manhood: Narratives of Homophobia and Fathering', *British Journal of Psychotherapy,* 22(1): 37–56.

Gallacher, J., Crossan, B., Leahy, J., Merrill, B. and Field, J. (2000) *Education for All? Further Education, Social Inclusion and Widening Access*. Glasgow, CRLL: Glasgow Caledonian University.

Gay, P. (1988) *Freud: A Life for Our Time*. London: Papermac.

Gerson, K. and Horowitz, R. (2002) 'Observation and Interviewing: Options and Choices in Qualitative Research', in T. May (2003) (ed.) *Qualitative Research in Action*. London: Sage.

Giddens, A. (1991) *Modernity and Self-Identity*. Cambridge: Polity.

Giddens, A. (1999) *Runaway World*. London: Profile Books.

Gilligan, C. (1982) *In a Different Voice: Psychological Theory and Women's Development*. Cambridge, MA: Harvard University Press.

Glaser, B. (1992) *Basics of Grounded Theory Analysis*. California: Sociology Press Mill.

Glaser, B.G. and Strauss, A.L. (1967) *The Discovery of Grounded Theory: Strategies for Qualitative Research*. Chicago: Aldine.

Glaser, B. and Strauss, A. (1968) *A Time for Dying*. Chicago: Aldine.

Gluck, S. (1979) 'What's So Special About Women? Women's Oral History', *Frontiers*, 2(2): 3–11.

Gluck, S. and Patai, D. (eds) (1991) *Women's Words, the Feminist Practice of Oral History*. London: Routledge.

Goffman, E. (1961/1968) *Asylums*. Harmondsworth: Penguin.

Goldberger, N. (1997) 'Preface', in M.F. Belenky, B.M. Clinchy, N.R. Goldberger and J.M. Tarule (eds) *Women's Ways of Knowing: The Development of Self, Voice and Mind*. (2nd edn). New York: Basic Books.

Good, F. (2006) 'Voice, Ear and Text', in R. Perks and A. Thomson (eds) *The Oral History Reader* (2nd edn). London: Routledge.

Goodley, D. (2004a) 'Gerry's Life Story', in D. Goodley, R. Lawthom, P. Clough and M. Moore, *Researching Life Stories: Method, Theory, Analyses in a Biographical Age*. London: Routledge Falmer.

Goodley, D. (2004b) 'Craft and Ethics in Researching Life Stories', in D. Goodley, R. Lawthom, P. Clough and M. Moore, *Researching Life Stories: Method, Theory, Analyses in a Biographical Age*. London: Routledge Falmer.

Goodley, D., Lawthom, R., Clough, P. and Moore, M. (2004) *Researching Life Stories: Method, Theory and Analyses in a Biographical Age*. London: Routledge Falmer.

Goodson, I. (ed.) (1992) *Studying Teacher's Lives*. London: Routledge.

Goodson, I. (1994) 'Studying the Teacher's Life and Work', *Teaching and Teacher Education*, 10(1): 29–37.

Goodson, I. and Sykes, P. (2001) *Life History Research in Education Settings: Learning from Lives*. Buckingham: Open University Press.

Gould, R. (2009) 'Contemplating Old Age: An Auto/Biographical Study of How it Feels to Get Old', PhD thesis, Canterbury Christ Church University, UK.

Gramling, L.F. and Carr, R.L. (2004) 'A Life History Methodology', *Nursing Research*, 53(3): 207–10.

Greenhalgh, T. and Hurwitz, B. (1998) *Narrative Based Medicine, Dialogue and Discourse in Clinical Practice*. London: BMJ.

Gribbin, J. (2007) *The Universe: A Biography*. London: Allen Lane.

Habermas, J. (1972) *Knowledge and Human Interests*. Heinemann: London.

Hammersley, M. (1995) *The Politics of Social Research*. London: Sage.

Hammersley, M. (1998) *Reading Ethnographic Research: A Critical Guide*. London: Longdon.

Hammersley, M. (2000) *Taking Sides in Social Research*. London: Routledge.

Hammersley, M. (2002) 'Research as Emancipatory: The Case of Bhaskar's Critical Realism', *Journal of Critical Realism*, 1: 33–48.

Hammersley, M. and Atkinson, P. (1992) *Ethnography: Principles in Practice*. London: Routledge.

Haraway, D. (1988) 'Situated Knowledges: The Science Question in Feminism and the Privilege of Partial Perspective', *Feminist Studies*, 14: 575–99.

Harding, S. (ed.) (1987) *Feminism and Methodology*. Indiana: Indiana University Press.

Haug, F., Andersen, S., Bünz-Elfferding, A., Hauser, K., Lang, U., Lauden, M., Lüdemann, M., Meir, U., Nemitz, B., Niehoff, E., Prinz, R., Rathzel, N., Scheu, M. and Thomas, C. (eds) (1987) *Female Sexualization: A Collective Work of Memory*, trans E. Carter. London: Verso Press.

Hodkinson, P., Hodkinson, H., Evans, K., Kersh, N., Fuller, A., Unwin, L. and Senker, P. (2004) 'The Significance of Individual Biography in Workplace Learning', *Studies in the Education of Adults*, 36(1): 6–24.

Hoggart, R. (1957) *The Uses of Literacy*. London: Penguin, in association with Chatto and Windus.

Holliday, A. (2007) *Doing and Writing Qualitative Research* (2nd edn). London: Sage.

Hollway, W. (1989) *Subjectivity and Method in Psychology: Gender, Meaning and Science*. London: Sage.

Hollway, W. and Jefferson, T. (2000) *Doing Qualitative Research Differently*. London: Sage.

hooks, b. (1984) *Feminist Theory: From Margin to Center*. Boston: South End Press.

Hopper, E. and Osborn, M. (1975) *Adult Students, Education, Selection and Social Control*. London: Frances Pinter.

Horkheimer, M. (1982) *Critical Theory*. New York: Continuum.

Horsdal, M. (2002) *Active Citizenship and the Non-Formal Education: Description of Competencies*. Copenhagen: FFO Højskolerne.

Howatson-Jones, L. (2009) 'Exploring the Learning of Nurses', PhD thesis, Canterbury Christ Church University, UK.

Hudson, L. (1966) *Contrary Imaginations: A Psychological Study of the English Schoolboy*. Harmondsworth: Penguin.

Humm, M. (1992) *Feminisms: A Reader*. London: Prentice-Hall Europe.

Humphreys, L. (1970) *Tea Room Trade*. London: Duckworth.

Humphries, S. (1984) *The Handbook of Oral History, Recording Life Stories*. London: Inter-Action.

Hunt, C. and Sampson, F. (2006) *Writing, Self and Reflexivity*. London: Palgrave.

Hunt, C. and West, L. (2006) 'Learning in a Border Country: Using Psychodynamic Perspectives in Teaching and Research', *Studies in the Education of Adults*, 38(2): 160–77.

Hunt, C. and West, L. (2009) 'Salvaging the Self in Adult Learning', *Studies in the Education of Adults*, in press.

Hutchings, M. (2007) 'Teach First: "A Cut Above the Rest"', paper presented to a Learning to Teach in Post Devolution UK Conference, Roehampton, March.

Hutchings, M., Maylor, U., Mendick, H., Menter, I. and Smart, S. (2006) *An Evaluation of Innovative Approaches to Teacher Training on the Teach First Programme: Final Report to the Training and Development Agency for School Student TDA*.

Jackson, B. and Marsden, D. (1966) *Education and the Working Class*. London: Pelican.

Jackson, D. (1990) *Unmasking Masculinity: A Critical Autobiography*. London: Unwin.

Johnston, R. and Merrill, B. (2004) 'From Old to New Learning Identities: Charting the Change for Non-traditional Adult Students in Higher Education', in *ESREA Proceedings: Between 'Old' and 'New' Worlds of Adult Learning*. Wroclaw: University of Wroclaw. pp. 153–66.

Jones, C. and Rupp, S. (2000) 'Understanding the Carer's World: A Biographical-interpretive Case Study', in P. Chamberlayne, J. Bornat and T. Wengraf (eds) *The Turn to Biographical Methods in Social Science*. London: Routledge.

Jung, C. (1933) *Memories, Dreams, Reflections.* London: Pantheon.

Kennedy, E.L. (2006) Telling Tales: Oral History and the Construction of Pre-Stonewall Lesbian History', in R. Perks and A. Thomson (eds) *The Oral History Reader* (2nd edn). London: Routledge.

Kincheloe, J.L. and McLaren, P. (2003) 'Rethinking Critical Theory and Qualitative Research', in N.K. Denzin and Y.S. Lincoln (eds) *The Landscape of Qualitative Research: Theories and Issues* (2nd edn). Thousand Oaks, CA: Sage.

King, E. (1995) 'The Use of Self in Qualitative Research', draft paper.

Kirby, S. (1998) 'The Resurgence of Oral History and the New Issues it Raises', *Nurse Researcher,* 5(2): 45–58.

Klein, M. (1998) *Love, Gratitude and Other Works, 1921–1945.* London: Virago.

Kleinman, S. and Copp, M. (1993) *Emotions and Field Work.* Qualitative Research Methods Series, 28. London: Sage.

Krieger, S. (1991) *Social Science and the Self.* New Brunswick, NJ: Rutgers University Press.

Lalljee, M., Kearney, P. and West, L. (1989) 'Confidence and Control: A Psychological Perspective on the Impact of Second Chance to Learn', *Studies in the Education of Adults,* 21(1): 20–8.

Lather, P. (1991) *Getting Smart: Feminist Research and Pedagogy with/in the Postmodern.* London: Routledge.

Launer, J. (2002) *Narrative-based Primary Care.* Abingdon: Radcliffe Medical Press.

Lawthom, R. (2004) in D. Goodley, R. Lawthom, P. Clough and M. Moore, *Researching Life Stories: Method, Theory and Analyses in a Biographical Age.* London: Routledge Falmer.

Lee, H. (2008) *Edith Wharton.* London: Vintage Books.

Levinson, D. (1978) *The Seasons of a Man's Life.* New York: Ballintine.

Lincoln, Y.S. and Denzin, N.K. (2003) 'The Seventh Moment: Out of the Past', in N.K. Denzin and Y.S. Lincoln (eds) *The Landscape of Qualitative Research: Theories and Issues* (2nd edn). Thousand Oaks, CA: Sage.

London School of Economics (LSE) (2006) *The Depression Report: A New Deal for Depression and Anxiety Disorders,* a report by The Centre for Economic Performance's Mental Health Policy Group, chaired by Lord Layard. London: LSE.

Lyon, T. (2004) *Guns and Guerilla Girls: Women in the Zimbabwean Liberation Struggle.* Trenton, NJ: African World Press.

McClaren, A. (1985) *Ambitions and Realisations: Women in Adult Education.* London: Peter Owen.

McKinney, J.C. (1966) *Constructive Typology and Social Theory.* New York: Appleton-Century-Crofts.

McRobbie, A. and Garber, J. (1976) 'Girls and Subcultures – An Exploration', in S. Hall and T. Jefferson (eds) *Resistance Through Rituals.* London: Hutchinson University Library.

Malcolm, I. (2006) 'Life History as Emotional Labour', paper presented at the ESREA Life History and Biographical Research Network Conference, Volos, Greece.

Marvasti, A. (2004) *Qualitative Research in Sociology.* London: Sage.

Marx, K. (1842) *Rheinische Zeitung* (Works1, 97).

Marx, K. (1843) *Deutsch-Französische Jahrbücher* (letter to Ruge).

Marx, K. (1845) 'Theses on Feuerbach', in F. Engels (1888/1934) *Ludwig Feuerbach and the End of Classical German Philosophy.* London: M. Lawrence.

Marx, K. (1852/1973) 'The Eighteenth Brumaire of Louis Bonaparte', in E. Fischer, *Marx in his Own Words.* Harmondsworth: Penguin.

Mason, J. (1996) *Qualitative Researching.* London: Sage.

Matza, D. (1964) *Delinquency and Drift.* Berkeley: John Wiley and Sons.

Matza, D. (1969) *Becoming Deviant.* Englewood Cliffs, NJ: Prentice Hall.

May, T. (2001) *Social Research: Issues, Methods and Process.* Buckingham: Open University Press.

Mead, G.H. (1934/1972) *Mind, Self and Society.* Chicago: University of Chicago Press.

Mead, G.H. (1982) *The Individual and the Social Self.* Chicago: University of Chicago Press.

Meltzer, B.N., Petras, J.W. and Reynolds, L.T. (1975) *Symbolic Interactionism: Genesis, Varieties and Criticisms.* London: Routledege & Kegan Paul.

Merrill, B. (1999) *Gender, Change and Identity: Mature Women Students in Universities.* Aldershot: Ashgate.

Merrill, B. (2001) 'Learning Careers: Conceptualising Adult Learning Experiences Through Biographies', paper presented at ESREA Biography and Life History Network Conference, Roskilde, Denmark.

Merrill, B. (2003) 'Women's Lives and Learning: Struggling for Transformation', in B. Dybbroe and E. Ollagnier, *Challenging Gender in Lifelong Learning: European Perspectives.* Roskilde: Roskilde University Press.

Merrill, B. (2007) 'Recovering Class and the Collective in the Stories of Adult Learners', in L. West, B. Merrill, P. Alheit, A. Bron and A. Siig Andersen (eds) *Using Biographical and Life History Approaches in the Study of Adult and Lifelong Learning.* Frankfurt-am-Main: Peter Lang.

Merrill, B. and Puigvert, L. (2001) 'Discounting "Other Women"', in *Researching Widening Access – International Perspectives,* Conference Proceedings, CRLL. Glasgow: Glasgow Caledonian University.

Michelet, J. (1847) *Histoire de la Révolution Française.* Paris.

Mies, M. (1991) 'Women's Research or Feminist Research?', in M.M. Fonow and J.A. Cook (eds) *Beyond Methodology: Feminist Scholarship as Lived Research.* Bloomington: Indiana University Press.

Miles, M.B. and Huberman, A.M. (1994) *Qualitative Data Analysis: A Sourcebook of New Methods.* Thousand Oaks, CA: Sage.

Miller, J. (1997) *Autobiography and Research.* London: University of London Institute of Education.

Miller, N. (2007) 'Developing an Auto/Biographical Imagination', in L. West, B. Merrill, P. Alheit, A. Bron and A. Siig Andersen (eds) *Using Biographical and Life History Approaches in the Study of Adult and Lifelong Learning.* Frankfurt-am-Main: Peter Lang.

Milner, M. (1971) *On Not Being Able to Paint.* London: Heinemann Educational Books.

Moore, M. (2004) 'Grounded Theory', in D. Goodley, R. Lawthom, P. Clough and M. Moore, *Researching Life Stories: Method, Theory and Analyses in a Biographical Age.* London: Routledge Falmer.

Morse, J.M. (1994) 'Designing Funded Qualitative Research', in N.K. Denzin and Y.S. Lincoln (eds) *Handbook of Qualitative Research.* Thousand Oaks, CA: Sage.

NESS (2005) *Early Impacts of Sure Start Programmes on Children and Families; Research Report NESS/2005/FR/013.* London: HMSO.

NESS (2008) *The Impact of Sure Start on Three-Year-Olds and their Families.* London: HMSO.

Oakely, A. (1979) *Becoming a Mother.* Oxford: Martin Robertson.

Oakley, A. (1981) *From Here to Maternity: Becoming a Mother.* Harmondsworth: Penguin.

Oakley, A. (1992) 'Interviewing Women: A Contradiction in Terms', in H. Roberts (ed.) *Doing Feminist Research.* London: Routledge.

Ollagnier, E. (2002) 'Life History Approach in Adult Education Research', in A. Bron and M. Schemmann (eds) *Social Sciences Theories in Adult Education Research.* Münster: LIT Verlag.

Ollagnier, E. (2007) 'Challenging Gender with Life History', in L. West, B. Merrill, P. Alheit, A. Bron and A. Siig Andersen (eds) *Using Biographical and Life History Approaches in the Study of Adult and Lifelong Learning*. Frankfurt-am-Main: Peter Lang.

Pahl, R. (1989) 'Is the Emperor Naked?', *International Journal of Urban and Regional Research*, 13: 711–20.

Parker, H. (1974) *View from the Boys: A Sociology of Downtown Adolescents*. Newton Abbot: David & Charles.

Passerini, L. (1990) 'Mythbiography in Oral History', in R. Samuel and P. Thompson (eds) *The Myths We Live By*. London: Routledge.

Perdue, T. (1980) *Nations Remembered: An Oral History of the Five Civilised Tribes, 1865–1907*. Westport, CT: Greenwood Press.

Perks, R. and Thomson, A. (2006) (eds) *The Oral History Reader* (2nd edn). London: Routledge.

Personal Narratives Group (1989) *Interpreting Women's Lives: Feminist Theory and Personal Narratives*. Bloomington: Indiana University Press.

Plummer, K. (1983) *Documents of Life: An Introduction to the Problems and Literature of a Humanistic Method*. London: George Allen and Unwin.

Plummer, K. (2001) *Documents of Life 2: An Invitation to Critical Humanism*. London: Sage.

Pollert, A. (1981) *Girls, Wives, Factory Lives*. London: Macmillan.

Popadiuk, N. (2004) 'The Feminist Biographical Method in Psychological Research, *The Qualitative Report*, 9(3): 392–412, http://www.nova.edu/ssss/QR/QR9-3/popadiuk.pdf

Portelli, A. (1990) 'Uchronic Dreams, Working-class Memory and Possible Worlds', in R. Samuel and P. Thompson (eds) *The Myths We Live By*. London: Routledge.

Portelli, A. (2006) 'What Makes Oral History Different?', in R. Perks. and A. Thomson (eds) *The Oral History Reader* (2nd edn). London: Routledge.

Postone, M. (1993) *Time, Labour and Social Domination: A Reinterpretation of Marx's Critical Theory*. Cambridge: Cambridge University Press.

Puigvert, L. and Valls, R. (2002) 'Political and Social Impact of "the Other Women" Movement', paper presented at the Second International Conference of the Popular Education Network, University of Barcelona, Barcelona, 27–9 September.

Ranson, S. and Rutledge, H. (2005) *Including Families in the Learning Community: Family Centres and the Expansion of Learning*. York: Joseph Rowntree Foundation.

Reid, H. and West, L. (2008) 'Talking with a Shared Purpose: Applying Auto/biographical and Narrative Approaches to Practice', *Constructing a Way Forward: Innovation in Theory and Practice for Career Guidance*, Occasional Paper. Canterbury, CCCU, pp. 29–38.

Reinharz, S. (1992) *Feminist Methods in Social Research*. New York: Oxford University Press.

Richardson, L. (1990) *Writing Strategies: Reaching Diverse Audiences*. Newbury Park: Sage.

Rickard, W. (2004) 'The Biographical Turn in Health Studies', *Biographical Methods and Professional Practice*. Bristol: The Policy Press.

Roberts, B. (2002) *Biographical Research*. Buckingham: Open University Press.

Roper, M. (2003) 'Analysing the Analysed: Transference and Counter-transference in the Oral History Encounter', *Oral History*, Autumn: 20–32.

Rosenthal, G. (1993) 'Reconstruction of Life Stories: Principles of Selection in Generating Stories for Biographical Narrative Interviews', in R. Josselson and A. Lieblich, *The Narrative Study of Lives*, Volume 1. Newbury Park, CA: Sage. pp. 59–91.

Rosenthal, G. (1995) *Erlebte und Erzählte Lebensgesichte. Gesalt und Struktur Biographischer Selbstbeschreibenungen*. Frankfurt: Campus.

Rosenthal, G. (2004) Paper presented to the ESREA Life History and Biography Network/ISA Conference. Roskilde, March.

Ross, F. (2003) *Bearing Witness: Women and the Truth and Reconciliation Struggle in South Africa*. London: Pluto.

Rustin, M. (2000) 'Reflections on the Biographical Turn in Social Science', in P. Chamberlayne, J. Barnett and T. Wengraff (eds) *The Turn to Biographical Methods in Social Science*. London: Routledge.

Salinsky, J. and Sackin, P. (2000) *What are you Feeling, Doctor?* Oxford: Radcliffe.

Salling Olesen, H. (2007a) 'Professional Identities, Subjectivity and Learning: Be(coming) a General Practitioner', in L. West, B. Merrill, P. Alheit and A. Siig Andersen (2007) (eds) *Using Biographical and Life History Approaches in the Study of Adult and Lifelong Learning:* Frankfurt-am-Main: Peter Lang. pp. 125–41.

Salling Olesen, H. (2007b) 'Theorising Learning in Life History: A Psychosocietal Approach', *Studies in the Education of Adults*, 39(1): 38–53.

Samuel, R. (1982) 'Local History and Oral History', in R.G. Burgess (ed.) *Field Research: A Sourcebook and Field Manual*. London: George Allen and Unwin.

Savage, M. (2000) *Class Analysis and Social Transformation*. Buckingham: Open University Press.

Sayer, A. (2005) *The Moral Significance of Class*. Cambridge: Cambridge University Press.

Sayers, J. (1995) *The Man Who Never Was: Freudian Tales*. London: Chatto and Windus.

Sayers, J. (2003) *Divine Therapy: Love, Mysticism and Psychoanalysis*. Oxford: Oxford University Press.

Schaff, A. (1970) *Marxism and the Human Individual*. New York: McGraw-Hill.

Schuller, T., Preston, J. and Hammond, C. (2007) 'Mixing Methods to Measure Learning Benefits', in L. West, P. Alheit, A. Siig Andersen and B. Merrill (eds) *Using Biographical and Life History Approaches in the Study of Adult and Lifelong Learning: European Perspectives*. Frankfurt-am-Main: Peter Lang.

Schutze, F. (1992) 'Pressure and Guilt: The Experience of a Young German Soldier in World War Two and its Biographical Implications', *International Sociology*, 7(2): 187–208; 7(3): 347–67.

Schwartz, J. (1999) *Casandra's Daughter: A History of Psychoanalysis in Europe and America*. London: Allen Lane.

Sclater, S.D. (2004) 'What is the Subject?', *Narrative Enquiry*, 13(2): 317–30.

Seabrook, J. (1982) *Working-Class Childhood*. London: Gollancz.

Seidman, I.E. (1991) *Interviewing as Qualitative Research*. New York: Oxford University Press.

Shaw, C. (1966) *The Jack Roller: A Delinquent Boy's Own Story*. Chicago: The University of Chicago Press.

Shilling, C. (1999) 'Towards an Embodied Understanding of the Structure/Agency Debate', *British Journal of Sociology*, 50(4): 543–62.

Silverman, D. (2006) *Interpreting Qualitative Data*. London: Sage.

Sinclair, S. (1997) *Making Doctors*. Oxford: Berg.

Skeggs, B. (1997) *Formations of Class and Gender*. London: Sage.

Slim, H., Thompson, P., Bennett, O. and Cross, N. (eds) (1993) *Listening for a Change: Oral Testimony and Community Development*. London: Panos Publications.

Smith, D.E. (1987) 'Women's Perspective as a Radical Critique of Sociology', in S. Harding (ed.) *Feminism and Methodology*. Bloomington: Indiana University Press.

Smith, L. (1994) 'Biographical Method', in N.K. Denzin and Y.S. Lincoln (eds) *Handbook of Qualitative Research*. Thousands Oaks, CA: Sage.

Smith, L. (1998) 'Biographical Method', in N.K. Denzin and Y.S. Lincoln (eds) *Strategies of Qualitative Enquiry*. Thousand Oaks, CA: Sage.

Smith, R. (2001) 'Why are Doctors so Unhappy?', Editorials, *BMJ*, 322: 1073–4.

Snodgrass, J. (1982) *The Jack-Roller at Seventy*. Lexington: Lexington Books.

Sork, T.J., Chapman, V.L. and St Clair, R. (eds) (2000) *Proceedings of the 41st Annual Adult Education Research Conference.* Vancouver: University of British Columbia.

Stadlen, N. (2004) *What Mothers Do: Especially When it Looks Like Nothing.* London: Piatkus.

Stanley, L. (1992) *The Auto/Biographical I: Theory and Practice of Feminist Auto/Biography.* Manchester: Manchester University Press.

Stanley, L. and Wise, S. (1993) *Breaking Out Again: Feminist Ontology and Epistemology.* London: Routledge.

Steedman, C. (1986) *Landscape for a Good Woman.* London: Virago.

Stones, R. (1996) *Sociological Reasoning: Towards a Post-Modern Sociology.* London: Macmillan.

Strauss, A.L. and Corbin, J. (1990) *Basics of Qualitative Research: Grounded Theory Procedures and Techniques.* London: Sage.

Swindells, J. (1995) 'Introduction', in J. Swindells (ed.) *The Uses of Biography.* London: Taylor and Francis.

Sztompka, P. (1984) 'Florian Znaniecki's Sociology: Humanistic or Scientific?', in P. Sztompka (ed.) *Masters of Polish Sociology.* Wroclaw: Ossolineum.

Tharu, S. and Lalita, K. (1991) *Women Writing in India, from 600BC to the early Twentieth Century.* New York: The Feminist Press at CUNY.

Thomas, W.I. and Znaniecki, F. (1958) *The Polish Peasant in Europe and America.* New York: Dover Publications. (First published 1918–1921.)

Thompson, B. (1990) 'Raisins and Smiles for Me and My Sister: A Feminist Theory of Eating Problems, Trauma and Recovery in Women's Lives', PhD dissertation, Brandeis University.

Thompson, E.P. (1978) *The Poverty of Theory and Other Essays.* London: Merlin Press.

Thompson, E.P. (1980) *The Making of the English Working Class.* London: Penguin.

Thompson, J. (2000) *Women, Class and Education.* London: Routledge.

Thompson, P. (2000) *The Voice of the Past* (3rd edn). Oxford: Oxford University Press.

Thomson, A. (1994) *Anzac Memories: Living with the Legend.* Auckland: Oxford University Press.

Tonkin, E. (1992) *Narrating Our Pasts: The Social Construction of Oral History.* Cambridge: Cambridge University Press.

Tucker, S. (1988) *Telling Memories among Southern Women: Domestic Workers and their Employers in the Segregated South.* Baton Rouge: Louisiana State University Press.

Vansina, J. (1985) *Oral Tradition as History.* Madison, WI: University of Wisconsin Press.

Viney, L. (1993) *Life Stories: Personal Construct Therapy with the Elderly.* Chichester: John Wiley and Sons.

Walmsley, J. (2006) 'Life History Interviews with People with Learning Disabilities', in R. Perks and A. Thomson (2006) (eds) *The Oral History Reader* (2nd edn). London: Routledge.

Weber, K. (2007) 'Gender, Between the Knowledge Economy and Every Day Life', in L. West, B. Merrill, P. Alheit, A. Bron and A. Siig Andersen (eds) *Using Biographical and Life History Approaches in the Study of Adult and Lifelong Learning.* Frankfurt-am-Main: Peter Lang.

Weinberg, M.S. (1966) 'Becoming a Nudist', *Psychiatry: Journal for the Study of Interpersonal Processes*, 29(1).

Wengraf, T. (2000) 'Uncovering the General from the Particular: From Contingencies to Typologies in the Understanding of Cases', in P. Chamberlayne, J. Bornat and T. Wengraf (eds) *The Turn to Biographical Methods in Social Science.* London: Routledge.

West, L. (1996) *Beyond Fragments: Adults, Motivation and Higher Education.* London: Taylor and Francis.

West, L. (2001) *Doctors on the Edge: General Practitioners, Health and Learning in the Inner City*. London: Free Association Books.

West, L. (2004a) 'Doctors on an Edge: A Cultural Psychology of Learning and Health', in P. Chamberlayne, J. Bornat and U. Apitzsch (eds) *Biographical Methods and Professional Practice: An International Perspective*. Bristol: The Policy Press.

West, L. (2004b) 'Re-generating our Stories: Psychoanalytic Perspectives, Learning and the Subject called the Learner', in C. Hunt (ed.) *Whose Story Now? (Re)generating Research in Adult Learning and Teaching. Proceedings of the 34th SCUTREA Conference.* Exeter, pp. 303–10.

West, L. (2005) 'Old Issues, New Thoughts: Family Learning, Relationship and Community Activism', in A. Bron, E. Kurantowicz, H. Salling Olesen and L. West, *'Old' and 'New' Worlds of Adult Learning*. Wydawnictwo Naukowe: Wroclaw.

West, L. (2006) 'Really Reflexive Practice: Auto/Biographical Research and Struggles for a Critical Reflexivity', paper to the SCUTREA Pre-Conference on Reflective Practice, Leeds, July.

West, L. (2007) 'An Auto/Biographical Imagination and the Radical Challenge of Families and their Learning', in L. West, B. Merrill, P. Alheit, A. Bron and A. Siig Andersen (eds) *Using Biographical and Life History Approaches in the Study of Adult and Lifelong Learning*. Frankfurt-am-Main: Peter Lang.

West, L. (2008a) 'On the Emotional Dimensions of Learning to be a Teacher: Auto/Biographical perspectives', paper presented to the ESREA Conference on Emotionality in Learning and Research, Canterbury, March.

West, L. (2008b) 'Gendered Space: Men, Families and Learning', in E. Ollagnier and J. Ostrouch (eds) *Gender and Adult Learning*. Frankfurt: Peter Lang.

West, L. (2009, in press) 'Really Reflective Practice: Auto/Biographical Research and Struggles for a Clinical Reflexivity', in H. Bradbury, N. Frost, S. Kilminster and M. Zukas (eds) *Beyond Reflective Practice: Professional Lifelong Learning for the 21st Century*. London: Routledge.

West, L. and Carlson, A. (2006) 'Claiming and Sustaining Space? Sure Start and the Auto/Biographical Imagination', *Auto/Biography*, 14: 359–80.

West, L. and Carlson, A. (2007) *Claiming Space: An In-depth Auto/Biographical Study of a Local Sure Start Project*. CISDP, CCCU.

West, L., Merrill, B., Alheit, P. and Siig Andersen, A. (eds) (2007) *Using Biographical and Life History Approaches in the Study of Adult and Lifelong Learning: European Perspectives*. Frankfurt-am-Main: Peter Lang.

West, L., Miller, N., O'Reilly, D. and Allen, R. (eds) (2001) 'Travellers' Tales: From Adult Education to Lifelong Learning and Beyond', *Proceedings of the 31st SCUTREA Conference*. London: UEL.

Whyte, W.F. (1943) *Street Corner Society: The Social Structure of an Italian Slum*. Chicago: University of Chicago Press.

Widgery, D. (1993) *Some Lives: A GP's East End*. London: Simon and Schuster.

Willis, P. (1977) *Learning to Labour: How Working Class Kids get Working Class Jobs*. Farnborough: Saxon House.

Wilson, A. (1978) *Finding a Voice*. London: Virago.

Winnicott, D. (1971) *Playing and Reality*. London: Routledge.

Wolcott, H.F. (1997) *Writing Up Qualitative Research*. London: Sage.

Woodley, A., Wagner, L., Slowey, M., Fulton, O. and Bowner, T. (1987) *Choosing to Lear.* Buckingham: SRHE/Open University Press.

Woods, D. (1993) 'Managing Marginality: Teacher Development through Grounded Life History', *British Educational Research Journal*, 19(5): 447–65.

Wright, E.O. (1985) *Classes.* London: Verso.

Wright, E.O. (1997) *Class Counts: Comparative Studies in Class Analysis.* Cambridge: Cambridge University Press.

Wright Mills, C. (1970) *The Sociological Imagination.* Harmondsworth: Penguin. (First published 1959.)

Wright Mills, C. (1973) *The Sociological Imagination* (3rd edn). Harmondsworth: Penguin.

Index

New Labour, 78
nurses and nursing, 50–1

Oakley, Ann, 29, 116, 173
object relations theory, 69–70
objectivist approaches to analysis, 142–3
objectivity, 180–1
Oevermann, Ulrich, 35
Ollagnier, E., 35
oral history, 3–4, 18–22, 25–8, 31, 35, 50–1, 54,
    180, 191
  definition of, 19
  and feminism, 21–2
Oral History Association, US, 20
Oral History Society, 20
oral tradition, 17–19

Park, Robert, 22–4
Parsons, Talcott, 27
participant observation, 26, 61, 174
Passerini, Luisa, 19
Patai, Daphne, 116
payment to research participants, 172
Pedder, Jonathan, 117
Personal Narratives Group, 30
Pineau, Gaston, 34
plagiarism, 156
Plummer, Ken, 16, 24, 32, 57, 104, 155, 159,
    162, 164, 167, 182, 184
Pollert, Anna, 29
Popadiuk, Natalee, 65
Portelli, Alessandro, 19–20
positivism, 27, 58–9, 104–5
postmodernism, 17, 65–7, 75, 167, 185, 192
post-structuralism, 11, 32, 163, 167, 180,
    185, 192
power relationships, 173–4
pragmatism, 184, 192
praxis, concept of, 186
proformas, use of, 137–40
pseudonyms, use of, 172
psychoanalytic theory and practice, 48, 69–75,
    101, 105, 117–19, 143, 175–6, 182, 186–7
psychology, 8–9, 32–6
Puigvert, L., 66

Qualidata, 173
qualitative research, 50, 104, 129; *see also*
    statistical methods of research
quotations, use of, 153

Rafael, Falk, 50–1
Rajan, Mrs, 44
randomised control trials, 50
realism, 58, 192

recording of interviews, 124–5
Red Brigade, 19–20
reflexivity, 180–2
Reinecke, Ruth, 42
Reinharz, Shulamit, 29
reliability of research, 164
research process, problems with, 103
research reports, structure of, 158
research topics, selection of, 98–103, 111
researchers, lives of, 188
Richardson, Laurel, 153
Rickard, Wendy, 51
Roberts, Brian, 48, 66
Romany peoples, 53
Roper, Michael, 20, 73
Rosenthal, Gabriele, 35, 106
Ross, Fiona, 53
Rousseau, Jean-Jacques, 185
Royal College of Nursing, 51
Rustin, Mike, 105, 150, 167, 188

Salling Olesen, Henning, 32, 48, 50, 54,
    72, 187
sample size, 104–6
sampling, 104, 164, 166, 188
  opportunistic, 79, 107
  purposive or theoretical, 79, 107–8;
    see also criterion sampling; snowball
    sampling
Sampson, Fiona, 149
Samuel, Raphael, 18
Sassall, John, 48–9, 170
Sayer, Andrew, 66
Schaff, Adam, 186
Schuller, Tom, 82, 108, 165, 189
Schutze, Fritz, 35, 136, 143
Schwartz, Joseph, 101
Seabrook, Jeremy, 72
Seidman, Irving, 173–4
selective memory, theory of, 19
self, concepts of, 60–1, 70
September 11th 2001 attacks, victims of, 153
Shakespeare, William, 105
Shaw, Clifford R., 24–8, 61, 104, 107, 183
Shilling, C., 95
Shipman, Harold, 84
significance of research, 164
Silverman, David, 129
Skeggs, Beverly, 66, 141
Slim, Hugo, 53–4
Smith, Dorothy, 64
Smith, Louis, 32–3, 38
snowball sampling, 108–9
social class, 4, 66–7
social constructivism, 167

Supporting researchers for more than forty years

Research methods have always been at the core of SAGE's publishing. Sara Miller McCune founded SAGE in 1965 and soon after, she published SAGE's first methods book, *Public Policy Evaluation*. A few years later, she launched the Quantitative Applications in the Social Sciences series – affectionately known as the 'little green books'.

Always at the forefront of developing and supporting new approaches in methods, SAGE published early groundbreaking texts and journals in the fields of qualitative methods and evaluation.

Today, more than forty years and two million little green books later, SAGE continues to push the boundaries with a growing list of more than 1,200 research methods books, journals, and reference works across the social, behavioural, and health sciences.

From qualitative, quantitative and mixed methods to evaluation, SAGE is the essential resource for academics and practitioners looking for the latest in methods by leading scholars.

www.sagepublications.com